Culture Bumps

TOPICS IN TRANSLATION

Series Editors: Susan Bassnett (*University of Warwick*)
Edwin Gentzler (*University of Massachusetts, Amherst*)
Editor for Annotated Texts for Translation: Beverly Adab (*Aston University, Birmingham*)
Editor for Translation in the Commercial Environment: Geoffrey Samuelsson-Brown
(*Aardvark Translation Services Ltd*)

Other Books in the Series
Annotated Texts for Translation: French - English
  BEVERLY ADAB
Annotated Texts for Translation: English – French
  BEVERLY ADAB
Linguistic Auditing
  NIGEL REEVES and COLIN WRIGHT
Paragraphs on Translation
  PETER NEWMARK
Practical Guide for Translators
  GEOFFREY SAMUELSSON-BROWN
The Coming Industry of Teletranslation
  MINAKO O'HAGAN
Translation, Power, Subversion
  ROMAN ALVAREZ and M. CARMEN-AFRICA VIDAL (eds)
Words, Words, Words: The Translator and the Language Learner
  GUNILLA ANDERMAN and MARGARET ROGERS

Other Books of Interest
About Translation
  PETER NEWMARK
Cultural Functions of Translation
  C. SCHÄFFNER and H. KELLY-HOLMES (eds)
Discourse and Ideologies
  C. SCHÄFFNER and H. KELLY-HOLMES (eds)

Please contact us for the latest book information:
Multilingual Matters Ltd, Frankfurt Lodge, Clevedon Hall,
Victoria Road, Clevedon, England, BS21 7HH

TOPICS IN TRANSLATION 10
Series Editors: Susan Bassnett (*University of Warwick*)
Edwin Gentzler (*University of Massachusetts, Amherst*)

Culture Bumps

An Empirical Approach to the Translation of Allusions

Ritva Leppihalme

MULTILINGUAL MATTERS LTD
Clevedon • Philadelphia • Toronto • Sydney • Johannesburg

Library of Congress Cataloging in Publication Data

Leppihalme, Ritva
Culture Bumps: An Empirical Approach to the Translation of Allusions
Ritva Leppihalme
Topics in Translation: 10
Includes bibliographical references and index
1. Translating and interpreting. 2. Allusions. I. Title. II. Series.
P306.2.L46   1997
418'.02–dc21   97-7446

British Library Cataloguing in Publication Data

A CIP catalogue record for this book is available from the British Library.

ISBN 1-85359-374-5 (hbk)
ISBN 1-85359-373-7 (pbk)

Multilingual Matters Ltd

UK: Frankfurt Lodge, Clevedon Hall, Victoria Road, Clevedon BS21 7HH.
USA: 1900 Frost Road, Suite 101, Bristol, PA 19007, USA.
Canada: OISE, 712 Gordon Baker Road, Toronto, Ontario, Canada M2H 3R7.
Australia: P.O. Box 586, Artamon, NSW, Australia.
South Africa: PO Box 1080, Northcliffe 2115, Johannesburg, South Africa.

Typeset by Bookcraft, Stroud.

ISBN 978-1-85359-373-4

Contents

v

Preface

The cultural turn taken by translation studies over the past 15 years is no doubt related partly to the increasing internationalisation of our world and the consequent need for more and better translation. In today's world it is easy to see that for a translation to work, we have to go beyond mere words. It is not enough to work out how best to render the *words* of the source text; it is much more important to work out what the words *mean* in a particular situational and cultural context.

The term 'culture shock', which describes the result of sudden contact with another culture, implies a shock to the entire system. For less serious upsets, the term 'culture bump' has been suggested. Carol M. Archer (1986) has used the term of problems in face-to-face communication, culture bumps occurring between speakers of different cultural backgrounds, but we may observe culture bumps in reading situations as well, when culture-bound elements hinder communication of the meaning to readers in another language culture.

Allusions are one type of culture-bound elements in a text. They are expected to convey a meaning that goes beyond the mere words used. George Steiner (1991) may deplore the fact that Britain is no longer, with pollution and the Channel Tunnel, *set in a silver sea*. This phrase will remind many of his readers of a passage in Shakespeare eulogising sixteenth-century England as a 'demi-paradise'. A Finnish industrialist talking about leadership styles will convey his meaning clearly to the vast majority of Finnish adults by urging managers to emulate *Koskela*, rather than *lieutenant Lammio*. These two characters in *The Unknown Soldier* are so well known in his country that no further descriptions are needed.

But as culture-bound elements, allusions depend largely on familiarity to convey meaning. To take an example: an American journalist discussing problems with the planned health-care reform in the United States compared the cost issue to *the Cheshire Cat*, explaining that 'it may sometimes vanish, leaving behind only a smile: the promise of new benefits. But the cat is still there – and it's rapidly growing into a tiger' (Peterson, 1994). The writer of this comparison clearly expects his readers to connect the image with an illustration in Lewis Carroll's *Alice's Adventures in Wonderland* (or very likely Disney's cartoon film), with its strange cat figure which slowly fades away, until only the smile is left. But if this article were to be translated for the readers of a business magazine in another country, targeting economists, engineers, executives, investors … what would their reaction be to the introduction of a foreign children's story to a serious article on a serious subject? Instead of the allusion making the meaning easier to grasp, it might confuse the issue when translated.

The translation of allusions thus involves two language cultures as well as literary and pragmatic aspects on the textual level. Allusions have meaning in the culture or subculture in which they arise but not necessarily in others.

Sometimes, of course, allusions present no particular translation problems. It *is* possible to allude across language barriers as there are bicultural readers as well as transcultural allusions, the latter shared by source and target culture alike. A mother, hoping to welcome the son missing for weeks in a distant corner of the globe on his round-the-world trip, may promise to *slaughter the fatted calf* when the *prodigal* returns. This biblical allusion can be used to describe her feelings in a number of languages, as long as the target language culture has been sufficiently influenced by the Bible. Similarly, it is easy to translate into English the opinion of the journalist who suggested in 1994 that the Finnish minister of agriculture should see his role as that of the *good shepherd* leading *his flock* to the *pastures* of the European Union.

The need for better intercultural communication and poststructuralist theories of literature have given better balance to our conception of the translation process. We see that the translator is not the only operator in the process: the readers too participate, using what they have learned to make sense of what they read. We see the importance of considering not just the relationship of source text and target text, which in the past led to fairly fruitless discussions of equivalence, and want a clearer focus on the target text and its readers in the target culture. It is no excuse that a text is 'correctly' translated, if the target text readers cannot *understand* it. In this book I emphasise the translator's need to be more aware of his/her responsibility to the readers of the target text, and the need to remember this when choosing translation strategies. A translation which disregards differences in cultural backgrounds runs the risk of being unintelligible, if only occasionally. Sometimes the culture bump is hardly perceptible; at other times it may hinder communication quite badly.

As the current trend in translation studies increasingly focuses on how translations work in the target language culture, it is, inevitably, and despite the logistical problems involved, to readers that we must go to learn how they receive target texts. If there is a subtext to my efforts, it is that readers deserve the best. It is a plea for creative and varied use of strategies, the competent translator recognising his or her role as cultural mediator and striving to produce a target-language version that will enable the target-text readers to participate in text production in their own way, seeing connections and meaning instead of stumbling over culture bumps.

In this book translators and readers are not discussed only in the abstract: interviews with practising translators bring in the professional's point of view, while readers answer open-ended questions and occasionally offer spontaneous comments on particular examples. The review of potential translation strategies for allusions is complemented by a presentation of actual choices made by the translators interviewed, and by the responses of target-language readers to a selection of these examples. Examples are discussed from a functional viewpoint, providing insights into the significance of allusions in their contexts; otherwise typologies are kept to a minimum. The prospect of teachers wanting to discuss allusions in the language or translation classroom is also kept in mind throughout the book.

This book is a revised version of my doctoral dissertation (1994). It grew out of experiences in teaching translation at the Helsinki University English department. Over and over again I was struck by the difficulty my Finnish students tended to have with source-cultural allusions in British and American fiction and journalism. 'Getting it' was a problem for most, and finding a translation strategy that would convey the half-hidden meaning to target-language readers was inevitably the next problem. I decided to try to explore the function and meaning of allusions in source texts as well as a translator's strategies for coping with them. I soon discovered that the topic spread out in many different directions, requiring not just analyses of source and target texts and endless verification of sources, but also interviews with translators and above all some contact with potential receivers of target texts, as with the genres involved, translators would not be translating for themselves – in order to solve intellectual puzzles – but for Finnish general readers. As a result this book is neither a comparative study of source and target texts nor a purely descriptive study of translation strategies used. I thought it important not to lose sight of the needs of the end-users (the target-text readers) and of the novice translators in the classroom.

Acknowledgements

I would like to express my heartfelt thanks to those who, in an official or in-official capacity, guided me in my research process. They were, above all, Professor Matti Rissanen, Associate Professor Andrew Chesterman, Professor Susan Bassnett, Professor Sonja Tirkkonen-Condit, Associate Professor Krista Varantola and Associate Professor Jan-Ola Östman. Professor Wolfram Wilss, Professor Gideon Toury, and the late Professor André Lefevere also took a kind interest in my work and offered help and encouragement, for which I am greatly indebted to them.

With warm feelings I acknowledge the support of all my friends and colleagues at the Helsinki University English department, the Kouvola department of translation studies, and other university departments throughout Finland. I would like to thank especially those who, as native speakers of English, gave me access to their responses to allusions. I also wish to express my sincere thanks for their cooperation to the translators Elsa Carroll, Liisa Hakola, Erkki Jukarainen, Kalevi Nyytäjä, Eila Salminen and Anna-Laura Talvio 'Elone, who kindly agreed to be interviewed for this study.

I am grateful to all the general readers who took the time and trouble to answer my questionnaires. I would also like to thank the students who were helpful in collecting general reader responses. The keen interest taken by my students in all aspects of my research has been a continued source of encouragement and has afforded me a chance of getting early feedback on a number of points.

I thank the British Centre for Literary Translation for the bursary which enabled me to do research at the University of East Anglia in November 1989. Likewise, I wish to thank the Alfred Kordelin Foundation for awarding me a grant which allowed me to take a term off teaching in 1991.

I would also like to acknowledge the following who kindly granted permission to reproduce copyright material in this book: Victor Gollancz Ltd for extract from *Bitter Medicine*, by Sara Paretsky (1987); The Peters Fraser & Dunlop Group for extracts from *The Best Man to Die*, by Ruth Rendell (Hutchinson/Arrow, 1969) and from *Penny Post*, by Susan Moody (Macmillan, 1985); HUI Corporation and Gelfman Schneider Literary Agents, Inc. for extracts from *Bread*, by Evan Hunter (1974); Curtis Brown Ltd for extract from *The China Governess*, by M. Allingham (Chatto & Windus, 1963); Penguin UK for extract from *Looking for Rachel Wallace*, by Robert B. Parker (1980); A.P. Watt Ltd for extract from *Foreign Affairs*, by Alison Lurie (Michael Joseph/Sphere, 1985).

A very special thank you goes to my family, without whose support I literally could not have completed my work. I dedicate this book with love and gratitude to Matti, Tuulia and Ilkka.

Abbreviations

GRT	general reader test
KLA	test held at Kouvola department of translation studies
KP	key-phrase
NS	native speaker
PN	proper name
SAC	semi-allusive comparison
SL	source language
ST	source text
TL	target language
TSE	test of students of English
TT	target text

The following abbreviations refer to dictionaries and encyclopedias listed among the works cited:

CDE	Collins English Dictionary
CDQ	Concise Dictionary of Quotations
COD	Concise Oxford Dictionary of Current English
DMQ	Penguin Dictionary of Modern Quotations
ODP	Oxford Dictionary of English Proverbs
OED	Oxford English Dictionary
PCE	Penguin Concise Columbia Encyclopedia
PDP	Penguin Dictionary of Proverbs
PDQ	Penguin Dictionary of Quotations
Pocket Treasury	Reader's Digest Pocket Treasury of Great Quotations
TDQ	Bloomsbury Thematic Dictionary of Quotations

The books of the Bible are referred to by their standard abbreviations.

1 Introduction

Culture-oriented Translation Studies

Around 1980, a gradual shift of emphasis began to be perceived in translation studies.[1] The new approach was interdisciplinary and culturally oriented. It is true that perceptive representatives of the earlier, more linguistic orientation had recognised the relevance to translation studies not only of different subdivisions of linguistics but also of other disciplines; but still, among its early proponents, the new trend was felt to be a reaction against a too constricting view of translation studies, and the 'semantic terrorism – afterbabble' (Lefevere, 1981: 44) of linguistic jargon. Bassnett-McGuire (1980: 6) saw translation studies as 'bridging the gap between the vast area of stylistics, literary history, linguistics, semiotics and aesthetics'. Snell-Hornby (1988: 2–3) placed translation studies into a somewhat different field of disciplines, but she too emphasised the interdisciplinary approach:

> translation studies, as a culturally oriented subject, draws on a number of disciplines, including psychology... , ethnology... and philosophy... without being a subdivision of any of them. Similarly, it can and should utilise relevant concepts and methods developed from the study of language... without automatically becoming a branch of linguistics

and pleaded for dropping rigid polarisations. Ingo (1992) sees translation studies related at least to philosophy, philology, literary studies, linguistics, information theory, sociology, pragmatics and cultural studies. Toury even calls translation studies an 'interdiscipline' (Snell-Hornby, 1991: 19). Opinions like these seem to reflect a general move away from excessive compartmentalisation in the humanities, and a desire to bring together ideas, concepts and discoveries from various disciplines so that old and new problems might be seen in a different light, and work with them might be more fruitful. A similar interest in an integrated approach is revealed in the writings of a number of linguists and literary scholars who may be less

1

concerned with translation but eager to see work on language from a wider angle. '[A]ny attempt to make a statement about language, its composition or its usage, draws on many disciplines' (Smith, 1987: 11); similar feelings are evident in, for example, Sell (1991), Schogt (1988) and Hickey (1989). As a result, much of the work that is currently being done in translation studies foregrounds social and cultural aspects of translation, with the emphasis on texts in their 'macro-context' (Snell-Hornby, 1991: 15): instead of simply pondering the translatability of source texts, there is concern with the functioning of the target text in the target language and cultural context. Applied translation studies frequently focus on cross-cultural communication, drawing on discourse analysis and pragmatics (cf. Delisle, 1988: 78–79). A long list of articles by practising translators and critics shows that practitioners, too, share this interest in the intercultural aspects of translation. This may be partly because of the increased translation into major languages of literary works written in languages of limited diffusion, and partly because of a psychological and pragmatic interest in cross-cultural phenomena. There is clearly a practical need for this trend: the increasing internationalisation of our world means that communication across cultures needs to proceed as smoothly as possible, without too many hitches and breakdowns.

The new interdisciplinarity shows that 'both the translator and the translation theorist are... concerned with a world *between* disciplines, languages and cultures' (Snell-Hornby, 1988: 35; emphasis in the original), and with texts in their larger context, situational and cultural. This requires a new approach, not the rigid categorisation of the exact sciences, but one 'admitting blends and blurred edges' (p.36).

Culture-bound Translation Problems

Interest in intercultural translation problems arises from a recognition that culture-bound concepts, even where the two cultures involved are not too distant, can be more problematic for the translator than the semantic or syntactic difficulties of a text (Cordero, 1984: 473). Some researchers have focused on mainly extralinguistic phenomena, from natural (topography, flora and fauna, etc.) to man-made (social institutions, buildings, trademarks, etc.). (For a typology, see for instance Nedergaard-Larsen, 1993.) Extralinguistic problems are often expressed as lexical: is there a word in the target language (TL) for a given feature of the source-language (SL) world? Others see culture-bound translation problems as mainly intralinguistic and pragmatic (involving idioms, puns, wordplay or ways of, for instance, addressing a person, complimenting him or her, or apologising).

Quite often intralinguistic problems involve indirect or implicit messages or connotations, the question being how the meaning of the source text can be made accessible to TL receivers, if 'just translating it' turns out to be inadequate. The emphasis tends to be on how well a translation functions in the receiving language culture.[2] Increased international contacts mean that this second type of problem is not merely academic. A translator of economic or political texts no less than the literary translator can hardly avoid coming across implicit messages grounded in the source culture, and vital interests may be at stake if misunderstandings occur.

Culturally oriented translation studies, then, do not see the source text (ST) and the target text (TT) simply as samples of linguistic material. The texts occur in a given situation in a given culture in the world, and each has a specific function and an audience of its own. Instead of studying specimens of language under laboratory conditions as it were, the modern translation scholar – and the translator – thus approaches a text as if from a helicopter: seeing first the cultural context, then the situational context, and finally the text itself. My special topic in this book is the translation problem caused by small stretches of other texts embedded in the text at hand, which interact with and colour it, but may be meaningless or puzzling in translation. Some such embedded texts or 'in-texts' (Nord, 1991: 102) are known as allusions.

Allusions – Culture Bumps?

'Allusion', a term current in literary studies, is given a slightly extended meaning in this study. The term refers here to a variety of uses of preformed linguistic material (Meyer, 1968) in either its original or a modified form, and of proper names, to convey often implicit meaning:[3]

(a) key-phrase allusions:

to separate the wheat from the chaff

to pee or not to pee

hung round his neck like an albatross

(b) proper-name allusions:

I felt *like Benedict Arnold*

I do my *Rumpelstiltskin* dance

a *Gadarene* rush by high-street retailers

The viewpoint adopted here focuses less on allusions as a literary phenomenon and more on them as translation problems requiring problem-solving and the use of appropriate strategies. For the use of allusions presupposes a particular kind of receiver participation. The words of the allusion function as a clue to the meaning, but the meaning can usually be understood only if the receiver can connect the clue with an earlier use of the same or similar words in another source; or the use of a name evokes the referent and some characteristic feature linked to the name. Some allusions have developed into clichés or been lexicalised so that they are no longer necessarily popularly linked with their original sources; others presuppose familiarity with esoteric sources and are recognised by a small minority of receivers only.

Allusions require a high degree of biculturalisation of receivers in order to be understood across a cultural barrier. It has been accepted for some time that translators need to be not just bilingual but bicultural in order to fully understand the ST and to be able to transmit it to the target audience (for example Straight, 1981: 41; Reiss & Vermeer, 1984: 26). But what about the TT readers? Is it realistic to expect them to be bicultural also? Is the receiver participation which the use of allusions presupposes possible when texts are transferred from source language culture to target language culture? Or do allusions in fact become *culture bumps* when they occur in translated texts?

The term 'culture bump' has been used by Carol M. Archer (1986: 170–1) of problems in face-to-face intercultural communication which are milder than culture shocks: 'A culture bump occurs when an individual finds himself or herself in a different, strange, or uncomfortable situation when interacting with persons of a different culture'. I have extended the use of her term to translation, for a situation where the reader of a TT has a problem understanding a source-cultural allusion. Such an allusion may well fail to function in the TT, as it is not part of the TL reader's culture. Instead of conveying a coherent meaning to TT readers, the allusion may remain unclear and puzzling.

As Snell-Hornby (1988: 41) has pointed out, the translatability of a text depends on the extent to which the text is 'embedded in its own specific culture' and also on how far apart, with regard to time and place, the ST and TT receivers are. In this study, the distance is not particularly great: the STs are contemporary English-language texts and the target audience is Finnish – people exposed to at least certain aspects of Anglo-American culture throughout this century, increasingly so in recent decades. Culturally, then, there is little distance, though linguistically there is more, as Finnish is one of the few European languages which are not Indo-European in origin. The STs considered here represent genres which are often translated ('middle-brow' fiction and quality journalism), and reflect contemporary concerns in a variety of ways. Their potential Finnish readers share much of the Western tradition and have access to international mass media and popular culture, frequently in English. They will often know some English, or even know it well. This would all perhaps suggest that culture-specific translation problems might not play much of a role when such texts are translated for such an audience; but in fact, a consideration of the material on which this study is based will show that potential culture-bound problems are by no means uncommon in it. This will also be borne out by the empirical data in Chapters 5 and 6.

If translation is seen as a form of intercultural communication, both partners in the translation process – the translator who produces the TT and the receiver who reads it – deserve attention. After the overview of theoretical concerns in Chapter 2, the approach adopted in this study will be largely empirical. Problems of ST analysis are presented in Chapter 3 with examples taken from a corpus of approximately 700 English-language allusions[4] collected from 21 fictional and 200 non-fictional British and American text. A presentation of translation strategies for allusions considers both potential strategies and those actually adopted by Finnish translators; and we also hear from the professional translators who had the task of translating some of those texts for publication (Chapter 4). Reader responses indicating that some translated allusions were received as 'culture bumps' by Finnish respondents are reported in Chapter 5. Hence in this study reference is made not just to scholars' visualisations of readers, but also to real readers and their reactions when they meet allusions to various foreign, source-cultural matters in texts translated into their mother tongue.

Finally, Chapter 6 takes us to the classroom and discusses the failure of target-cultural students (in the role of novice translators) to spot and understand source-cultural allusions and their function and meaning in SL texts, and some pedagogical implications of this.

At this point it may need to be emphasised that allusions are not a rarity. On the contrary, they are common in both literary texts and journalism, perhaps particularly in English (Lass *et al.* 1987: vi), though there is, of course, variation in frequency between genres as well as authors. Allusions may not always be recognised as an actual translation problem by practising translators (cf. Chapter 4) but they are a recurrent and often significant feature of many types of text to be translated.

The Concept of Allusion

The etymology of the term 'allusion' shows a connection with the idea of play: *ad + ludere → alludere*. While not all use of allusion is playful, humour is clearly one of its functions. In the long rhetorical tradition allusion has had a place among such other tropes or figures of speech as allegory, hyperbole, metalepsis, irony etc. (Fontanier 1968: 498–9). Standard definitions in literary studies share the idea of 'reference to something':

> ALLUSION. Latin *alludere*, to play with, to jest, to refer to. A reference to characters and events of mythology, legends, history. (Scott, 1965)

> ALLUSION. Tacit reference to another literary work, to another art, to history, to contemporary figures, or the like. (Preminger, 1965)

> A reference, usually brief, often casual, occasionally indirect, to a person, event, or condition presumably familiar but sometimes obscure or unknown to the reader. (Shaw, 1976)

> a reference, explicit or indirect, to a person, place, or event, or to another literary work or passage (Abrams, 1984)

Such reference is made in order to compare A and B:

> An allusion is a figure of speech that compares aspects or qualities of counterparts in history, mythology, scripture, literature, popular or contemporary culture. (Lass *et al.*, 1987)

Allusion is not only a literary phenomenon, however; there are allusions in non-fictional writing, and also in music, painting, film etc. Thus a line of dialogue or the brief appearance of an actor in a film may allude to an earlier film, and audience recognition of this is expected. (See, for instance, Eco [1988] for examples.) More extended use of the term is made for example by Freud, who sees dreams as containing allusions to the dreamer's experiences when awake; and Lively (1992), who in a work of fiction, repeatedly speaks of the physical present-day London containing allusions to its earlier epochs (p.9, 88 etc.).

The definitions and uses cited show that the definers and users are willing to accept considerable latitude for the term. Indeed, the use of the term 'allusion' varies to a certain degree from scholar to scholar. Allusion is more or less closely related to such terms as reference, quotation or citation, borrowing (even occasionally plagiarism)[5] and the more complex intertextuality, as well as punning and wordplay (for modified allusions); but precisely in what relationship such terms stand to one another is seldom made clear. Definitions are mostly based on common intuition rather than a theoretical analysis (Ben-Porat, 1976: 105–6). Compilers of an extensive annotated allusion bibliography (Perri *et al.*, 1979) sometimes comment that in a particular work 'allusion' is used synonymously with 'quotation' (p.221), or that some scholars use the term 'generically' (p.215) or 'quite loosely' (p.213). They appear to have wished that there were less terminological vagueness. As against this, Wilss (1989: 13), in his study of approximately 2000 German allusions (mostly in journalistic texts), states that for allusions, intuition is more important than definitions.

The following may serve as a brief indication of the range of allusion studies in literary criticism and theory. It is a list of the descriptive adjectives premodifying the word '*allusion(s)*' which occur in the titles of and annotations to books and articles in Perri *et al.* (1979):

Aesopic, ambiguous, applied vs. organic, artistic, astronomical, Balzacian, biblical, biographical, Catholic, Christian, classical, comic, conspicuous, contemporary, cultural, current, Dantean, deliberate, direct vs. indirect, evaluative, evocative, exegetical, fictional vs. literal, functional, heroic, hidden, historic(al), Homeric, illusive, implicit vs. explicit, intertwined, involuntary, ironic, literary, liturgical, local, mathematical, medieval, metaphoric, modern, moral, musical, mythic, mythological, obscure, overt, parodic, Platonic, political, proverbial, pseudo-contemporary, satiric, scientific, scriptural, Shakespearean, significant, stylistic, tonal, topical, topical vs. textual, veiled, verbal, Virgilian, visual.

In her introductory remarks to the bibliography Perri affirms that the treatment of allusion in literary studies is amorphous (p.171); that statement is surely borne out by the quoted list, and if updated to the 1990s, the list would doubtless be even longer. In general terms it might be said that the trend in allusion studies has been from the annotative identification of sources towards an analysis of the thematic and structural aspects of allusion.

Among the purposes of literary allusion researchers have noted a desire to call attention to one's learning or wide reading (Preminger, 1965: 18); to enrich the work by bringing in new meanings and associations, 'a wealth of experience and knowledge beyond the limits of plain statement' (Shaw, 1976: 14); an attempt to characterise people, or suggest thoughts or unconscious impressions and attitudes in characters (Hall, 1971: 534–5); or to increase the significance of one's work by generalising or suggesting universality (Weisgerber, 1970: 39). The first of these is no longer thought of as an important reason for alluding in literature but may feature in interpersonal communication as one of the power games people play. (See Chapter 3 for a closer look at the functions of allusions.)

An important aspect in alluding is the capacity of literature 'to create new literature out of old' (Johnson, 1976: 579), that is, to involve the reader in a re-creation by hinting at half-hidden meanings which the reader is expected to recover and then use for a deeper understanding of the work. The increased interest of literary studies during the 1980s in reader reception and the role of the reader in general has made this a specially relevant point. Similarly, Wilss (1989) sees the function of an allusion generally as making a text more attractive (*zugkräftiger*): the conventional meaning and the new meaning provided by the allusion 'react chemically' (p.63; my translation) upon each other. He emphasises the intellectual joy of the receiver who perceives another unexpected instance of what can be done with language. On the macro-level, an entire text may play upon receivers' familiarity with another text: Stoppard's *Rosencrantz and Guildenstern Are Dead* is a different play altogether for those who know *Hamlet* and for those who do not.

Discussions on intertextuality (the term was coined by Kristeva in 1969; to attempt even to summarise the literature on this wide topic is beyond the scope of my book) have emphasised that it is a more complex phenomenon than mere borrowing of words from earlier texts. What is important is the function of the insertion in the new text and a recognition that all texts owe something to other texts which colour and may even transform them. For a non-literary (semiotic) discussion of intertextuality see Hatim and Mason (1990: 120–37), for whom intertextuality is a 'signifying system which operates by connotation' and extends the boundaries of textual meaning (p.129).

From a communicative point of view, the use of allusion is linked to such linguistic and pragmatic phenomena as implicature (Grice, 1975), inference and relevance. If communication is seen primarily as an inferential process, an allusion can be thought of as a message or stimulus which the communicator sends, and it is up to the receiver to find the intended referent – to fill in the gaps in the text (Gutt, 1990: 139–41, speaking of inferencing with no specific mention of allusion). A 'shared cognitive environment' (p.145) is needed for this to work, so that if the receivers are grounded in another culture, they may well be unable to draw the intended inference.

Hatim and Mason (1990) in their semiotic approach distinguish between active (strong) and passive (weak) intertextuality; the former 'activates knowledge and belief systems well beyond the text itself' (p.124), involving experience of other 'texts' (in a wide sense); while the latter, using the device of co-reference (synonymy, substitution etc.), simply ensures the internal coherence, intelligibility, of a text. Weisgerber (1970) speaks of the use of borrowed material, which may be seen to include the use of borrowed words on the one hand, and the use of 'patterns, situations, plots, or characters' on the other (p.37). This study sees the former of both divisions worth more attention from the translation point of view; and therefore focuses on allusion (to other texts) expressed through borrowed, or, as I prefer to say, preformed material. Use of preformed linguistic material includes many other types of borrowing than literal quotations, as the borrowing of words in allusion need by no means be literal: allusions are often modified, twisted out of their original wording.

An evoked[6] 'text' does not necessarily mean a written text: television soundbites and advertising slogans are typical oral texts that often give rise to modified allusions; and with proper names, the concept of text may need to be widened further, to include names of real-life or fictional characters and features associated with such names.[7] I also share Ben-Porat's (1976: 110) view that even an idiom or a collocation can be alluded to.

Granted, not all instances of borrowed words in English are true allusions where echoes of the evoked context are assumed to colour the new context for the receiver.

Ben-Porat's (1976: 113–16) examples of two 'transformations' of the same line of Marlowe illustrate the difference between allusions that activate the evoked text and hence enrich the interpretation of the alluding text, and those that do not:

This is the nose *that launched a thousand* battles

This is the smell *that launched a thousand* barbecues

Both examples allude to Marlowe's line *Is this the face that launched a thousand ships?*, and in both, the modifications are similar (a change from interrogative to declarative, and the replacement of the same two nouns by others). In the context, however, the first allusion, which occurred in a British cinematic version of Edmond Rostand's *Cyrano de Bergerac*, will, if its source is recognised by the receiver, actualise Marlowe's *Dr Faustus* and therefore allow for a rich interpretation involving both mock-heroism and tragedy. Contrast the second allusion, in a cheese advertisement, which is not meant to activate the evoked text but simply to suggest that those who recognise the referent should buy the advertised product 'because it is a special product for special (intelligent) people' (p.116). Ben-Porat (1976: 115–6) believes that there is a tacit agreement between sender and receiver in journalism and advertising to discourage further interpretation, which might even, as in this instance, have a 'grotesque' effect.

Limiting this study to the sophisticated interplay of evoked and al-luding texts in literary allusion would, however, bypass the problems caused for translators also by the less evocative examples common in many genres. A decision to focus on literary allusion alone might make the results of this study less useful for translators as both allusions in general and liter-ary allusions cause translation problems.

This study, then, will consider various types of allusions found in fiction and journalism. Typologies will largely be bypassed,[8] as I tend to agree with Pasco (1973: 467) that classifications of allusions are inadvisable: they may foreground what is external rather than the importance of the context for each allusion.

Special terminology will be limited to the following:

(I)   Allusions proper:

(A) Proper-name (PN) allusions = allusions containing a proper name:

Think I've become a *Raffles* in my old age?

(B) Key-phrase (KP) allusions = allusions containing no proper name:

Apparently taxis all *turn into pumpkins at midnight*.

Both of these classes are further divided into:

(a) Regular allusions = an unmarked category of 'prototypical' allusions:

Someone's got to stand up and say *that the emperor has no clothes*.

(b) Modified allusions = allusions containing a 'twist', that is, an al-teration or modification of preformed material:

Where have all the old Hillman Imps *gone? In the* scrap yards, *every one*.

(II) Stereotyped allusions = allusions in frequent use that have lost their freshness and do not necessarily evoke their sources; also clichés and proverbs:[9]

We were *ships that pass in the night*.

By analogy with metaphors, one is tempted to speak of dead or dying al-lusions, but there is naturally no clear 'time of death', no distinct boundary between live and dead allusions. Instead, there are various degrees of life and death as noted, too, by scholars on metaphor translation. Note that phrases commonly used in a stereotyped way are occasionally 'reani-mated', becoming allusions proper.

Little attention will be paid later to examples of a more marginal character:

(III) (A) Semi-allusive comparisons (SACs) = superficial comparisons or looser associations :

> *Like the land of Oz,* technology has good and bad witches.

(B) Eponymous adjectives (adjectives derived from names) which do not form fixed collocations with their current headwords:

> *Orwellian* images; in her most *Jamesian* manner

Excluded are eponyms in fixed collocations (*a pyrrhic victory, draconian measures, a Pavlovian response*); other lexicalised eponyms, which have become lexical items in their own right: for example *an odyssey* 'a long, (potentially hazardous) journey', *a Casanova* 'any man noted for his amorous adventures; a rake' (CDE); and institutionalised allusions – Newmark's (1988: 201) 'familiar alternatives' (*the Emerald Isle* = Ireland; *the War to End All Wars* = First World War).

The sources of the allusions in Chapter 1

to separate the wheat from the chaff: 'He will ... gather his wheat into the garner; but he will burn up the chaff with unquenchable fire.' (Matt. 3: 12)

to pee or not to pee: a modification of *to be or not to be (Hamlet). (Glamour,* 1995)

hung round his neck like an albatross: 'the Albatross / about my neck was hung' (S.T. Coleridge, 'The Rime of the Ancient Mariner')

Benedict Arnold: 1741–1801, American Revolutionary general and traitor.

Rumpelstiltskin: a character in one of Grimm's *Tales.*

Gadarene (swine): Matt. 8: 28–34.

Rosencrantz and Guildenstern: minor characters in *Hamlet.*

Is this the face that launched a thousand ships? Asked by Dr Faustus (regarding Helen of Troy) in Marlowe's play of the same name.

Raffles: the hero of Ernest William Hornung's novel *The Amateur Cracksman.*

turn into pumpkins at midnight: this happened to Cinderella's carriage in the fairytale.

the emperor has no clothes: H.C. Andersen, *The Emperor's New Clothes.*

Where have all the [soldiers] gone? In the graveyards, everyone: Pete Seeger's song 'Where Have All the Flowers Gone?'

ships that pass in the night: H.W. Longfellow, 'Tales of a Wayside Inn'.

the land of Oz: L. Frank Baum, *The Wizard of Oz.*

Orwellian: George Orwell.

Jamesian: Henry James.

Notes

1. The term 'translation studies' (Holmes, 1972) is used as a neutral term for the discipline throughout this study, without implying adherence to any particular school of thought. See Lambert (1991: 26–30) for a critical look at the term and its alternatives.
2. The term 'language culture' is used by Hewson and Martin (1991) to emphasise that language and culture are indissoluble.
3. The sources (referents) of the allusions used as examples are given at the end of Chapters 1–4 before the Notes, in the order in which they occur in each chapter, unless the information is given in the text itself.
4. As well as c.160 more marginal examples, of types (III) (A) and (B) (see later).
5. Bradbury (1988: 52) more or less playfully has a character comment, in reference to a charge of plagiarism: 'Alas that no one had whispered in that noble ear the simple word "intertextuality".'
6. The terms 'alluding text' and 'evoked text' are suggested by Ben-Porat (1976).
7. If an idea is called 'about as likely as *Boy George joining the SAS*' (Moody, 1985: 131), receivers need to recognize the name as that of a singer and to know that, at the time the alluding text was written, he presented an exaggeratedly feminised appearance, at odds with the image of professional soldiers in the Special Air Service.
8. Typologies of various sorts have been constructed both by literary scholars (for example Fontanier, 1968, Morier, 1961) and by linguisticians (for example Ditt-gen, 1989 on wordplay). Wilss (1989: 18) found, while considering his large corpus, that the immense variety of allusions means that it is not possible to construct an abstract ideal typology.
9. The inclusion of stereotyped allusions can be justified on the grounds that a translator who is unaware of the allusive origin of such a phrase might be puzzled or even misled by the seemingly inexplicable meaning of one of its component parts (such as the adjective *fell* in *at one fell swoop*) in the alluding context.

2 Translational Issues

Translation as Communication

The purpose of this chapter is to outline the development of ideas for this study, to acknowledge debts and to clarify the positions taken on certain relevant issues. It builds on the brief introductory remarks in Chapter 1.

Approaches to translation

Hewson and Martin (1991: 34–8) in their somewhat abstract review of theories of translation compress existing translation theories into two approaches, the universalist and the relativist. The former is based on an ideal of 'contractual transaction' (p.34, emphasis deleted), where signification is transferred through equivalents, and some degree of universality is assumed (that is, there are thought to be universal ideas that can be expressed in a number of different languages). The question is how to achieve an optimal realisation of meaning (van den Broeck, 1992: 115). The latter approach sees signification as non-universal and non-transferrable, and translation as 'production within an interactive structure' (Hewson & Martin, 1991: 37, emphases deleted). For the latter, '[s]ignification is always potentially plural. There is no original meaning, but rather an interplay... of original meanings' (Benjamin, 1989: 44). This second approach is more receiver- and target-text oriented: instead of fidelity to the ST, the translator is urged to see the implications of an audience of individuals with different, individual interpretations, and to acknowledge that his/her translation is but one such interpretation. The relativist approach is to some degree in sympathy with such contemporary trends as deconstructionism in literary criticism.

This book is based on the idea of translation as communication, not just involving the communication of messages across a cultural-linguistic border but including the subsequent functioning of the translated text as communication within the target cultural-linguistic context (Toury 1980: 15–16). This implies a more TT- than ST- oriented approach, but I would

13

nevertheless like to preserve a balanced position between the two. Radical attempts to totally devalue the ST have come in for (in my view) justified criticism, for example Wilss (1990: 23–4) speaks strongly against the opinion that the ST has no intrinsic value of its own; but then many of the controversial issues in translation studies are perhaps controversial mainly because of a desire of some scholars to generalise overmuch, to state general principles as if they applied across the board, instead of accepting that translation occurs in widely different situations and that what may be valid in some situations may well not apply to others.

The ST or TT orientation of approaches and translations (cf. Newmark, 1988: 45–8 on semantic and communicative translation) is closely related to the function of the TT. Is it, for instance, intended to reveal a 'sacred' text, for example a religious or philosophical text of another culture, to a group of TL readers willing to make the effort of processing unfamiliar information, in which case ST orientation is appropriate? Or is it meant to convey practical information on how to operate a household appliance – in which case TL culture norms on instructions written for such a purpose should be observed, and the translation needs to be TT oriented? Even when the functions of ST and TT are nearly the same, for instance in the case of crime fiction published to provide general readers with a few hours' relaxation or escape from work and family concerns, TT readers differ from ST readers in that they live in another language culture.

Gutt (1990: 144) notes the interdependence of the meaning ('explicatures and implicatures') of a text with the cognitive environment in which the communication is processed. A translation may share most, or only a few, of the explicatures and implicatures of the original text, not all of them, as the communication situation is always different for ST receivers and TT receivers. To summarise Gutt (1990: 157):

> What the translator has to do in order to communicate successfully is to arrive at the intended interpretation of the original, and then determine in what respects his translation should interpretively resemble the original in order to be consistent with the principle of relevance for his target audience with its particular cognitive environment. Nothing else is needed.

Gutt's comment that it is a mistake to think that the total meaning of the ST can be communicated to *any* target audience, no matter how different the cognitive environment, is particularly relevant for the translation of allusions. The translator has to select: communication 'crucially involves determining what one *can* communicate to a particular audience, given their particular background knowledge' (p.146; emphasis in the original).

(See also the section on receivers later in this chapter.)

Delisle sees translation as a re-expression of concepts or ideas. He urges that the contextual and referential parameters of a text should be examined as a necessary step towards interpretation, as the meaning of a text does not simply equal the sum of the significations of its words. For two excellent brief illustrations of this, consider Hewson and Martin's (1991) comments on the texts *Cette semaine on tue le cochon*[1] (pp.114–121) and *We just can't say cheese*[2] (pp.105–110), where, obviously, word-for-word translations would lead to TTs that would be impenetrable for readers in other cultures. A message has its language component but it has many non-linguistic components as well, such as being linked to a time and place and requiring a certain degree of extralinguistic knowledge, usually intuitively accessed by ST receivers. Comprehension thus requires a close intra- and interlinguistic analysis as a prerequisite for interlingual operations. This analysis is the responsibility of the translator.

Senders and receivers

Any communicative situation presumes a sender and receivers.[3] Nord (1991: 42–47) makes a distinction between sender and text producer. These roles are often fused (typically with signed texts), but can be differentiated, for example, when the text is an advertisement, sent by a company and produced by a copywriter. Translation complicates the communicative situation in that the translator, a receiver of the ST, becomes the text producer of the TT – not its sender, though, for as Nord points out, the 'instructions' of the sender/author limit the translator's free choice of textual strategies, at least under certain circumstances. Translations of European Union (EU) administrative prose met with violent criticism in Finland in the mid-1990s because the EU's instructions were objected to among those concerned with the development of the Finnish language. The EU is thought to have made it clear that the syntax of the English or French EU regulations and directives had to be retained; this led to TTs that departed in obvious ways from the norms of comparable Finnish texts.[4] Concerns were expressed that the clumsy and unnatural syntax used in EU translations would eventually be harmful to Nordic conceptions of democracy and equality (Kallio, 1993: 11, Karvonen, 1995: 3) and increase the distance between administrators and citizens (Ylikangas & Koivusalo 1994: 2). It was felt that the situation threatened the rights of citizens as well as downgraded the professional skills of translators: 'Translators have been blindfolded and gagged before being set to work' (Lyytikäinen 1995: 130, my translation).

A distinction can further be made between primary or ST receivers and secondary or TT receivers. For the sender/author, ST readers are doubtless the primary target group in mind during the writing process, and the eventuality of a TT readership is a secondary consideration. Even the possibility of a section of primary readers belonging to another language culture than the majority may not often be taken into account by senders even though Western societies are becoming increasingly multicultural. One example of belated recognition of such cultural variety in readers (of untranslated texts) occurs in an article (Maddox, 1992) in the scientific journal *Nature*, commenting on a recent experience of communicative failure in that journal. The playful caption *Prides and prejudice* on the front cover referring to a story on lions had led a Japanese reader of the journal to inquire what the significance of the caption might be. Granting that the caption might perhaps have meant very little to some British readers as well,[5] Maddox concluded that for a journal 'whose readers include perhaps 40 per cent for whom English is not their first language, allusive writing is a disservice and should usually be avoided'. Such considerations may turn into economic ones as well when an international journal is attempting to increase its attraction for audiences in non-British language cultures.

Differences in cognitive environment thus lead to communicative problems. One attempt at an explanation of how this happens is the channel model in Nida and Taber (1969). In this model, a message is 'designed to fit the channel capacity' of its receivers (p.164). An intralingual message is assumed to pass through the channel without trouble – though a critic might observe that there are also intralingual misunderstandings, not to mention the pluralities of meaning referred to earlier. In interlingual communication, according to the model, the message cannot always pass through because the channel capacity of the receivers is too narrow and the message has not been adjusted accordingly. If it is so adjusted (by reformulation), the message can again flow through smoothly enough. Di Jin (1989), who has worked with Nida, grants that this model is simplistic; he argues, however, that the receiver's channel capacity is 'conditioned by his own language and cultural background' and that the content must necessarily change to some degree – 'will never remain identical' – through the translation process (p.157). The extent of the adjustments has always been a practical problem, with some scholars demanding 'fidelity', that is, 'faithfully' rendering '*all* the relevant features of the source text' (Nord, 1991: 22; emphasis added). It is, nevertheless, hardly possible to follow such instructions to the letter. There is usually a need to establish a hierarchy of features/messages in the text, reflecting the hierarchy of the values the translator wishes to preserve, which in turn is based on a translationally relevant text analysis (Koller, 1989: 104). These features are then included in the translation by working from the top down, that is, starting with those that have been deemed the most important.[6] At some point or other it is usually recognised that all the features cannot be included in the translation. The importance of individual items in the text should be 'decided by their relevance in the larger context of text, situation and culture' (Snell-Hornby, 1988: 36).

This is brought out clearly in Holmes (1988), where various translations of a 15th century French poem are examined to see to what extent they are either retentive (retaining aspects of the ST) or re-creative (seeking 'equivalents'). Aspects or features under study in the article include lexical items, metre and sociocultural imagery. (Others could be added.) Only one of the translations, a historicising one written in mock Middle English, is retentive with regard to most of these, and even that one has substituted a TL verse pattern for the French one, and chosen partially to ignore the rhyme scheme.

I do not want to go further into the age-old argument between proponents of faithful and free translation, but I am in sympathy with Nord's ethical and moral concept of the translator's loyalty, to both ST sender and TT receiver (Nord, 1991: 28–29). Indeed, it may be claimed that 'loyalty to the author is meaningless if it does not coexist with a loyalty to the receptors' (Di Jin, 1989: 163). Chesterman's (1993: 8) accountability norm adds the commissioner (that is, the person on whose initiative the translator carries out a translating task) to the list of those to whom a translator must be loyal.

An alternative to adjusting the message to fit the channel capacity of TL receivers is the widening of their channel through exposure to SL culture and through education in general. It is an approach that has been used and is doubtless still being used under certain circumstances: for instance Hrala (1989: 30) speaks of the important role played by translated literature 'as a means of democratisation of education' in the early days of the Czech national revival (the late 18th and the early 19th century), and similar trends could be observed in Finland about half a century later (cf. Chapter 5). Historians of translation have also noted changes in familiarity with distant cultures over relatively short periods of time. For instance Bödeker (1991) notes that the increasing familiarity with American society and culture in Germany during the 20th century is reflected in translations of Jack London dating from different decades. Mass media play an important role in this in a world where the smallest village in Papua New Guinea is not without a TV set to enable villagers to watch *Dallas* (Kulick, 1992: 145). The aim of enriching the TL by translation from languages considered superior models is a common stage of historical development – English went through this stage in the 16th and 17th centuries. Blake (1992) links this development with the status of the translator: it is high as long as the TL is thought to be in need of such enrichment and expansion, and falls when this is no longer the case.

The Translator as Competent Reader and Responsible Text Producer

The role of the translator needs special emphasis in a problem-restricted study of translation because whatever translation scholars may write, it is ultimately the translator who must decide how to solve each individual problem occurring in the process of translating a text. Without a translator, there would be no translation.[7]

The extent of the emphasis on the translator in the literature is dependent on the nature of each scholar's general approach to translation. If translation is seen mostly as transcoding, there is little interest in the translator, whose work is seen as semi-automatic: Sorvali (1990: 145) has noted that there is practically no mention of the translator in Catford (1965). Hewson and Martin (1991: 116) make the more general statement that in theories, the translator 'simply disappears'. Strongly ST oriented views of translation tend to imply that whatever the translator does, s/he can never hope to produce anything quite as good as the ST. The translator's autonomy is questioned by those who think of him/her as a monkey, 'with no choice save to make the same grimaces as his master' (Briere 1988: 36, citing Coindreau, 1974: 22).

Others take issue with what they see as the traditional role assigned to the translator, describing it in terms of humility and invisibility, as hiding behind the ST. Venuti (1995a: 1–17) sees translators as culturally marginalised and economically exploited and underpaid. Their work is seldom given due recognition, eclipsed as it is – even to some extent in law – by a conception of the author's text as original and authentic, and the translator's as a mere copy: 'derivative, fake' (p.7). After all, it is undeniable that the author's text owes its very existence in the TL to the translator and the translation. Recognition of this has led to radical reappraisals of the translator's role (from various perspectives, such as the feminist one) and critiques of the cultural assumptions that restrict his/her autonomy in decision-making.

The vast need for translation in today's world has made it easier to see the translator in a social context, responding to a social need as someone particularly qualified to deal with language and communication. The frequently cited work of Holz-Mänttäri (1984) has emphasised the role of the translator as a qualified professional.

Basically, the translation process consists of three stages where the translator is the operator. They are: (1) analysis of the ST and of the translation task in question; (2) problem-solving (on various levels); and (3) reverbalisation. What actually happens in the translation process is a central area of research which can and will fruitfully be further explored both by translation scholars and researchers in other disciplines (including neurophysiology) as well as by translators themselves who set down their reflections. The translator–scholar James S. Holmes (1988) is a pre-eminent example of both; as regards the practitioner, there have been several volumes representing the craftsman approach (for instance Arrowsmith & Shattuck, 1971). Professional journals, too, afford examples of insights shared in this way. Bassnett (1991: xiii–xvi) remarks that translators' prefaces and other statements on their work reflect the views on translation held by their communities, and offers some intriguing examples of how metaphors for translation have changed in the course of time.

Lörscher (1991), however, has questioned whether translators can really describe what has become to them an automatised process. Empirical research into the aspect referred to as 'what goes on in the heads of translators' (Krings 1986) uses the think-aloud protocol method combined with observation of translators at work and performance analysis (for example Lörscher, 1991), and it has, for instance, found differences in the way professional and non-professional translators operate (Jääskeläinen & Tirkkonen-Condit, 1991; see also Fraser, 1996).

Instead of trying to illuminate the nature of the translation process itself, this study focuses on problem-solving and decision-making with regard to the intercultural problem of translating allusions. The translator is seen in an active role as a cultural mediator[8] and decision-maker. S/he is thought to be an independent and competent professional, a language and communication expert serving both author and reader, who are equally in need of his/her special skills. The notion of serving does not imply a subservient role.

The keywords in my conception of the translator as cultural mediator and decision-maker are 'competent' and 'responsible'. These roles are of crucial importance in the translation of allusions. A writer (mostly) writes for people who share a certain amount of cultural background information with him/her. It is therefore not necessary, and would in fact be counter-productive, to make all such information explicit in the text – consider newspaper commentaries on topical issues, and how they take it for granted that readers already possess a considerable amount of background knowledge. TT readers, however, have a different cognitive environment from ST readers, which means that the translator will need to consider also the implicit part of the message – the contextual and referential part – and to decide whether it needs to be explicated in the TT. All meaning is, after all, culturally conditioned (Larson, 1984: 441).

In the translation process, as we have seen, the translator functions both as receiver and interpreter of the ST and producer of the TT. His/her 'job description', the list of skills needed to carry out these functions in a competent and responsible manner,⁹ might take the following form:

In order to be a competent ST reader (one of a large number of such readers), the translator needs not only language skills to comprehend the linguistic part of the message, but also extralinguistic knowledge of the source language culture. In other words (with regard to allusions), s/he needs to be sensitive to what is implied by the use of sociocultural and intertextual elements. However, hypersensitivity to this aspect may be detrimental to interpretation – witness Delisle's (1988: 58) example and his comment on overtranslation caused by seeing allusions where none exists, or at least where allusive interpretation obscures the main message. A holistic approach combined with intelligence and reading experience is required in order that the translator may arrive at an interpretation that is based on a consideration of a maximum number of clues given, not just those that are explicit.¹⁰ The translation, in turn, is based on that interpretation.

The translator's communicative competence includes both intercultural awareness and strategic or problem-solving competence (Wilss, 1990: 26). The first is needed for anticipating TT reader responses. Translators, as experts in intercultural communication, would need to be aware of TT readers' needs and to take into account the expectations and background knowledge of potential TT readers in order to make decisions on appropriate translation strategies. (Sadly, in practice there is often not enough data to allow this.) Knowing the source and target languages and cultures is not enough, the translator must also work out the correspondences and equivalences between them (Straight, 1981: 41). A metacultural capacity helps to analyse similarities and differences between cultures. In fact, what is required is a kind of contrastive cultural analysis, however intuitive. Strategic competence enables a translator to make appropriate decisions on which strategy to adopt with regard to a particular problem. Associative skills and creativity will also be needed by the translator as competent producer of the TT.[11]

In view of all this, it is not surprising that the Finnish term for a translator, especially one working in administration or industry, *kielenkääntäjä* ('translator', literally 'turner of language'), should occasionally have come under some criticism. The term foregrounds linguistic skills, bypassing cultural and metacultural competence, and even suggests that the 'turning' is a fairly automatic process.[12]

My view of responsibility, the second keyword, is in agreement with Chesterman's (1993) ethical norm of accountability, which requires that a translator should follow 'professional standards of integrity and thoroughness' (p.8) and accept responsibility for his/her translation. To me, this behaviour is motivated by respect for both the ST and its author and the TT and its readers, and leads to a willingness to take trouble (both as reader/interpreter and as text producer) in order to serve them well.

The Invisible Target Text Audience

We cannot proceed without having a quick look at the remaining participant in (almost) any translation event: the TT audience. In the communicative process, the role of the receiver is equally necessary as that of the sender. But while the TT reader's communicative importance is generally granted in theory, in practice his/her role is nebulous. In subject indexes to a number of translation studies, receivers either do not occur,[13] or reference is to one page only, where perhaps a schematic representation of the translation process is given.

As regards the actual production of translations, too, the neglect of readers' requirements and expectations has been called one of 'the most glaring defects of many translations' (Dejean Le Féal, 1987: 210). The ethically laudable fidelity to the ST may inadvertently lead to a disregard of the expectations, and one may be tempted to say, the rights of the TT readership.

In literary studies there has been a 'return of the reader'(cf. Freund, 1987), which sees the reader (even the reader of translations) not just as a passive receiver of instruction and education but as a participator, a co-author almost, or even the 'real author' (Genette, 1980: 262) without whose interpretation a text does not exist. Linked with the communicative model of translation, this has led to more receiver-oriented translation studies, where the ST is not thought superordinate, nor TTs only pale imitations, necessarily poorer than the original. Rather, the ST is seen as a communication which also needs to reach its secondary addressees, the readers of the TT, whose sociocultural situation is different.

An alluding author (as we saw with *Prides and prejudice*) is unlikely to consider TT readers in the course of the literary process, but will allude mostly to what s/he assumes are well-known texts (de Beaugrande & Dressler, 1988: 186), with native-speaker (NS) readers in mind. Yet it is clear that TT readers, who have grown up in a different culture, will often be quite unable to recognise the names or phrases used and to make the necessary connections in order to make sense of TT passages in which source-cultural allusions occur. Allusive names and phrases may carry meaning which is instantly perceived by members of the source culture[14] but which may convey nothing to TT readers in whose culture allusions are provided by different texts altogether.[15]

It may be helpful to distinguish between different levels of understanding at this point. Enkvist (1991: 7–8) explains that a message is 'intelligible' if it is understood on the phonological, lexical and syntactic level; 'comprehensible' on the semantic level; and 'interpretable' on the pragmatic level. An extract like the following:

There was a lot more dust in here. Plus cobwebs and woodworm. Penny looked round. 'Who's your decorator?' she said. '*Miss Havisham*?' (Moody, 1985: 129)

is both intelligible and comprehensible[16] to anyone with a basic command of English, but interpretable only if the receiver can recognise elements in the description which link with the name of a character in Dickens, and amount to a witty comment on the state of the room.

According to Enkvist (1991: 1), readers will generally try their utmost to make sense even of inexplicable messages: 'human beings are programmed to look for information, even desperately, in anything they suspect might be a message'. This leads directly to the question of receiver participation raised earlier. It is a crucial point that in an intercultural situation (translation), the needed receiver recognition of connotative and contextual meaning is necessarily often lacking. This in turn means that readers will search for meaning without the ability to recognise the clues. An informed reader of the sentence:

Unlike Sairey Gamp, this nurse did not tipple gin (Peters, 1977: 190)

is expected to react by making the connection to the drunken midwife in Dickens's *Martin Chuzzlewit*. A less well-informed ST reader, but also most readers of the TT, if the text is translated, will be unable to make this connection, and are likely to shrug off the reference as puzzling or irrelevant.

It may be thought by some that such losses are negligible. I would argue, however, that texts (of the type and function considered in this study) tend to be impoverished if allusions are neglected. It is unlikely that writers (of the genres considered in this study) wish to send inexplicable messages. They may choose to 'keep some readers out, let others in' (Weldon, 1985: 131), but they are also likely to feel that 'writing must be in some way a shared experience between reader and writer' (p.97). The conception of a reasonably well-informed or competent readership who are to be 'let in' to share the experience may well fail to apply in an intercultural situation, with secondary receivers. A monocultural TL reader, who cannot be familiar with the same source-cultural background knowledge as SL readers, will at times need the intervention of a competent and responsible translator.

   While acknowledging that there is a multiplicity of possible individual interpretations for texts, I nevertheless believe that with the particular problem of allusions in the genres of the STs considered here, experienced and competent ST readers will tend to arrive at some kind of consensus meaning. We accept that a poetic metaphor, for example a winter land-scape, may signify sickness or death to one reader, the loss of the creative vision to another, war to a third, despair to a fourth, etc. (Nikula, 1991). With allusions, however, there is a more collective and culture-specific type of understanding. In this sense, a reference in an English text to a capi-talised *White Rabbit* is an allusion to Carroll's *Alice*; it can doubtless be assumed to have been intended as such by the ST author and received as such by the collective ST audience, even though individual ST readers can be found who do not make the connection, either because of lack of general reading experience or because they happened not to meet *Alice* in print or as a film or TV version in their formative years. Such an allusion has a more or less definable, culture-specific meaning in the English-speaking world, but not necessarily in other cultures. The translator, in his/her role as cul-tural mediator, needs the necessary degree of biculturalism to recognise such meanings, and the awareness to see with which allusions and in which contexts the choice of translation strategy will need special atten-tion, either because of the importance of the allusion in the context, or because of the difference in cognitive environments.

   In his concern for loyalty to readers, Di Jin (1989) warns against the dan-ger of opaque translation, that is, the inclination not to consider the average reader's 'channel capacity' when translation decisions are made. The con-cept of 'average reader' is of course extremely vague, and the use of the singular form 'reader' in many translation studies may misleadingly sug-gest a generic uniformity among readers. For a translator, the problem is that in the absence of feedback from readers, s/he can only make

assumptions regarding the communicative background of readers and
their likely reactions to various features of the text, neither overstretching
nor understretching (Nord, 1991: 53) their capacity. Often such assumptions are little more than guesswork. Studies of reader response (for
instance Jauss, 1982) have foregrounded the importance of reader expectations, but for these to be taken into account in translation, much work re-
mains to be done not only on differences between the expectations and
cognitive environment of ST and TT audiences, but also on subgroups
within them. The admittedly modest attempts at measuring the responses
of actual readers in this study (Chapter 5) must be read against this background, that is, as small steps towards a still elusive but potentially useful
goal.

The Concept of Translation Strategy

The work of the competent and responsible translator involves the application of translation strategies to translation problems. Before we can
examine translators at work and discuss translation strategies for allusions,
the concept of translation strategy itself may need some clarification.

Problem-solving translating

Wilss (1983: 145) calls translation strategy a 'rather diffuse concept'; he
deals with it quite briefly, seeing the term as referring to 'the general transfer perspective or transfer concept for a particular text' like Cicero's
oratorically oriented strategy. Lörscher (1991: 67–81) examines the notion
of strategy from its military origins onwards, notes that it is often used
without precise definition in many different senses, and distinguishes it
from such related notions as method, plan, rule and tactics, defining it as 'a
potentially conscious procedure for the solution of a problem which an individual is faced with when translating a text segment from one language
to another' (p.76). His analysis of the constituents of the concept clarifies
that in non-technical use, strategy implies (1) procedures carried out by an
individual (as opposed to supra-individual methods);[17] (2) planning; (3)
goals; and (4) a sequence of actions for reaching a goal. His focus being on
translation as a mental process, Lörscher uses the term 'translation strategy' descriptively, to indicate what considerations a translator 'does in fact
make' (p.72) while translating.

If we try to visualise a translator at work, we can perhaps see his/her use
of strategies a little more clearly as follows: A translation problem occurs
and is identified as a problem ('What do I do about this?'). There is a need
and a wish to solve the problem. There is a goal: a translation which works.

To specify the goal and to make a plan, the translator has to consider a number of extra- and intratextual factors and make a number of decisions on both macro- and micro-levels. ('Who wrote this and why?' 'Who is addressed?' 'What is the function of the TT?' 'Why did the author put these words here?' 'What does this mean in its situational and textual context?' etc.) (See Nord [1991] for a comprehensive account of translation-oriented text analysis.) Next the translator considers different ways of solving the problem. S/he may either consider strategies in abstract terms (asking him/herself for instance: 'Literal translation? Replacement by target cultural material? Footnote?') or try out different possible solutions for the problem at hand. S/he then makes a decision: determines on a strategy and evaluates the result, trying to see whether or not the goal has been reached. Later, the result may perhaps be evaluated by a publisher's reader, an editor, a teacher – or general readers of the TT.

The translator may not always be conscious of using strategies.[18] Lörscher (1991) makes a distinction between strategic or problem-solving translating, and non-strategic translating, aiming at 'accomplishing tasks' (p.119). I hesitate, however, to accept this idea of non-strategic (phases of) translation. I would prefer to see the smooth, no-problem translating of professionals as a process where the use of strategies has been automatised to such an extent that there is less frequent need to stop to think consciously about problem-solving; also, due to the automatisation, the translator may not find it easy to comment on what happens during the process. A non-professional translator, on the other hand, may be unaware of what s/he is doing for other reasons. S/he may have a very limited number of strategies at his/her (individual) disposal, or may make use of a limited number of them only. This is seen often enough in the work of inexperienced translators in the classroom. Such a translator may, for instance, make a minimum change on purely linguistic considerations, making the obligatory linguistic changes[19] but not considering for example contextual aspects.

A particular strategy, then, can be chosen either consciously, with the translator carrying out a series of operations judging various linguistic, contextual and cultural factors, or intuitively; the latter alternative again may either represent a blueprint developed by an experienced translator for use in a certain type of situation, or result from an inexperienced translator's lack of alternatives. Reasons for adopting a particular strategy also vary. A translator may, for example, choose omission responsibly, after rejecting all alternative strategies, or irresponsibly, to save him/herself the trouble of looking up something s/he does not know. The application of strategies does not therefore necessarily result in optimal solutions:

translators choosing from a range of strategies sometimes choose well, at other times unwisely.

As a translator often works under time pressure, s/he needs to develop 'minimax strategies' (Levý, 1967), using a minimum of effort to arrive at a maximum of effect. The automation developed by experienced professional translators can be thought of as a quick, often unconscious way of reviewing existing strategies and coming to a decision.

In translator training, where such automation has not yet developed, it often makes sense to consider and evaluate alternative strategies in class in the hope of raising students' awareness of the range of existing strategies and helping them develop problem-solving and decision-making faculties. The examples in later chapters of this book may provide material for exercises on this.

A descriptive or prescriptive concept?

Translators should not only have latitude to make innovations and alterations where such are required but also to estimate such necessity themselves. Evaluation both of potential strategies and of their realisations in specific instances easily slides into what is often perceived as undue prescriptiveness: a desire to dictate what strategies *should* or *must* be used. (These modals are said to represent the 'We Know Better' approach which Toury [1992: 67] argues should be rejected in translator training.)

Lörscher's (1991) main criticism of earlier uses of the term 'strategy' in translation studies (such as Hönig & Kussmaul, 1982 and Wilss, 1983) is that they have been prescriptive, a form of giving instructions to the translator. It seems to me that this focus is linked to the interest of researchers in the teaching of translation and need not be altogether avoided. From a pedagogical perspective especially, translating involves problem-solving and decision-making (Wilss, 1990), and the term 'translation strategy' is a useful tool to apply descriptively both in a narrow sense (for what an individual translator does or decides to do) and in a broader sense (for what procedures or choices are in principle available to translators). But a descriptive look at strategies develops into implicit prescriptiveness when strategies are evaluated as effective or ineffective: for example Séguinot (1991) is interested in whether students can be taught to use better (more effective) strategies and thus to become better translators. She assumes that good translators and poor translators may well use different strategies and speaks for instance of strategies 'associated only with ineffective translators' (Séguinot, 1992: 40). Neubert and Shreve (1992: 53) suggest that strategies should be offered 'as heuristics, even prescriptions, for good translation practice'. Lörscher (1991: 230) himself, despite his criticism of the prescriptive attitude, speaks of 'successful and unsuccessful translation strategies'.

Use of the term strategy both in a descriptive and a more or less implicitly prescriptive sense seems appropriate in the kind of translation research which hopes to have practical and pedagogical implications. An approach with such aims requires of necessity some degree of generalisation and systematisation. Instead of the translator dealing with each allusion (or other translation problem) on a case-by-case basis, use of the concept of strategies means that the various potential ways of solving such problems can be grouped under a manageable number of headings (such as explanation, substitution, omission, etc.). In teaching translation, discussion of such general strategies is more useful than consideration of specific examples only, in that this may help students learn something that can be applied to other cases as well. As Wilss (1990: 28) puts it, 'translators must learn to develop problem-solving procedures [and] produce competent decisions'.

I shall thus allow myself to write for example of the strategy of omission, descriptively, that it is rarely used for allusions in the TTs examined in this study; and further (still descriptively) that there seems to be a norm in Finnish translation practice, recognised by the translators themselves (cf. Chapter 4), that omission should be used only as a last resort. As Chesterman (1993: 14) observes: '[I]f a given strategy turns out to be regularly used by competent professional translators, it will *de facto* take on the status of... a *normative law*' (emphasis in the original); this again has 'prescriptive force for members of a given translating community'.

It would also be legitimate for a teacher of translation to note, for instance, that the omission of an allusion is seldom the optimal alternative, as it necessarily results in loss of the message conveyed by the allusion; the seriousness of the loss could then be gauged with regard to other factors in the translation situation. An analysis of strategies which takes into account a number of factors for a given type of problem, prioritising certain of them, and perhaps even leading to the development of a possible method of dealing with such problems, can be defended against accusations of undue prescriptiveness. After all, it makes sense to encourage students to develop an awareness of the range of existing strategies and of translation involving problem-solving and decision-making. At no place in this study is it implied, though, that its proposals should be taken as generalisable to all allusions or all genres; on the contrary, it is emphasised that such factors as context and functionality are always pre-eminent. There is thus no desire to develop 'rules' which could be applied mechanically to individual problems. Rather, it is recognised that in the present state of the art it is the translator who needs to decide, in each individual case, whether a strategy is applicable to the problem at hand or not.

A 'necessary subjective element' (House, 1989: 160) is part of the individual translator's evaluation of the best strategy. Indeed, the concept of strategy centrally involves 'subjective optimality... : translation strategies are the means which the translator, within the confines of his or her existing knowledge, considers to be *best* in order to reach the goals set by the translation task' (Jääskeläinen, 1993: 111; emphases altered). Jääskeläinen clarifies that this does not mean prescriptiveness in the rigid sense of 'determining in advance which strategies a translator *should* use' (emphasis in the original). Rather, she resolves the conflict by postulating a cumulative qualitative analysis of individual examples eventually leading to more objective and generalisable evaluation: 'By analysing the (subjectively optimal) strategies used in translation processes in relation to the quality of the products of these processes, it will be possible to identify strategies that are likely to be optimal objectively, too, and *can be recommended for use in similar situations*' (Jääskeläinen, 1993: 112; emphasis added). Hence, knowledge of translatorial norms which are based on descriptive analyses of translations helps translators to find the most effective way to act. Chesterman (1993: 15) further accepts that the 'conditions under which each method would be the most appropriate one' can be specified. In this book, the discussion of potential and actual translation strategies for allusions (Chapter 4) and of the reader responses recorded to both minimum change and other strategies (Chapter 5) may take us some way in the direction of identifying such conditions with regard to the translation of allusions.

But in chronological terms, problem-solving is preceded by an analysis of the ST and its problems. This involves a number of issues, and to clarify them, a look at a number of examples in their contexts is indicated. We need, therefore, first to study allusions as they occur in STs.

The sources of the allusions in Chapter 2

Prides and prejudices: an allusion to Jane Austen's novel *Pride and Prejudice,* modified by plural use of *pride* for a group of lions.

Miss Havisham: a character in Dickens's *Great Expectations* – the archetypal jilted bride. She wears bridal clothes and has kept her rotting wedding feast intact for decades.

Sairey Gamp: a character in Dickens's *Martin Chuzzlewit* – a drunken midwife.

The White Rabbit: a character in Lewis Carroll's *Alice's Adventures in Wonderland.*

Notes

1. 'This week one kills the pig' — an annual notice in French butcher's shops inviting customers to purchase fresh pork at special offer prices.
2. This text of a Lufthansa advertisement showing a photograph of a half-smiling cabin attendant alludes to photographers' habit of inviting customers to mimic smiling by asking them to say 'Cheese'.
3. *Receiver, receptor* and *recipient* are all used synonymously in the literature.
4. In fact, there is a government resolution (of 1 August 1982) in Finland which requires that civil servants producing texts addressed to the public — provisions and documents of various sorts — must ensure that they are written in intelligible language so that citizens can understand what is required of them and on what grounds decisions that concern them are made. To what degree this objective is met is a matter of opinion; but generally speaking, the syntax of Finnish administrative prose does resemble that of ordinary language more than do corresponding EU texts.
5. Maddox's comment that many of those puzzled by the caption 'may *shamefully* have been' Britons (p.475; emphasis added) reveals that he has not realised that no monolithic national culture can be assumed; instead, there is a large number of subcultures.
6. Hönig and Kussmaul (1984: 40) state that deciding what the function of the TT is, is at the top of hierarchical decision-making, and the choice of individual words comes last, as a consequence of higher-ranking decisions. The functions of allusions on macro- and micro-level vary (see Chapter 3).
7. Disregarding machine translation; but even there, the production of a translation is only possible after a great deal of human time and effort has been put into developing the necessary software.
8. Hewson and Martin (1991) also stress this role of the translator, but I developed my emphasis independently of theirs (Leppihalme, 1990). (They mention allusions only in passing.)
9. It is a fact of life that not everybody who translates meets the high requirements set for successful performance — at least not at all times and in all situations. The list of requirements, then, must be thought idealised in the same way as, for instance, advertisements for vacant positions: 'Exceptional interpersonal skills, drive and enthusiasm are essential in order to succeed in this progressive world-wide organisation', '[f]luent communication and analytical skills will enable you to represent the Agency at the highest levels, negotiating with confidence both at home and abroad... The capacity for clear and concise presentation of technically complex issues is therefore essential' (advertisements for executive opportunities in *The Sunday Times*, 3 Jan. 1993, 2: 10–11). The skills listed are thought necessary for superlative performance; in practice, for most translators and executives alike, these are goals to aim for rather than descriptions of a state already achieved and in permanent possession. Meeting such goals is more fruitfully seen as a life-long process.
10. While I accept that a translator's reading is (frequently) one of many possible ones (cf. Hatim & Mason [1990: 11], who are more definite on this point), I believe that this is more often true of texts of certain more challenging genres (like poetry) than the texts of my corpus. Even so, there has been some variation in interpretation of some of my examples when these have been discussed in the classroom or with colleagues. Lack of sufficient context (the respondents usu-

ally not having read the books providing the examples) may have been one reason for this variation, preventing consideration of a maximum number of clues.

11. This discussion of the competence required of the translator is meant to highlight the skills and qualities needed in the translation of allusions. A different emphasis might have led to the foregrounding of different skills.

12. The term *kääntäjä* 'translator' is neutral and widely used. Literary translators often prefer the term *suomentaja*, which could be rendered as 'Finnisher'; this may have higher status and suggest inborn skills and creativity.

13. This may, of course, on occasion be a conscious decision to avoid burdening the index with terms that 'constantly occur' (Wilss, 1992: 245; my translation).

14. Or, quite often, a particular subculture. Within a family, for instance, a parent may be sensitive to literary allusions whose sources are part of the academic canon, and a son or daughter to allusions to rock lyrics or cult movies.

15. 'Text' must be understood throughout this study quite widely, to include TV programmes, political and commercial slogans, strip cartoons and the like.

16. The distinction between the two is best seen in nonsensical texts, where intelligibility involves understanding of syntactic structures, for instance that in *my beamish boy* (Carroll, 'Jabberwocky'), *beamish* is a premodifier; but comprehensibility would require ability to assign a meaning to the word *beamish*.

17. He does not, however, describe the distinction between individual 'strategies' and supra-individual 'methods' in absolute terms, but sees strategies as 'more individual' (Lörscher, 1991: 68).

18. The term 'has been used to refer to both conscious and unconscious procedures' (Séguinot, 1991: 82); see also Lörscher's (1991) definition cited earlier ('potentially conscious').

19. For instance changes in word order, or rendering prepositions by suffixes indicating grammatical case: 'Where *is* the book?' (inversion) 'The book is *on* the table' (preposition) = Finn. *Missä kirja on?* (direct word order) *Kirja on pöydällä* (adessive case). Minimum change translations are often unobjectionable, but examples where the strategy leads to translationese, that is, to clumsy or unnatural translations, are frequent enough.

3 Analysis: Hide-and-Seek

A translator who examines a text with a view to translating it will have a number of concerns. Among them allusions are likely to play a subsidiary but not negligible role: whenever the translator (as a competent reader) notices an allusion, a decision will need to be made on how it will be dealt with. The sections of this chapter are necessarily interlinked: recognisability depends at least partly on familiarity with sources, modifications of form may hinder recognition; but above all, a translator needs to consider the function of allusions in their contexts. Identifying the function is an important step towards deciding what translation strategy will be appropriate for the allusion in question.

Functions of Allusions

Function and effect

To establish an exhaustive list of mutually exclusive categories of functions that allusions may have would be difficult, even impossible. There is bound to be some leakage between them. For instance humour has many functions; descriptions may be of thematic importance (illuminating the theme of the text as a guide to interpretation); use of stereotyped allusions may be a device in characterisation, etc. The different functions are more usefully seen as a continuum, or even better, as a number of partially overlapping, non-concentric circles. Elaborate systems of classification seem inadvisable and even misleading when studying a phenomenon which is 'an internal process. Each example exists only as it occurs within a particular work' (Pasco, 1973: 467). It is therefore essential not to lose sight of the context in which each allusion occurs.

However, a useful distinction might be drawn between allusions operating mainly on the micro-level of the text and those operating on the macro-level. Simply put, the macro-level involves the internal structure of the entire text and its interpretation: its narrative and poetic structure, dramatic intrigue and authorial comment (Lambert & van Gorp, 1985: 52) – we might speak of structural and thematic use of allusion. The micro-level, on the other hand, is the lexico-semantic and stylistic level (pp.52–53). In their quest for a comprehensive scheme, Lambert & van Gorp (1985) also distinguish 'the broader systemic context' of intertextual and intersystemic relations as a separate level (p.53), but in my more modest, applied scope I would prefer to limit my focus to 'author; translator; readers; texts; micro- and macro-levels' (p.50).

As regards the author, Makkonen (1991: 16) states categorically that researchers of intertextuality are not interested in the author's intention, that attempts are not made to discover whether borrowed material is used on purpose or not, or what that purpose might be – 'court-of-law terminology (theft, apology, evidence) is not needed' (my translation). Both ST readers and translators are usually unaware of the motives and intentions of the author except to the extent that they can be inferred from the text. On infrequent occasions, indeed, an author may directly address the question of why allusions are used. Fay Weldon (1985: 17–18) explains her use of an allusion[1] as follows:

> When I refer to 'the riches of the years' I hope to convey the whole feeling-tone (as Freudians say of dreams) of the poem, both the power and the slight absurdity; *all* the poem in fact, in the five words of his that I choose, for the benefit of my sentence. Call it plagiarism, call it fellowship between writers, or resonance (since you're in a Department of English Literature). I don't suppose it matters much ... Words are not simple things, they take unto themselves, as they have through time, power and meaning: they did so then, they do so now.

A whole range of factors, including social class, gender, education, personal reading history, situational and cultural context, etc. are no doubt involved in an individual sender's choosing to communicate via allusion. A sender must judge each communicative situation subjectively to decide whether or not an allusion is the optimal strategy for achieving the desired effect in that situation (Wilss, 1989: 58). There are no rules telling a sender how to allude – creative alluding is individual and non-predictable. There are also fashions in alluding, but following of set formulae soon destroys the individuality and creativity which is characteristic of true allusions.

The interaction between author and reader can be described as hide-and-seek (Meyer, 1968: 79, Wilss, 1989: 49) or as the setting and solving of a puzzle (Weisgerber, 1970: 43). A reader who recognises a creative allusion achieves a deeper understanding of a passage or text, which means that he or she is somehow participating in the creation of the text and may consequently be rewarded by a sense of achievement and self-congratulation. In essence, s/he may feel that s/he has passed a test with flying colours, showing that s/he is part of an in-group of readers, on the same wavelength as the author. Redfern (1984: 30) quotes a correspondent as saying that he likes puns partly because of the 'intellectual snobbery' that shows an 'ability to think laterally' and partly because understanding someone else's pun 'implies a rapport'. If true of puns, this must be even more so of many allusions:

Kate shivered. She pulled her gauzy grey wrap closer round her shoulders. Under it she wore a black dress. She looked like the sort of thing *Whistler had flung in the public's face in 1877.* (Moody, 1985: 176)

This is a clear example of the puzzle aspect of alluding: the receiver is given a clue, both in the form of the name Whistler and in the phrase *flung in the public's face;* but the readers who do not know their art history (and many non-native readers will fall in that category, being more familiar with their national art) will have difficulty with the comparison. They will wonder who Whistler was, what it was that he flung in the public's face, whether it was flung literally or metaphorically, and if the date is of any significance? Those who solve the puzzle are likely to feel some sort of kinship with the writer, having filled in the gap in the message. To resolve the problem the reader must identify Whistler as the American artist James McNeill Whistler (1834–1903); and remember one of his best-known works, variously known as 'Portrait of the Painter's Mother' or 'Artist's Mother: Arrangement in Grey and Black No. 1' (1871). The identification of that widely known painting as the source of the allusion is strongly suggested by the adjectives *grey* and *black* in the immediate context, and by the description of Kate's clothing which resembles that of the figure in the portrait. When some of Whistler's portraits and landscapes were shown in London in 1877, they 'were so fiercely assailed by Ruskin... that Whistler retaliated, suing his critic for libel... ' (*Everyman's Encyclopedia*, 1978: 475). The wording *flung in the public's face* is clearly an allusion to Ruskin's attack: '[I have] never expected to hear a coxcomb ask two hundred guineas for flinging a pot of paint in the public's face' (quoted in CDQ 255).[2] If solved, the puzzle functions as a description of Kate, but that is in passing only, on the micro-level, and adds little to what is said overtly about her in the context – the painting referred to has no specific connotations. The main function of the allusion is to challenge the reader to solve the puzzle.

In a sense, of course, any allusion is a puzzle for readers who notice it without recognising it. More generally, allusions become puzzles when they cross a cultural divide. This may occur within a language as national borders are crossed (for instance allusions to many British television programmes would be unfamiliar to American audiences); or within a country, in the case of national subcultures, each demographic group alluding to its own texts; or equally when translation takes place. However, it would seem, on the basis of the examples I have studied, that to be a puzzle is seldom the main *function* of an allusion.

Nord (1991: 47–8) sees function and effect as two sides of a coin, with the difference that function can be defined before reception, while effect can only be judged after reception. Lack of empirical data on reception means that any discussion of effect is bound to be largely speculative. Schaar (1991) speaks of mental and physical responses to texts (associations, emotions, shivers, tears etc.) using the term 'energy' for the force that causes such responses. He makes a distinction between 'free semantic energy', which is experienced by the majority of receivers (often hearers, as this type of response has connections with orality) and is 'spontaneously induced, unaided by context' (p.175) and therefore often vague in meaning; and 'latent semantic energy', which involves reflection, has connections above all with literacy, and is experienced by the minority who have the special knowledge required. Without such knowledge, the response is 'puzzlement and non-understanding' (p.175). A receiver may thus enjoy certain high-sounding fragments of a text, but reflection and knowledge (for example of the sources of allusions) will lead to a deeper understanding and convey meaning that is not immediately apparent. This development is familiar to all who have been guided by more experienced receivers to see deeper meaning in a text or film. Schaar sees no 'rigid polarity' (p.175) between the two types of energy but believes that latent energy can also be transformed to free energy as an individual receiver no longer needs reflection before a particular text can cause an emotional response.

In general, it may be said that allusions are used because of the extra effect or meaning they bring to the text by their associations or connotations. Hatim and Mason (1990: 129) rightly make a distinction between the two, seeing associations as subjective and arbitrary, connotations as requiring social (collective) knowledge. The difference can be illustrated by the following example, where a lovely evening in the country is disrupted by the discovery of a grisly scene (emphases added):

> Underfoot there were leaves which crackled like cornflakes as they walked. The air was warm with residual heat. Beneath the trees were shadows. *Lovely, dark and deep.*
> 'Country living,' said Emerald. 'I never knew I was a deprived child until Kendal brought me here.' She scuffed up leaves. She breathed deeply.

'Good grief,' said Penny.
A square of ground had been fenced off. Thin white posts. Barbed
wire. It was grotesquely upholstered with the corpses of small creatures.
Grey squirrels were tied in rows by their tails, paws curled against
their chests. Crows hung upside down, wings spread, beaks open.
There was a weasel, its sharp white teeth bared as though sucking back
a scream. Rats and voles and rabbits lay crucified on the wire. More
crows swung from the branches of nearby trees *like broken umbrellas*.
'Fun, isn't it?' Emerald sounded apologetic.
'*Only man is vile*,' said Penny. She tried not to look at a vixen spread
like a jumble-sale tippet along the barbs, tail threaded between the wire
strands. There was a long-dried drip of blood at the corner of the half-
open mouth. Here and there, white bone showed through rotting flesh.
(Moody, 1985: 37)

As part of the empirical tests carried out for this study, half a dozen
teachers of literature in university departments of English in Finland (all
native speakers of English) were asked to read a somewhat longer text including this passage and to mark the allusions they noticed. Those that
were verifiable (*lovely, dark and deep; only man is vile*) received a number of
recognitions, but one informant also underlined the broken umbrellas image, explaining that while not an allusion, it was obviously a reminiscence
of D.H. Lawrence's poem 'Bat'.[3] The poem certainly contains the same image: 'wings *like bits of umbrella*'; but whether *broken umbrellas* could be said
to generally connote Lawrence's bat in the English language community
would be highly debatable. What is clear is that the image evoked an association with 'Bat' for that one reader and did not do so for his colleagues.
The presence of allusions may be a contributory factor for associations: in a
text teeming with allusions, a reader may be temporarily sensitised to intertextual material and prepared to look for more. It is also possible that the
author's use of the image was, in fact, an unconscious allusion to Lawrence's poem.

As against such personal and subjective associations, the other italicised
phrases in the example are generally accepted in the English language community (witness dictionaries of quotations) as preformed linguistic
material. If doubted, this can be verified by comparison with the evoked
texts. The effect of such phrases is reinforced by this communal awareness
of their preformed nature; we are thus speaking of connotations collec-
tively associated with a particular name or phrase. It is clear, however, that
there are degrees of cultural literacy and reading competence among

native-speaker (NS) readers. Some would receive little more than the surface meaning of *only man is vile*, that is, '(some, or all) men/people are vile',
while others would link the phrase with its religious source, and perhaps
remember the line preceding it there (*Though every prospect pleases*), and
hence be more strongly aware of the contrast between Moody's idyllic
wood and the instance of human cruelty revealed there.

From the point of view of translation, what is important is that the analysis of the ST requires recognition of connotative meaning by the translator.
Of course it is not possible to put subjective associations and collective connotations into totally separate compartments. Nevertheless, it can no doubt
be accepted that while the translator cannot control, and should not even
attempt to control, the subjective associations and interpretations of individual readers, s/he needs to be aware of and sensitive to the more
collective connotations – the 'socially constant meaning' (Turk, 1991: 123) –
of allusive names and phrases.

To speak of a language community, language culture or source culture
may falsely suggest a uniformity of culture among native-speakers of a language. The term 'source culture' and its synonyms are therefore used in
this study, as in translation studies generally, as a convenient construct to
highlight intercultural differences linked to SL and TL, without a desire to
imply uniformity within a language culture. The same proviso naturally
applies to the use of the term 'target culture' as well.

As each subculture will be familiar with different sources of allusions, it
follows that some ST allusions are known to a far larger proportion of NSs
than others. For instance many biblical and proverbial allusions in English
are said by NS informants to be better known than certain literary ones.
Many of the latter would only be recognisable by a small élite. A later discussion of the function of the allusions below is therefore not intended to
suggest that *all* NS readers would recognise each allusion and interpret it in
an identical way. Still, for the purposes of this study it is assumed that each
allusion is part of the text in which it occurs, and offers possibilities of interpretation for a larger or smaller section of the NS audience. Sometimes this
would be fairly automatic interpretation, as in the case of commonly used
allusions; in other cases access to such half-hidden information would be
open to a minority of readers only. Nor is the situation constant with regard
to any given allusion. Some topical allusions are short-lived and never even
make it to works of reference, while social change and the passage of time
will eventually deprive many if not most allusions of their evocative
power. At any given time the allusions with which an individual or a
demographic group will be familiar will differ from those familiar to

others. The TT-receiver-oriented nature of this study means that little attention is paid here to such differences among ST audiences. It is accepted that some allusions will be better recognised by academics, others by people who follow politics or parents who read aloud to their children, or young movie-goers; but a translator is often expected to serve all of these, and cannot therefore simply bypass the implicit information that allusions may convey to NS receivers.

The following sections present some (partly overlapping) creative functions of allusions: a suggestion of thematic importance on the macro-level; parody and irony, and other humour (mainly on the micro-level); the use of allusions for characterisation; and allusions as indicators of interpersonal relationships in fiction. The discussion is illustrated by authentic examples.

'Creative' is contrasted with more stereotyped use, that is, clichés and proverbs as well as dead and dying allusions. As will be seen from some of the examples, the same allusion can be found at times in stereotyped use, and at other times re-animated.

For the convenience of readers who are not at home in the source-language culture, the sources of the allusions used as examples are given at the end of each chapter, in the order in which they occur in the text, unless such information is given in the text itself or requires an endnote. Information on alluding texts (that is, the texts that supplied the examples) is mostly given in the text after each example except where this would hamper readability. In such cases details are omitted if they are not thought to merit an endnote; the information can, in any case, be found in the dissertation version of this study (Leppihalme, 1994).

Thematic allusions

On the macro-level the use of creative allusions often brings in a suggestion of universality, a heightening of emotion, a desire to imply that there is something about a situation or character in the alluding context that is more important than the reader would otherwise assume, and which may be of thematic importance for the interpretation of the text as a whole. This function of reinforcing themes has been the focus of much attention in literary criticism and there are countless excellent examples in the literary canon. This function is also reflected in the choice of allusive titles for journalistic pieces as well as for literary and scholarly works. To name just two examples of scholarly use, there are for instance *The Madwoman in the Attic: The Woman Writer and the Nineteenth-Century Imagination* (Gilbert & Gubar, 1984) and *Ain't I A Woman? Black Women and Feminism* (hooks, 1982).

For an illustration of thematic use of allusions in lighter fiction than is often considered in literary analyses of allusion, let us consider an extract from a crime novel. In the text, the allusions are used to give significance to the story of the killing of a truck-driver with criminal tendencies, to indicate that his attitude to life and his solid friendship with a childhood pal could be seen in a less sordid light than the mere facts of the case would seem to permit. That it is the author's intention to invite this kind of interpretation is made clear, for example, in the following allusive passage (and it is perhaps the presence of such overt explanations that makes the realisation of the plan somewhat unsatisfactory from a literary point of view. A more subtle approach might have been more effective – but then, the author's visualisation of her readers is not accessible to us). The man's tearful young widow, an ordinary young woman, speaks in clichés:

> 'We always went out together. We was like – like inseparable... He was a husband in a million, a good kind man, a wonderful man to his friends. You ask anyone, ask Jack ... . He was one in a million!' (Rendell, 1981: 89)

The well-read chief inspector to whom this is addressed, however, hears echoes of a grief more eloquently expressed, for the passage continues with a Shakespearean allusion (emphasis here and in other examples below added):

> *Oh! withered is the garland of war! The soldier's poll is fallen...* Strange, Wexford thought, that when you considered Charlie Hatton you thought of war and soldiers and battles. Was it because life itself is a battle and Hatton had waged it with unscrupulous weapons, winning rich spoils and falling as he marched home with a song on his lips? (Rendell, 1981: 89)

The last few pages of the novel underline the soldier image: a chessman (a knight), which symbolises Charlie, is smashed to bits. By way of summing up the friendship theme, there is also an allusion to the story of David and Jonathan on the penultimate page, where the loss of the dead man is seen through the eyes of his friend:

> Had [Charlie] recognised himself at the head of that scarlet army [of chessmen]? *And the Philistines slew Jonathan ... How are the mighty fallen and the weapons of war perished!* (Rendell, 1981: 184)

On a lexical level, there are supporting references to *soldiers of fortune* (pp.89, 185) and *comrades-in-arms* (p.185). The allusions and imagery thus guide the competent reader towards a macro-level interpretation.

Still, even a single allusion may be of thematic importance:

There was a poignancy in the way they assaulted the pavement with their long-legged strides; something in their attitude reminded me of a painting I had seen *of Adam and Eve being ejected from the Garden*, the urgency of their situation sweetened by the sharing of it. (Godwin, 1985: 43)

This comparison of an elderly couple to Adam and Eve in an expulsion painting reinforces the repeated hints in the text that the couple are living in some sort of exile, possibly self-inflicted.

Journalistic texts may contain very serious allusions for the heightening of emotion which are perhaps comparable to the thematic use of allusion in literary texts. Such allusions tend to be found either at the beginning or the end of texts for added emphasis. An article praising a lynched boy's mother for courageously seeking justice makes such use of allusions. The mother herself is introduced first with a biblical allusion and then a literary one, contrasting her heroism with the conventional view of heroes:

Some heroes are not *swift or strong* and they do not look like *Sir Lancelot*. This one is old and tired and overweight... (Ivins, 1988)

The crime itself is described with an allusion which makes it clear that it was an act of racism:

They found his body hanging from the tree *like a strange fruit* on a cold Mobile morning in March of 1981. A 19-year-old black man-child named Michael Donald, shy outside his family, a student at the state technical school who worked part-time at the local newspaper. (Ivins, 1988)

With less obvious emotion, a scientist writing to the scientific community on the plight of Bosnia and Croatia in the early 1990s concludes with a historical allusion (thinly disguised as a scientific source reference) that puts part of the blame for the events on the West:

For those unfamiliar with the theory of symmetry of culpability, it was originated by *Neville Chamberlain* and published in *Munich in 1938*. (Pravdic, 1992)

An allusion may sum up the drift of an article: after criticising men in high positions for urging workers to show restraint in their demands for pay raises while they raise their own salaries, an editorial concludes with two allusions:

And the more they get, the more they seem to want. Small wonder their
pleas for restraint are *falling on barren ground. If gold rusts, what shall iron
do?* (The *Guardian*, 1989)

There is even anecdotal evidence of allusions being used in real life as final 'exit lines' – a kind of reinforcement of the theme of one's life, perhaps:

> [*Peter Pan's*] first producer, the American showman Charles Frohman,
> who was killed in the sinking of the *Lusitania*, is reported to have cried
> as the ship went down, *'To die will be an awfully big adventure!'* – Peter's
> curtain line in act 3. (Lurie, 1990: 131–2)

Humour in allusions

Conversely, allusion may also be used parodically or ironically, to detract from the importance of a situation or character. Bakhtin (1988: 147)
convincingly argues that parody has lost ground in modern literature because we no longer have much sacred writing. This suggests to me that
some allusions may be parodic of the literature taught at school – the 'complex and multi-leveled hierarchy of discourses, forms, images, styles' (Bakhtin, 1988: 147) of set books and required reading. Such literature is
different from the users' own idiolects, and it may therefore be tempting for
many to make fun of memories of the schoolroom – and it is usually in the
schoolroom that a general reader first meets complex literature.

Macro-level parody occurs where a text as a whole is a parody of another
text. When there are parodic elements on the micro-level, these tend to
make use of frequently anthologised poetry ('canonised' works of literature):

> They climbed up a steep bank. At the top was the churchyard, full of
> the usual churchyard stuff. Bird-lime. Plastic flowers. Long grass with
> tottering headstones. *Rude forefathers* lay beneath epitaphs of the sort
> that make the comic verse collections. Très *Stoke Poges*. (Moody, 1985:
> 40)

> She thought of going for help. But that would endanger Emerald even
> more. It was up to her. She hadn't saved Kendal. But she'd save Emer-
> ald. Somehow. *No coward soul is mine*, she told herself. She turned back
> up the dark drive. (Moody, 1985: 216)

But there is a certain ambiguity between humour and seriousness in the
second example, as the character is truly in danger of her life and still
makes the decision not to flee.

Nash (1985: 45–6) discusses some examples of parodic allusion in advertisements (a genre not included in my corpus), and notes that 'the advertising slogan is the new wit-object, to be tasted, twisted, turned, much as the Elizabethans manipulated commonplace puns'. Most general readers are doubtless more familiar with advertisements than with the literary canon, which makes ads attractive raw material for wordplay.

Political attacks in newspapers are often spiced with ironic allusions, sometimes involving lexical substitution and similar modifications. Wilss (1989: 63–9) even sees aggressiveness as a special dimension beside emphasis and irony.[4]

> There is a bit of the *Richard Nixon* in [Quayle]. He turns legitimate questions about his national guard service into an attack on the press and talks of his reserve duty behind a typewriter as if it had been *winter at Valley Forge...* His defense of national guard service has been one long *Checkers* speech. Will he soon produce *a dog*? (Cohen, 1988)

Politicians may also find their own slogans turned against them. George Bush was not allowed to forget the invitation to *Read my lips:*

> The markets gave the US budget a universal sneer, mainly because Mr Bush had *read his own lips* all too well. No new taxes, a freeze on military expenditure and modestly increased spending on education, homelessness and drug abuse. (*The Guardian Weekly,* 1989)

> *Dread My Lips (Time,* 1989)

> His *lips say no.* His eyes – and his aides – say maybe. (Gleckman, 1989)

but the allusion was extended to other situations and other politicians as well:

> 'America's political landscape will never again be the same... To politicians who oppose choice, we say, *Read our lips.* Take our rights. Lose your jobs.' (Carlson, 1989)

Visualisations of Bush as a *kinder, gentler George* (alluding to a campaign speech in 1988) are also unlikely to have been taken at face value: they were very probably read as ironical by the majority of readers.

In this connection it may be worthwhile to have a look in passing at the techniques of humorous allusion. Nash (1985: 164ff.) and Wilss (1989: 49) both note the use of 'frames' in wordplay. A frame is a combination of words that is accepted in the language community as an example of preformed linguistic material. Modification of a frame can be either situational or lexical. If a frame has undergone little or no linguistic modification, its effect (laughter, surprise, shock etc.) may be due to the incongruity of the borrowed words and their connotations in the alluding context, as in the following examples. In the first one, a fictional burglar defends himself with the words of Richard Nixon during the Watergate affair:

They sent me out to shake down this place. It's my job. *I'm not a crook.* This is my job. You don't have to shoot me. (Cunningham, 1987: 122)

In the second, a husband and wife are in bed after a reconciliation, when the husband's mother comes 'stamping up the stairs':

'Alexander, where are you? Didn't you hear me calling?'
   '*The voice of the turtle is heard in the land,*' Sarah murmured. 'Let's hide under the covers.' (MacLeod, 1980: 108)

While the couple may be disposed to think of the Song of Songs with reference to themselves, the mother-in-law's voice is unlikely to sound to them like that of a turtle-dove. In a situational modification, what was poetic or seriously meant in the evoked context may well become a parody or be trivialised in the alluding context.

Lexical modification of the frame can take the form of substitution, where instead of the expected keyword, another lexical item is introduced. In the following, the frame is given first, with the keyword in square brackets, followed by an authentic example of modification, used in a journalistic text (published in 1988–89). The substitution is usually context-linked, so that a well-known frame can give rise to any number of variations. The syntax of the frame, on the other hand, can vary only slightly if the frame is to retain its recognisability:

By their [fruits] ye shall know them. (Matt. 7: 22)
By their ads *shall ye know them.*

they shall beat their [swords] into [ploughshares]. (Isa. 2:4)
Collecting plastic: *they shall beat their* cafeteria trays *into* flowerpots.

Those that live by the [sword] shall die by the [sword]. (Matt. 26: 52)[5]
I like to *live by the sword.* But I didn't say I want to *die by it.*
He who has *lived by the* word will *die by the sword.*
Those who *live by the* punchline *die by the* punchline.
Those who *live by the* procedural device must be prepared to *die by* it...

Recognition of the frame allows the receiver to recall the original wording and to note the contrast achieved. But alterations within frames are perhaps too mechanical to always produce the sort of associative delight which may ensue in situational twists. The well-known frame:

> *there is some corner of a [foreign] field that is for ever [England]*

can be altered through lexical substitution for example to:

> *There is some* part of a Roman *field that forever* shall be Mussolini's

but the following, where the words are unaltered but the situation is vastly different, is surely funnier because of the incongruity (and the scatological elements) of the situation:

> Due to hitherto undetected EEC apricot mountain, baby has runs – i.e., baby sits, I run. Result: this postcard written under low cloud formed by fall-out from nappies incinerating in *some foreign field that is forever England*. (Tweedie, 1983: 92)

All allusive humour does not make use of frames. Connections between evoked text and alluding text can be spelled out. In King (1991), one of a cavalcade of bit players is presented as living in the fictional world created by another writer, Ed McBain. The character is introduced as a colleague of McBain's Steve Carella of the 87th precinct:

> The New Yorker was Edward M. Norris, lieutenant of police, detective squad, in the Big Apple's *87th Precinct*. This was his first real vacation in five years. He ... planned to tell that sour son of a bitch *Steve Carella* that it was possible to take your wife and kids some place by car and have a good time. (King, 1991: 68)

The effect is then due to a reader noticing the unusual linking of two fictional worlds.

Sometimes a humorous allusion is offered in code, as it were, for readers to decode; there is neither a frame nor explicit linking of texts:

> She set off up a side street towards the beach. Yeoman walked beside her, swinging his bag. The slight rise of the roadway hid the sea ahead, but she knew it was there, all right. She could hear it crunching and slobbering as it gnawed away at the shingle. Ready to sock it to any smart-ass who showed up with a crown and an armchair, looking for a spot of direct confrontation. (Moody, 1984: 9)

The personalising of the sea, and the identification of the smart-ass with a crown and an armchair as a king on a throne may activate memories of the story told of the 11th century Danish king of England, Canute, ordering the waves to recede. The story is well-known in Britain ('any British primary school child would recognise it', according to a British informant), but for readers not raised in Britain it would be much more difficult to unravel.[6]

(The idea of a confrontation with the sea does not fully convey the lesson Canute is said to have wanted to teach: 'Confess how frivolous and vain is the might of an earthly king compared to that great Power who rules the elements' [*Story of British People* s.a.: 38; see also the illustration on that page].)

Allusive humour is only one area of wordplay, a wide subject worth separate attention (see for instance Nash [1985] and Redfern [1984] as well as Delabastita [1996]). Here, I have limited myself to brief remarks and illustrations only; further examples of allusive humour are discussed in the sections below (for example p.46 and the modified allusions on pp.60–2).

Use of allusions for characterisation

Allusions are often a fast and economical aid to characterisation. Characters who allude are shown to be well educated, literate and quick-witted, and their allusions reflect their interests, as when a central character, who is a professor with 'a well-established reputation in the expanding field of children's literature' (Lurie, 1986: 1) frequently alludes to Lewis Carroll and other children's classics. Naive or ignorant characters, on the other hand, fail to catch allusions as addressees, and if they use allusions themselves, these are trite and hackneyed. Characterisation with the help of allusions can occur on both the macro- and the micro-level, depending for instance on whether an allusion (or a series of them) is used to shed light on a central character, or whether the allusion occurs in connection with the sole appearance of a minor character. On the macro-level, the use of a series of allusions for characterisation is not much different from their use for conveying themes:

'Somehow whenever I fantasised being rescued, it was never the police, it was always you ... And you did it the way I expected you would. You bashed in the door and shot two people and picked me up and took me away. *Tarzan of the Apes*,' she said. (Parker, 1987a: 219)

The elliptical comparison of the addressed private eye, Spenser, with Tarzan may evoke simply brute force, and if the reader is mainly aware of the struggle for dominance discernible in the relationship between Spenser and the speaker, Rachel, the kidnapped feminist whom he has just rescued, this interpretation of the remark makes sense. It could be construed as expressing either Rachel's frequently stated disapproval of strong-arm tactics, or a veiled apology for this disapproval, now that it has been proved that Rachel herself was helpless and needed to be rescued by violent means; or it could also be seen as Rachel's way of trying to gain her equilibrium and independence after a shocking experience by returning to her former habit of putting down Spenser and all men who use violence. But when other allusions in the text connected to Spenser are considered, a possible alternative reading emerges. The connotations of Tarzan might be summed up naively as physical action, courage, strength, directness, being on the side of justice. And in fact, these characteristics are part of the connotations of the other allusions used when Spenser is described by his lover Susan or by Rachel, both of whom claim that he sees himself as a knight on a white charger (Parker, 1987a):

'What he won't say,' Susan said, 'and what he may not even admit to himself is that he'd like *to be Sir Gawain*. He was born five hundred years too late... '
'Six hundred years,' [Spenser] said. (p.29)

'I assume you think *you were some kind of Sir Galahad* protecting my good name when you punched that poor sexist fool at the library. Well, you were not. You were a stupid thug... ' (p.49)

'You're employed to keep me alive, not to exercise *your Arthurian fantasies*.' (p.85)

Susan said, 'If you want to give me your old clothes, I can put them through the wash for you. *Lancelot here* has all the modern conveniences.' (p.212)[7]

Spenser himself neither agrees nor disagrees with the imputations. When he uses allusive comparisons for himself, his concern is on a joking level with how well he measures up to more modern role models:

'[My father's name] was assigned me. Spenser. I had no choice. I couldn't say I'd rather be named Spade. *Samuel Spade*. That would be a terrific name, but no. I had to get a name like an English poet. You know what Spenser wrote?' (p.32)

At five o'clock I had seven pages of notes, and my eyes were starting to cross. If I weren't so tough, I would have thought about reading glasses. I wonder how *Bogie* would have looked with specs. *Here's looking at you, four-eyes*. (p.128)

Hence it is up to the reader to decide how much importance to give to the imputations of Arthurian fantasies. The text can be read purely for its action by those who like a good guy bashing up bad guys; or it can be seen (and this is perhaps clearer if several Spenser books are read as a series) as an episode in a quest for a resolution of the contradictions in Spenser's life,

caused by his high medieval ideals for himself and his daily struggle
against criminals in a modern American setting, as well as his problems
with love and trust towards Susan, an independent professional woman.
This rather romantic reading depends to a great extent on the presence of
the allusions; but it is supported by overt comments in the dialogue in the
Spenser series, as for example:

> 'It makes you better than other men,' Paul said. '... But it also traps
> you. Machismo's captive. Honor, commitment, absolute fidelity, the
> whole myth.' (Parker, 1987b: 160)

> Susan smiled at me slowly. 'That's what it really is, isn't it?' she said.
> 'You are one of the three or four most romantic diddles in the world... '
> (Parker, 1990: 68)

Not all use of allusions, however, involves this kind of consideration of
lengthy context. There are brief scenes where characters suddenly come
into focus through the use of an allusion in narrative or dialogue:

> 'Mother, lunch is ready,' said Monica, appearing in the doorway,
> looking rather harassed.
> 'Ah, our good *Martha*,' said Father Benger.
> He and Mrs Beltane moved slowly into the house, as if conscious of
> *being the ones who had chosen the better part*. (Pym, 1979: 144)

For a clergyman to address a girl who has toiled to provide him with a
meal, as *Martha*, with biblical reference, could be thought of as a sincere expression of gratitude, were it not for the narrator's allusive remark that
follows, which presents the clergyman's patronising attitude in an ironic
light.

Allusions as indicators of interpersonal relationships

Relationships between characters can be further illuminated through
the use of allusions in dialogue. This function will be dealt with in some detail here, as it is a recurrent one in fictional texts, and one that a translator
ignores at the peril of obscuring crucial relationships. The coherence of a
dialogue between a fictional sender and a fictional receiver involves awareness on the part of the reader of what may be a form of a bid for power or
dominance between characters. Nash (1985: 74) has commented on allusions as 'a device of power', linking this to the folklore belief that to know
a secret name is to have power (p.146). In the texts examined, the alluder is
often foregrounded. His/her dominance may derive from superior intelligence or education, or occasionally, better self-control (that is, not being

emotionally involved, unlike the 'alludee').[8]

In the following example one speaker uses an allusion as a cliché, and her interlocutor, Kate (a professor of English), takes it up and discusses the meaning of the phrase in its historical context, thus puzzling the first speaker:

> 'Well,' Gladys Geddes said, sipping her sherry (she did not, she had explained, drink the hard stuff), 'I thought Ted was far too tolerant of all that anti-youth stuff. Of course *to be young is very heaven* – didn't someone say that?'
>
> Since Gladys had paused, apparently for an answer, Kate said, 'Yes, but *when* you were young seemed to have something to do with it, and then it was remembered heaven, our old friend nostalgia. When Byron actually fought in a revolution, he was thirty-four, which he considered the very brink of desiccation, and his hair was going gray. He didn't live to be a really old man to talk about it, unlike Wordsworth.'
>
> Gladys looked puzzled. 'I don't actually follow you,' she said. 'What have Wordsworth and Byron to do with it? It's just better to be young than old; I'd have said that was obvious.'
>
> Kate tried very hard not to blame men for their wives, but she rarely succeeded. (Cross, 1985: 113; emphasis on *when* original.)

Here, power is very much in the hands of Kate, who feels intellectually superior to Gladys because, unlike Gladys, she is aware of the context in which Wordsworth originally used the words.[9] Kate's intellectual snobbery may well forfeit her the sympathies of many readers, however.

Some of the alludees in the corpus are shown to be aware of the power-play aspect and to interpret the use of an allusion in dialogue as an attempt on the part of the speaker to impress his/her interlocutor. The alludee hastens to cap the allusion or to name the source:

> 'Simply leave the hemlock beside my bed and I'll know what to do with it.' He spoke briefly in Greek.
> 'What?'
> 'I said *we owe a cock to Aesculapius.*'
> 'You and *Socrates,* huh?' (Moody, 1985: 171)

> 'Yes – I'd almost got to thinking of Eagle House as our own *private place.*'
> '*Like the grave,*' said Viola.
> '*Ah, yes, where none embrace,*' said Dulcie, catching the allusion. (Pym, 1979: 199)

On occasion the response may be minimal: a grunt or laugh, perhaps after a few seconds' reflection which is needed to make the connection:

> 'I was just looking for a taxi.'
> Mr Mumpson stares out across the empty, rain-sloshed, light-streaked pavement. 'Don't seem to be any here.'
> 'No.' She manages a brief defensive smile. 'Apparently they all *turn into pumpkins at midnight*.'
> 'Huh? Oh, ha-ha. Listen, I know what. You can come on the bus with us... ' (Lurie, 1986: 22)

The alludee's not catching the allusion is often presented as a sign of sociocultural inferiority. His/her ignorance can be revealed either by a carefully neutral reply, which does not fool the alluder:

> 'As I've always said, you're the perfect husband.'
> Even Penelope ought to have choked on that piece of hypocrisy, he thought. 'Sounds to me as if we'd start favourites for *the Dunmow flitch*.'
> 'I'm sure you would.'
> He was convinced she hadn't understood the reference. (Ashford, 1986: 53)

or an inappropriate reply:

> ' A year or two ago we did have a loaf in church, quite a beautiful thing [but] it was made of *plaster*. I thought that very wrong. You couldn't send a plaster loaf to the hospital, could you?'
> 'I suppose not – it would indeed be a case of *asking for bread and being given a stone*.'
> 'Well, Miss Mainwaring, it would be being given plaster, wouldn't it... ' (Pym, 1979: 34)

Asking for an explanation, on the other hand, may also label a character as naive:

> '... If you're not getting ahead every goddam minute you feel as if you're sliding back.'
> '*Like the Red Queen*.'
> 'Yeh?' Chuck blinks at her. 'What queen was that?'
> 'In *Through the Looking-Glass*.'
> 'Oh, yeh? I never read that. You think I should?' (Lurie, 1986: 168)

Even the absence of a reply may be part of the characterisation, indicating either that the alludee is not clever enough to register the contemptuous use of an allusion but takes it at face value, or that s/he is struck dumb by it, registering the insult but being unable to respond in kind.

In terms devised for the analysis of real-life interactions, it could be said that the alluder's alleged claim to sociocultural superiority is often seen as a face-threatening act (Brown & Levinson, 1987) by the alludee, who may overreact in self-defence and challenge the alluder. Some of the ensuing pacifications by alluders seem to suggest that the author has been carried away by his/her own linguistic usage and must provide the character with a feebly plausible excuse for being so literate: one policeman declaiming: 'Eternal vigilance is the price of liberty' explains: 'My kid's taking U.S. history' (Parker, 1987a: 152); another, after alluding to *Alice*, says 'My wife teaches English at Columbia. It rubs off' (Cunningham, 1987: 159). In scenes where responses to allusions are inappropriate or aggressive, the author appears to be inviting the reader to be a member of an in-group of educated persons chuckling over the comic lack of education or sophistication of others, as the effect of the inappropriate response is humorous:

> Nancy could hardly believe a letter would make her so happy. '… She is nothing to us. We each *possess one world. Each hath one and is one.*' Hath, she decided, must be a typing error, but the thought was there. (Rendell, 1970: 85)

More generally an alluding author and an appreciative reader can be said to form an in-group, with the reader flattered at being included. Such in-groups can be based on familiarity with a genre, for instance readers of crime fiction will appreciate allusions which are genre-specific, as it were, as in the earlier King example.

Shared recognition of allusions, especially of less common ones, very brief ones, or creatively modified allusions (all more challenging than their opposites), seems to be a pleasurable experience in fictional interactions, stressing 'in-group knowledge and commonality of attitudes' (Brown & Levinson, 1987: 28, speaking of on-record irony). This will lead to laughter and expressions of friendliness:

> 'White or black, they're all the same to me, they *all* stink. That's bigoted?'
> 'That's not even *equal but separate*,' Carella said, and Ollie burst out laughing… 'I like you guys,' he said, 'you know that? I really enjoy working with you guys.' (McBain, 1984: 190)[10]

The unrequested explanation of an allusion can be resented as condescending, with the alludee moving quickly to interrupt it:

'It's from *The Mikado*. Pitti-Sing was the –'
'We're quite conversant with the works of Gilbert and Sullivan,
thank you,' I said crisply. (Babson, 1988: 99)

In the following examples, the lack of certain aspects of cultural literacy
of two fictional characters (both of them medical doctors) is commented on
but not illustrated in dialogue, and explained in a more sympathetic way,
as resulting from a deprived childhood:

But Lionel had not read *Alice*; he had never read most of the children's
and semi-adults' books that formed the background to her own mental
landscape. The reading matter available in his own childhood home
had been largely polemical... (Tindall, 1983: 127)

What moved and astonished me most was that he knew no nursery
rhymes and fairy stories. He had read Dostoevsky, Proust, he read Ar-
istotle and Sophocles in Greek. He had read Chaucer and Spenser...
But he didn't know Humpty Dumpty, Little Miss Muffet, the Three
Bears, Red Riding-Hood. He knew the story of Cinderella only through
Rossini's opera. And all that sweet lyricism of our Anglo-Saxon childhood, a whole culture with rings on its fingers and bells on its toes, had
been lost to him in that infancy of slums and smelly drains, rats and
pawnshops, street prostitutes, curses, rags and hacking coughs, freez-
ing bare feet and no Prince Charmings, which had still been the lot of
the really poor in the years between the first and second world wars. I
had never before realised how the very poor people of the cities had inevitably been deprived of their own simple folklore of childhood.
(Spark, 1988: 178)

In each of these cases the powerplay aspect is lost sight of as the character with the more fortunate background is the man's lover:

At night, I used to sing nursery rhymes to William. I told him fairy stories ... They were part of our love affair. (Spark, 1988: 178)

Creative versus stereotyped use of allusions

A historical study might show a development where a commonly used
allusion is less and less often used with the purpose of reactivating particular contexts. By frequent repetition, such allusions may slowly come to lose
much of their allusive power and fade into stereotyped expressions or
idioms, in the end losing practically all of their contact with the original
context and becoming lexicalised.

The use of such allusions today seems to indicate mostly that a particular word or topic is associated in the mind of the writer with an often-heard phrase, which is repeated with little thought of the meaning it had in the original source context. In newspaper headlines for instance any news about Ireland or even a person with an Irish name may well be titled with some variation of the phrase *Irish Eyes Are Smiling;*[11] a story on an aging actress and animal lover and her many pets is called *Beauty and Her Many Beasts* without any implication (one trusts) of a love story developing between them; and a story on the inadequacy of British butchers' shops when compared to Continental ones is called *Unkind cuts come close to the bone* – surely with no thought of the context of the phrase *the most unkindest cut of all* in *Julius Caesar*. As pointed out by Ben-Porat (1976: 115–6), the activation of the evoked text in journalism and advertising would often lead to grotesque interpretations.

Stereotyped allusions could perhaps be called 'dead allusions' by analogy with dead metaphors. The death of an allusion can be assumed when a phrase is used in a context diametrically opposite to the original source context. As an example, consider *at one fell swoop*, which in its original source context refers to a father's anguish at the news that his wife and children are dead at the hands of his enemy. This often quoted phrase is found in a fictional text (Marlow, 1986) where a woman who is dying after giving birth to twins comments on the birth of two babies *in one fell swoop*. It may possibly be argued that her own imminent death darkens the scene and thus makes the allusion slightly more appropriate than it would otherwise be in such a context. When, however, a character in another text speaks of having to *buy a whole wardrobe at one fell swoop* (Cross, 1985: 99), this may be taken as conclusive evidence of the death of the allusion – except that things are seldom conclusive in analyses of this kind, and it is just possible that the phrase is intended to suggest superficiality or lack of facility with words in the minor character using the expression. Note, too, an example where the context (but not the tone, which is quite light-hearted) is equivalent enough to the source context in *Macbeth*. Interestingly, the speaker in that text (a newspaper column, written in parody of a diary), visualising the reactions of her husband to the potential death of his wife and children in a potential air disaster, does not use the phrase *at one fell swoop* but chooses to reactivate (and parody) the father's grief in *Macbeth* by alluding to the line immediately preceding that phrase in the play:

> Feel sorry for Spouse, about to receive devastating blow. *What all his pretty chickens and their Dam.* (Domum, 1989)

Reanimation of a normally stereotyped allusion sometimes occurs. The phrase *rise from the ashes* affords an example. As used in a newspaper article where the prediction is made that *Labour will never rise from the electoral ashes until ...* , it is to all intents and purposes an idiom. However, the idea of the mythical phoenix first burning itself to ashes and then rising again is reanimated in an emotionally charged scene in a fictional text:

> He wasn't sure what would happen. He wasn't sure that it was the right thing to do. He was working on instinct, a blind instinct which insisted that something good had to *rise, like a phoenix triumphant, from the ashes* of the day.
>
> ... He understood that now, and as he looked at her trusting, resolute face, he saw that Havers – reading his intention in their destination – had built *the funeral pyre* herself and was perfectly determined *to strike the match* that would put to the test the promise of *the phoenix*. (George, 1989: 319–20)

Admitting such possibility of reanimation, I still venture to give as examples some frequently dead or dying allusions encountered mostly in headlines: *Search and ye shall find* (used in my material in connection with the employment of clergymen); *Forgive us our debts* (on the financial pages); *Out, damn spot* (introducing a new household cleaner); *A tale of two cities* (on Anglo-Irish relations in one case; in another on the contrast between official Washington, DC and the black District of Columbia). In my corpus dead or dying allusions are used more often in non-fiction than in fiction, perhaps reflecting the pace of journalistic work, where the search for a novel turn of phrase is sometimes of secondary importance; what matters is that stories get written fast. No doubt the use of allusive and/or punning headlines is also thought to serve as an attention-getting device, that is, to evoke interest and encourage readers to read the item.

In fiction, the rare uses encountered of allusions normally dead are ironical:

> '... This machine here is doing the work that was done last year by twelve men.'
>
> '*Oh brave new world*,' said Robyn, 'where only the managing directors have jobs.' (Lodge, 1988: 85)

The irony is not so subtle as to go unnoticed by the director in the context (whose lack of literary knowledge is an important part of the theme of the novel). But then, the exclamation, originally alluding to Shakespeare's *The Tempest*, has mostly been used ironically since Aldous Huxley gave it this sense in his novel (Lass *et al.* 1987: 32).

Indeed, it is likely that any dead or dying allusion can be reanimated, which shows that their allusive roots are alive. Dead, dying and live (creative) allusions form a continuum. A translator needs to be alert to the function of even the most inert-seeming allusion.

Clichés and proverbs

At the time of the Renaissance, commonplace books constituted 'an important literary genre' where people could find 'grains of wisdom and glimmers of hope' (Schaar, 1991: 166). Increasing numbers of dictionaries of quotations continue this tradition; proverbs, maxims, aphorisms, some of them anonymous, many quotes from what are popularly known as great writers, pithily express old truths in concentrated form, and guide readers by suggesting how their problems and joys should most profitably be seen: *The only sure thing about luck is that it will change; nothing succeeds like success; fear of death is worse than death itself.* One period may prefer morally elevated sayings; for another, cynicism is closer to truth: *A woman has to be twice as good as a man to go half as far; every decision you make is a mistake.* What was profound in one century may be a platitude in another: *United we stand, divided we fall; blood is thicker than water.* For this reason Partridge's (1962: 3) radical distinction between proverbs and clichés ('Proverbs are instances of racial wisdom, whereas clichés are instances of racial inanition') seems to hold only synchronically at most.

While some may deplore the unoriginality of thought of those who need to borrow, others propose that '[i]t is a good thing for an uneducated man to read books of quotations [. They will] when engraved upon the memory give you good thoughts' (Churchill, 1958: 114). The compilers of such books assure that we all 'love to use an apt quotation to enliven conversation or score a point in an argument' (*Pocket Treasury* 1988:5). Proverbs are used to 'give a word of advice or of warning, or a wise general comment on a situation' (Seidl & McMordie, 1978: 241). In fact, Gutt (1991: 151) believes that proverbs have an effect precisely because they 'express popular insights' and that if they are not recognised as proverbs, they will often be imperfectly understood (for instance by children or foreigners, who do not see that they have a metaphorical meaning). To use Schaar's (1991) terms, the 'free semantic energy' of maxims is experienced by the majority of receivers, who have come to know them as they are repeated (as opposed to the 'latent' energy of more literary fragments which are transparent only to the minority who are aware of the source context).

Clichés and proverbs are thus one more category of preformed linguistic material, with the 'unwritten' literature of proverbs corresponding to the store of quotations from written literature. This point is made by Meyer (1968: 69–70) who, when discussing the use of citation in *Don Quixote*, observes that Sancho Panza's 'brilliant use of popular expressions and proverbs' corresponds in an antithetical way to Don Quixote's use of high-style quotations, though occasionally the two men change styles.

The repeating of stereotyped sayings is also criticised as 'an alarming symptom of cultural weariness and debility' (Meyer, 1968: 19). Proverbial expressions become stereotyped not by losing touch with their sources (provenance is usually immaterial with this type of saying, cf. Schaar, 1991: 165) as happens with the death of allusions, but by having their effect worn down by constant repetition. The unexpectedness that is a quality of alluding at its most successful is lost. There is a feeling of staleness, and hence it is not surprising that this use of allusions is not common in print. Authors are understandably not eager to use stereotyped expressions for their own thoughts. A true-crime writer, describing the speech habits of an actual person, shows how such use of clichés can be interpreted:

> Diane didn't read much. He was surprised to find that she often spoke in platitudes and homilies, sounding like a school girl's C- theme. ('You can lead a horse to water, but you can't make him drink', 'Everything always turns out for the best.') At first, he thought she was joking, and he laughed aloud. But she was serious. It was as if Diane didn't really understand the way humans were supposed to feel and used her trite quotations to guide herself. (Rule, 1988: 332–3)

When this type of allusion is found in fiction, it usually has the function of indicating that a character is unintelligent or conventional:

> 'She knew I'd never write, Mrs Fielding. We were – what-d'you-call-it? – *ships that pass in the night*. She never even said a proper good-bye, but I'm not breaking my heart over it.' (Rendell, 1984: 38)

> 'It wasn't very nice of the old gentleman to ask it but *everything's fair in love and war*, isn't it? You two have got to stand up for yourselves... ' (Allingham, 1986: 94)

There are 'uncultured, little-reading' persons in real life who see stock phrases and think them 'apt and smart' (Partridge, 1962: 2). Such use in fiction is thus not truly stereotypical, but a characterising device. When characters who are pictured as quick-witted and sharp on the uptake use the 'old truths', they tend to do so ironically or in unexpected contexts, with lexical or situational modifications:

> 'Really, Jeff, when I consider what Mother has introduced you to. *You can lead a horse to* champagne *but* he'd rather *drink* warm beer.' (Piercy, 1987: 184)

He collected his own glass and helped himself equally liberally. When he sat, he did so much more heavily than he'd intended and a little cognac slopped over the edge of the glass. He licked his hand. 'As my mother always taught me, *waste not, want not*.' (Ashford, 1986: 11)

Wilss (1989: 69) has noted instances in his German material where the truth of proverbs is questioned through cynical additions.[12]

As regards non-fiction, Hewson and Martin (1991: 224), in their criticism of the translation of an article in *Le Monde* for the *Guardian Weekly*, note that articles in the British press do not usually start with a proverb. In that translation, the French *l'adage* had been translated as 'the old saw' (p.223), which has negative connotations. If proverbs have negative connotations as stereotyped material for journalists in the English language culture generally, this may explain the dearth of proverbs in the non-fictional texts examined.[13] Reanimated proverbs are another matter as reanimation is creative: one article made thematic use of a reanimation of the proverb *a man's house is his castle* (ODP, 21), contrasting a man's house with a woman's body, said to be 'rarely her own' (Steinem, 1989: 41, speaking of abortion).

As stressed many times earlier, the kind of delineation of the functions of allusions given in this study can only ever be an approximation. Lack of interest in taxonomy as such and a desire to see each allusion above all in its context led to the decision not to prioritise categorisation. What the presentation of the functions of allusions even in this fluid shape has shown, I hope, is that ST allusions are not irrelevant elements from the point of view of the text as a whole but have significance of various sorts, depending on their function in the context. In translation, there may well be losses if this significance (as well as that of other implicit messages) is not gauged and taken into account as part of the analysis of the ST. Appropriate translation strategies are needed so that whatever the function of an allusion, either on the macro-level or on the micro-level, it is not lost unnecessarily.

Forms of Allusions

The form allusions take is much less crucial than their function for the translator. At least with regard to English and Finnish, it appears that while similar forms exist in both languages, the function and meaning of the ST allusion may often not be conveyed by corresponding TL words. The simple classification of allusions given in Chapter 1 made use of such formal criteria as the presence or absence of a proper name (PN versus KP allusions) and the degree of fidelity to the preformed wording (regular versus modified allusions). On the lines of metaphor studies (Brooke-Rose, 1958),[14] other possible criteria could be, for example, the wordclass or phrase type of the allusion, leading to such categories as noun phrase allusions *(these latter-day Sam Spades);* verb-phrase allusions *(you've porlocked me);*[15] adjective phrase allusions *(sear and yellow),* etc. Or classification could be based on syntactic function, with such categories as premodifying allusions *(her Cheshire grin);* subject complement allusions *(you were a very parfit gentil knight),* etc. Another possibility would be to divide allusions into phrases versus clauses *(our sceptred isle; there are stranger things in this world than in all your philosophies, Horatio).* Rhetorical terminology might also provide elements of a typology (cf. that constructed by Heibert [1993: 98–104] for wordplay). Categories could also take into account the difference between a single KP embedded in the alluding text:

> *Stable doors,* he thought. Regrets, apologies, but the boy is gone and I am here too late, with too little. I can say nothing that will provide either comfort or hope... (Gosling, 1992: 208)

and paragraphs of what might be termed matching text, with little repetition of lexical words but similar rhetorical structure:

Alluding text

> *It was the best of* crimes, *it was the worst of* crimes; *it was* born of love, *it was* spawned by greed; *it was* completely unplanned, *it was* coldly premeditated; *it was* an open-and-shut case, *it was* a locked-room mystery; *it was* the act of a guileless girl, *it was* the work of a scheming scoundrel;... a man with the *face* of a laughing boy *reigned in Washington,* a man with the *features* of a lugubrious hound *ruled in Westminster...*
> *It was the Year of Our Lord nineteen hundred and sixty-three...* (Hill, 1993: 9)[16]

Evoked text

> *It was the best of* times, *it was the worst of* times, *it was* the age of wisdom, *it was* the age of foolishness, *it was* the epoch of belief, *it was* the epoch of incredulity, *it was* the season of Light, *it was* the season of Darkness, *it was* the spring of hope, *it was* the winter of despair...
> There were a *king* with a large *jaw* and a queen with a plain *face,* on the *throne of England* ; there were a *king* with a large *jaw* and a queen with a fair *face,* on the *throne of France...*
> *It was the year of Our Lord one thousand seven hundred and seventy-five.* (Dickens, 1906: 5)

However, the construction of a typology based on isolated formal aspects is hardly useful, as the almost limitless variety of actual examples could hardly be exhausted by any kind of formal analysis. The function of allusions or their connotations are not dependent on syntax. As Lefevere (1992: 56–7) observes:

> allusions point to ... the real untranslatable, which does not reside in syntactic transfers or semantic constructions, but rather in the peculiar way in which cultures all develop their own 'shorthand,' which is what allusions really are. A word or phrase can evoke a situation that is symbolic for an emotion or a state of affairs. The translator can render the word or phrase and the corresponding state of affairs without much trouble. The link between the two, which is so intricately bound up with the foreign culture itself, is much harder to translate.

The translation of allusions being the main focus of this study, I shall illustrate the striking variety in form, which may be of some relevance as far as the recognisability of allusions is concerned, by taking up two particular aspects only. These are the range of syntactic variety in allusive expressions of comparison (chiefly involving proper names), and different ways of modifying allusions (mostly key-phrases).

Expressions of comparison

When allusions compare 'aspects or qualities of counterparts in history... , literature, popular or contemporary culture' (Lass *et al.*, 1987: v–vi), as they frequently do, such comparison is expressed by a variety of linguistic means. There is at least the simile, with its variations: 'that man is like Onassis', 'he reminds me of Onassis', the metaphor 'he is an Onassis', the appositive expression 'my neighbour, that Onassis', the premodifying allusion, 'an Onassis type' and the vocative allusion, 'It's easy for you to say, Onassis!' – all attested (with different names, of course) in my corpus. We may look at some examples of similes to see whether it is true that the form an allusion takes has little bearing on its function. Many similes can be categorised as semi-allusive comparisons (SACs, see Chapter 1) – a marginal category – but it needs to be noted that others may well be truly allusive, even on the macro-level. Contrast the use of allusive similes in two crime novels, Moody (1985) and Haymon (1984). Moody, who spreads hers all over different characters and situations in the text, uses them as SACs, creating an eventually tiresome firework display of humorous comparisons, while in Haymon the similes tend to concentrate on one person, the central character of her novel, the deceased Appleyard of Hungary. This fact gives many of her similes a thematic importance: by frequently comparing Appleyard to heroic characters of the past, Haymon both sets him up as a hero and prepares the reader for the shocks to come, which motivate the crimes in the book. It can therefore well be argued that the comparisons

of Appleyard to Nelson, Lawrence of Arabia, King Solomon etc. (all similes) are comparable to the comparisons in the form of metaphor of Parker's
(1987a) detective Spenser to Arthurian knights and have a similar thematic
or characterising function. (It may be relevant that the three texts are all
crime novels. Crime fiction may well make more use of allusions than some
other types of text because the genre requires that the reader should actively search for clues; and this may make readers more prepared to work
at uncovering other types of implicit messages.)[17]

The slight logical problem caused by the metaphoric use of PNs is often
circumvented by an indefinite article or a limiting pre- or postmodifier. 'He
is Onassis' is seldom true in the literal sense, but 'he is an Onassis' only
means that he is one of a class of men like Onassis. A negative, interrogative
or exclamatory sentence structure likewise circumvents the logical
problem:

> Who am I, Mrs Rockefeller, I have time to sit with my ear stuck to the
> radio? (Piercy, 1987: 55)

> 'I'm not Marshal Dillon out there in Dodge City, shooting it out with some
> lunatic ...   That's not what I'm paid for.' (Cunningham, 1987: 177)

The speakers thus deny comparison with rich women, or fearless sher-
iffs on the screen.

In appositive allusion, one of the phrases in apposition not uncommonly
acts as a key to the other, clarifying the allusive image:

> This was his Rubicon, the moment when he betrayed his principles. (Ash-
> ford, 1986: 148)

or an allusive image may be the second appositive, suggesting what attitude or feelings are linked to the first:

> Then, at nineteen, she transferred from Smith to Barnard and finally
> made it to Manhattan, the glittering Oz of her childhood where she had al-
> ways known she really belonged. (Piercy, 1987: 23)

Premodifying allusions may be eponymous adjectives (derived from
names), with or without adjectival suffixes: Cassandrian speeches, Nelsonian
indifference, Maurice Chevalieresque English, their Anne Frank haircuts (referring to children 'we intuitively recognise as concentration-camp inmates'
[Clemons, 1988]). Comparison is then compressed and therefore often perhaps more effective: instead of a statement, for example In their full anti-riot
gear, the policemen looked like Darth Vader in Star Wars,[18] the premodifying allusion Darth Vader riot policemen (Iyer, 1988) is more unexpected, engages

the reader's imagination, and has him/her participating in the creation of the image.

In vocative allusions, where character A is addressed or referred to as B, the comparison is implicit. The well-known name B is mostly seen as a role model for A; A is thus being compared to B in the world of the text (usually by an interlocutor), and, in most cases, thought to fall short of the model. The mode of address is usually ironic or aggressive in tone:

> 'Ah, there you are, *Maigret!* ... Pay attention, *Sherlock!...* . Don't say I didn't warn you, *Poirot!*' (Haymon 1984:49)

Socially, the ambiguity between attack and compliment can be useful:

> 'What do you propose doing, *Nancy Drew?*' (Paretsky, 1987: 275)

> 'I hope *Nancy Drew* Warshawski here knows what she's doing – ' (Paretsky, 1987: 281)

To compare an adult private detective to the teenage heroine of mystery stories for girls is a subtle putdown, but if challenged, the speaker could claim to be speaking admiringly. Cf. Brown and Levinson (1987: 211) who point out: 'If a speaker wants to do a [face-threatening act], but wants to avoid the responsibility for doing it, he can do it off record and leave it up to the addressee to decide how to interpret it.'

In a further form of allusive comparison the allusion consists of a verb and its PN object, as in: *to do a Sarah Bernhardt, to play Pollyanna.*

Ways of modifying allusions

This section will not provide a full typology. Even those whose attempts to do so are more ambitious admit that 'language in its reality of use is richer than all attempts to present it exhaustively on the basis of abstract criteria' (Heibert, 1993: 98; my translation). (He distinguishes 27 techniques of wordplay.) The ways of modification noted here are perhaps of more interest to translators than to linguists – after all, modification complicates the translator's task as it may, for example, remove from the allusion precisely the words that would help locate the allusion in a reference work.

It was noted in the earlier discussion of allusive humour that modification of allusions can be either situational or lexical. Basically, in situational twists, familiar words belonging to a particular sphere or context are applied to a dramatically different one, with the desired effect of, for example, surprise, laughter or shock. There is little or no change in the wording itself. (Without such difference in contexts, the allusion would not be modified at all.) The situationally modified allusion often uses the borrowed words parodically, in other words subverts them. The effect of shock, by contrast, is achieved when an utterly serious or more literal interpretation of what was earlier thought of mainly as a metaphoric cliché is made clear by the new context. The headline *Eyeless in Gaza* in itself evokes Milton, but when it is used for an article on the work of a surgeon trying to help the wounded in the refugee camps in the Gaza strip, it achieves a graphic reality (Ang, 1989).

A common technique in lexical modification is the use of frames, where the operative word is replaced by another. Frames were discussed as illustrations to the comic function of allusions, but it can be added that they work not only with KPs as in the earlier examples, but also with PNs:

to out-Herod Herod → to out-Truman Truman Capote

O Liberty, what crimes are committed in thy name! → Ah, Hemingway, what nonsense is committed in thy name (Piercy, 1987: 240)

While context-linked substitutions in or out of frames are in a sense unpredictable (*days of wine and roses → days of swine and Porsches* [Hill, 1995: 8]), substitutions are usually motivated by the context: for example the frame *a storm in a teacup* can become *a tempest in a soda bottle* when the subject is the Pepsi Corporation (*Newsweek,* 20 March 1989). Some regularities can also frequently be noted in the choice of a substitution. Words may be replaced by their antonyms:

It's a *small step (a giant tumble for mankind)* from private health, education, and Neighbourhood Watch schemes, to vigilantism. (Ellmann, 1989)

Two key words may be transposed:

If perfect *fear* casteth out *love,* perfect shame can cast out even agony. (Fussell, The *Guardian,* 1989)

Changes from male to female, or vice versa, illustrate both of these techniques:

'We haven't seen as much of you lately as we should like.' It was the very phrase he used to church backsliders.
I have married a *husband* and therefore I cannot come, Alice nearly said. (Rendell, 1984: 35)

(a *woman* works from sun to sun, but a *man's* work is never done) (McBain, 1984: 97)

Transpositions may also involve changing affirmative sentences into negative ones or vice versa:

Penny sighed. '*I always make passes at men who wear glasses.*' (Moody, 1985: 68)

An author may move very quickly from one frame to another, making lexical modifications:

Where are they now, the Hillman Imps *of yesteryear? In the* scrapyards, *every one*, or nearly. (Lodge, 1988: 11)

or use a punning modification where perhaps only one letter changes:

... now, standing *amid the alien porn* of Soho, six thousand miles from home ... he thinks, 'Why not?' and ducks into the very first strip-joint he comes to ... (Lodge, 1979: 112)

[Sir] Kendal put a hand on the back of [Emerald's] neck. It was one of the more overtly desirous gestures Penny had ever seen. *Tender is the knight.* (Moody, 1985: 66)

Puns are especially common in newspaper headlines. Often they are dropped after serving the purpose of catching the reader's eye; but a pun can also be reinforced in the body of the text: *Life in the Faust lane* (headline to a story on the athlete Ben Johnson's doping scandal in 1988; Dyer, 1988) was followed up by a mention of *Mephistophelian chemists*. Not all puns get such reinforcement: a story on the English Schools Championships at Wigan was headlined:

Merry has no *Wigan peer* for sprint title (*The Daily Telegraph*, 7 July 1989)

but there was no further allusion to Orwell's social critique in the 1930s. This example again serves as a reminder of Ben-Porat's (1976) assumption that journalistic use of allusions in headlines is seldom intended to evoke the original context at any depth.

Among the unpredictable but context-linked alterations in wording, there are both additions:

But he still had enough of a singing head to fail to notice that... the change was not only *in the bloodshot eye of the beholder.* (Dickinson, 1985: 99)

and substitutions:

[The surgeon said:] 'It won't be noticeable ... Your boyfriend may see a faint line when he kisses you, but if he's that close he probably won't be

looking.'
Sexist asshole, I said, but to myself. No point in *biting the hand that sews you.* (Paretsky, 1987: 85)

Syntactic modification, on the other hand, tends to be slight, usually involving only the changes made necessary by embedding the allusion in a new sentence. Too much syntactic change in addition to lexical modification would soon endanger the recognisability of the allusion.

Not only do modified allusions make demands on the translator, who is unable to identify them unless s/he recognises their preformed nature even in their veiled state of modification, but they also presuppose a high degree of interaction between the author and the reader, so that the reader truly participates in the literary creation instead of passively receiving what the author has seen fit to offer. Perri (1978: 299) speaks of the reader 'actively and comprehensively' completing the allusion's unstated significance. In Weisgerber's (1970: 44) apt image, 'the author designs the jigsaw puzzle, the reader fits its pieces together'.[19] For this reason, modified allusions present a particular challenge to translators, who, if they are to be loyal also to the TT readership, must ensure that TT readers have something to work with. Some of the empirical results in Chapter 5 will show that this does not always happen automatically, without giving some thought to appropriate strategies.

The Recognisability of Allusions

A name may signal allusion by itself (for example in the case of vocative allusion, where addressing a person as *Sherlock* or *Florence*[20] instead of his/her real name invites comparison with the source). Even if the name is unfamiliar, the receiver is likely to see the allusive intention, though s/he may miss its point. The recognition of a KP allusion as an allusion (that is, registering the presence of an allusion but not necessarily knowing its source) may be more strongly dependent on familiarity. The preformed phrase 'rings a bell'. The musical metaphor is appropriate as music, too, may make use of borrowed material to evoke echoes of an earlier composition.

Psychologically, familiarity with particular phrases is reinforced both by repetition and by exposure at an early age. Thus phrases a reader has heard repeatedly since childhood ought to be among the most easily recognisable ones to that individual; nationwide, the same goes for phrases that are generally repeated in the presence of children and young people: in stories read to them, in books they read at home and at school, in church (if regular attendance is the norm), and in the songs they listen to and the films and television programmes they watch (though the allusion-generative potential of such material may not always be long-lived). The more homogeneous a society is, the more agreement there will be on what texts every child should be exposed to, partly in order to build up a store of preformed linguistic material s/he can expect to need to be familiar with throughout his/her life. The growing diversity of American culture is partly the cause of the debate on cultural literacy in the United States (Armstrong, 1988: 29); one of its initiators (Hirsch, 1988), while agreeing that literate culture must 'keep up with historical and technical change' and press for 'greater representation of women and minorities and of non-Western cultures', nevertheless argues that cultural conservatism is valuable because it enables people to communicate with each other over barriers of age, race, geography, political leanings and class (Hirsch, 1988: xii–xiii). The sources that proved to be most fruitful of allusions in my material (the Bible and Shakespeare) not surprisingly reflect this cultural conservatism and the consequences of exposure to these sources over many generations in the English-speaking world. Absence of familiarity with traditional culture has even been seen as partly responsible for national economic decline due to lack of communication skills (Hirsch, 1988: 5); hence 'shared literate information is deliberately sustained by national systems of education in many countries because they recognise the importance of giving their children a common basis for communication' (p.14).

Thus, the recognition of allusions, at least at a superficial level, is reinforced by the exposure of sections of the population, in one way or another, to a common store of names and phrases recalling shared experiences. In some countries (such as Britain), much of the population has been exposed at school to a solid core of literature, 'which even comics of the Benny Hill genre expect to be well enough known to use in their shows' (Hatakka, 1990: 1). Nevertheless:

> there must ... be millions of literate, intelligent people ... who had never read *Jane Eyre* or *Wuthering Heights*, though it was difficult to imagine such a state of cultural deprivation. (Lodge, 1988: 141)

An individual reader can expect from time to time to meet an echo-evoking phrase in reading or conversation. The familiarity of such a phrase may be enhanced – or, if there is no familiarity, the phrase may be signalled – by deviations in spelling, lexis, grammar or style (such deviations serving to distinguish the allusion from its context). Additionally, at times, there may be an introductory phrase, quotation marks or some other such 'extra-allusive' device.

The length of an allusion may sometimes also be a factor here: a line or two of (perhaps even rhyming) poetry, or an entire sentence which departs from the context in a noticeable way will ring a bell more loudly than a phrase reduced to one or two words – though, as can be seen in some of the examples used, even the briefest KP can function adequately as an allusion. The following examples illustrate these techniques.

Allusions referring to older sources often contain linguistic features that are no longer current in contemporary English. Orthographical variation in written allusions may preserve 14th century spellings:

> What he said was, that you were *a very parfit gentil knight* (Haymon, 1984: 215)

and poetic elision:

> He had the furrowed look of someone whom the Almighty Power had just hurled *flaming from th' ethereal sky.* (Moody, 1985: 116)

> Lexical surprises involve the use of rare and archaic or dialectal words:

> *'A chiel's among ye, taking notes,'* said Wexford (Rendell, 1981: 178)

or words which the reader's knowledge of the world reveals to have a non-literal sense:

> 'I don't know that we've got any *fatted calves* in the cupboard, but you look as if you ought to eat something. And you could do with a bath.' (Bawden, 1987: 175)

> Uttered by a contemporary father to his son, the mention of *fatted calves* only makes sense as a biblical allusion to the story of the prodigal son.

Differences in word order and verbal inflexion stamp the following example with the unmistakable flavour of the 17th century:

> 'I said to Kathleen only yesterday, *Blessed is he that sitteth not in the seat of the scornful.'* (Rendell, 1984: 113)

The disappearance of the second person singular from among contemporary standard English pronouns makes the borrowed phrase in the following example stand out as an allusion:

> 'Ah,' Reed said. 'And her advice to me would be, *go thou and do like-wise...* ' (Cross, 1985: 16)

Deviations in style may be evident, for instance, in the use of imagery. In the following example the Donne allusion departs from the otherwise un-poetic assurances of the happiness of a young couple and lifts their love to a higher plane:

[Emerald] stood with Kendal, his arm about her. They didn't match. Not at all. Yet you could tell they wouldn't need a reminder-card about the till-death-do-us-part bit.
'*Twin compasses*,' Penny said. '*Like gold to airy thinness beat.*'
'Huh?'
'Emerald seems very happy.' (Moody, 1985: 60)

In the following, there is no striking grammatical or lexical oddity,[21] yet the rhythm reveals that the character is speaking poetry:

'Perhaps he just parked here for a bit,' Burden said. 'Walked up this way for – well, a natural purpose or just because he needed air... '
But Wexford looked at the view and said presently, '*Where every prospect pleases, and only man is vile.*' (Rendell, 1981: 150)

Occasionally, too, an allusion may be signalled by rhyme (in this example also by word order):

The three cops investigating the case knew very little about high-level business transactions involving astronomical figures. They knew only that *tangled are the webs we weave when first we practise to deceive*, and they further knew that nobody invests a million bucks hoping merely to break even. (McBain, 1984: 175–6)

The length of an allusion has less importance as a signal than might be thought, mathematically. An allusion can be reduced to the briefest phrase and still evoke the necessary echo. To speak of *tilting at windmills* always evokes Don Quixote for the competent reader; any non-ornithological mention of an *albatross* is likely to be an allusion to Coleridge's 'Ancient Mariner'. But in both of these instances (as with *fatted calves* above), the low frequency of the key word or collocation helps reserve the phrase, as it were, for allusive use: albatrosses and people tilting at windmills are not part of most English speakers' experience in the literal sense (contrast *albatross* with *robin* or *duck*). Only Noah ever *built an ark.*

The tendency for allusions to signal their allusivity by some sort of contrast explains why those allusions which are unremarkable in the ways discussed in this section are easily overlooked (Chapter 6):

She spoke seriously, without contempt, *her voice gentle and low – an excellent thing in woman.* But ... (Dickinson, 1985: 147)

Allusions can also be signalled, not by contrast alone but overtly, with the use of quotation marks or an introductory phrase such as 'they say', to underline the preformed nature of the words:

How did that bit go – about there being *more joy in heaven over one repen-
tant sinner than for ninety-nine* law-abiding citizens. (Haymon, 1984:
210)

They say that *hell hath no fury like a woman scorned* ...   (Cunningham,
1987: 122)

This rarely occurred in the corpus, however; no doubt because allusion
is more effective when it is not underlined in such ways.

This discussion of the form and the recognisability of allusions concerns
the translation problem central in this study, as awareness of what forms an
allusion can take and how allusiveness is signalled is part of a translator's
source-cultural and reading competence. If a translator does not recognise
an allusion, s/he will not pause to consider which translation strategies
would be appropriate for that allusion. The translators interviewed for this
study all knew that allusions 'ring a bell' in some way but found it difficult
to be more specific. They also thought that novice translators might have
difficulty spotting allusions. This assumption was confirmed in my experiments with students of English (Chapter 6).

Sources of Allusions

This section will give some idea of what types of sources (referents) a
translator of contemporary English STs can expect to meet and hence need
to be familiar with. An overview of common sources of allusions will indicate the range of the cultural competence required of a translator. While
some allusions are transcultural (shared by both source and target culture),
many others are culture-specific, and can only be understood by people
sufficiently familiar with the culture in question. While the broad categories of sources are unlikely to differ much from one selection of texts (of
the same date and genre) to another, a different selection of texts would no
doubt have produced a different group of individual allusions from those
sources. The generalisations of this section should be seen in this light.

Proper-name allusions

Both real-life and fictional figures may be alluded to by name. The
international names of entertainers or politicians who are familiar on
target-culture TV screens as well present no translation problem. The
famous names of past generations tend to be those of leaders of men, or of
writers and painters: both generals and artists have had a better than average chance to make their names memorable. The rare woman who leads
men to war is particularly well remembered: Fraser, in her study of Warrior

Queens (1989), calls Boadicea, the first-century AD Queen of the Iceni in Britain, 'one of the most powerful figures in our history in terms of popular imagination' (p.3), and states that 'it would be a rare day which did not produce at least one [allusion] to her in the British press' (p.4) – a claim borne out by her library research (p.337), and of course partly explained by the association of Boadicea with Margaret Thatcher. Allusive references in the corpus to real places and events are mostly references to war and politics: *Hastings* (1066), *Valley Forge* (1777–78), *El Alamein* (1942).

Biblical PN allusions tend to be names associated with dramatic scenes and confrontations, where memory may be aided not only by written popularisations but also by visual representations seen at an early age in book illustrations, paintings in museums or films: for example David and Goliath, Samson and Delilah.

Allusions to figures of myth and antiquity are less numerous today than some centuries ago, reflecting changes in fashions and education. Rissanen (1971: 116 ff) lists classical sources of Shakespeare's imagery in *Macbeth* and argues that Shakespeare would hardly have used so many had he not thought that the meaning of such images would be understood by most of his audience. This no doubt means most of the learned part of the audience; but it is possible to link Shakespeare's language with Schaar's (1991) idea of free and latent semantic energy and to speculate that only the learned sections of the audience received the classical images as recognisable items worth reflection, while the enjoyment of 'the mixed and noisy crowds' (Harrison 1954: 73) was not dependent on understanding the meaning of the allusions. Rissanen (1971: 116 note 2) lists nine typical examples, and points out that 'most of the images derived from classical sources occur in passages of deep emotion, often with reference to horrid and unnatural deeds'.

Few present-day speakers of English allude to figures of antiquity at times of emotional stress. Fashions in English literature have changed: witness Coleridge's (1906) recollection that his school master, James Bowyer, rebuked him as a boy for making too much use of the classical images then in fashion[22] – advice which did not prevent the poet from using some of these forbidden terms in his mature writing.[23] According to Hazlitt (1991: 187), the French revolution of 1789 had a revolutionary effect on English literature: among other things, a classical allusion came to be considered as a 'piece of antiquated foppery'. With the further decrease in attention in schools to classical myths and literature in this century there has also been a decrease in the relative size of the audience who is capable of readily understanding such allusions. Many of those that are still used are used less as allusions than as standard items of vocabulary, thus references for instance to *Hercules* or *Sisyphus*. Again, it is the dramatic scenes that are remembered best: *Midas*, whose touch turned everything to gold, *Nero* fiddling while Rome burned, and sailors trying to choose whether to sail closer to *Scylla* or *Charybdis*.

The list of literary characters alluded to in the corpus mostly contains characters in texts that are widely read and studied at school and university in English-speaking countries; there is observable variation between British and American texts in that the allusions to American literature mostly occur in American texts, no doubt because of differences in school curricula. Names of characters in Shakespeare (*Ariel, Horatio, Ophelia*) and Dickens (*Gradgrind, Miss Havisham, Little Nell*) are frequent, but there are also allusions to popular culture: film and television (*Dixon of Dock Green, Educating Rita* and *She Who Must Be Obeyed*). Children's classics like *Alice in Wonderland* and the stories of Perrault and the Brothers Grimm are traditional sources of allusions. They are complemented by more modern material, such as characters in comic strips (*Dennis the Menace, Popeye*). Sometimes, again, it is children's films rather than books that are being alluded to; this is evident, for example, from the reference to a particular song in Walt Disney's *Snow White and the Seven Dwarfs* (1937) or to the change from black and white to colour in the middle of the 1939 film version of *The Wizard of Oz*.

Titles of books, songs, films and the like are used in comparisons, sometimes modified.

Key-phrase allusions

It is commonplace to say that the Bible is the source of countless allusions in English. Bradley (1957: 219) states that the Bible has 'for centuries been the most widely read and most frequently quoted of books' for speakers of English. The Bible is of course central to the cultures of most Western societies, but according to Bradley, 'phrases used with conscious allusion to Scriptural incidents' are much more common in English than in the languages of predominantly Catholic countries, 'where the Bible is directly familiar only to the learned' (p.223). In Lutheran Finland, the language of the Bible is well-known only to the minority who are what is called 'religious', and while some biblical phrases are used allusively in Finnish, the number of those in frequent use is not particularly high. By contrast,

> biblical phrases lie embedded in many pages of English prose from the seventeenth century to the present day. But they remain always a thing apart from the movement of the writer's own prose. He knows, and his

audience knows, that he is citing Scripture. To both reader and writer the words are so familiar that quotation marks are unnecessary. (Gordon, 1966: 101)

It is therefore no surprise that the Bible is the most common single source of key-phrase allusions in the corpus. Allusions were more often to the New Testament than the Old. Psalms (*the paths of righteousness*) and Ecclesiastes (*the race is not to the swift, nor the battle to the strong*) were the Old Testament books most often quoted; in the New, Matthew (*the meek shall inherit the earth*) was the most common source (but where the same wording occurs in more than one book of the Bible, I have only noted the source given in standard works of reference). The Book of Common Prayer (*in the midst of life we are in death*) and various hymns and religious songs (*sheep may safely graze*) also provided sources for allusions.

KP allusions to figures of classical myth and literature seldom occur. In this corpus there is only the occasional mention of a knife hanging, or a huntress and the moon.

Other literary sources of KP allusions in the corpus would form a small dictionary of quotations. Shakespeare of course heads the list (after the Bible) in terms of frequency (*oh, my prophetic soul; that way madness lies; this sceptred isle* and many more). Most of the allusions are to the texts of authors who wrote in English (exceptions include translations of Villon and H.C. Andersen, and Proust, untranslated). Nineteenth and 20th century sources are more common than earlier ones (with the exception of Shakespeare). Allusions to 20th century material are more often to prose (*only connect*) than to poetry (*miles to go before I sleep*). Few allusions later than Shakespeare were repeated in the corpus, however, which makes generalisation difficult. Nursery rhymes and children's tales are also alluded to (*three blind mice, pumpkins at midnight*). There are allusions to songs, both popular songs (*I never promised you a rose garden*) and prestigious and patriotic songs ('Rule, Britannia', 'The Star Spangled Banner'). The infrequent historical allusions go back to the Middle Ages (*to die of a surfeit of lampreys*), taking in the second world war (*never was so much owed by so many to so few*), and space-age exploration (*one small step for a man, a giant leap for mankind*).

Allusions to well-known films and topical television programmes were not numerous, but some may well have been missed in the compilation of the corpus. Among slogans, some political ones were in vogue at the time the journalistic texts of the corpus were written, thus there were repeated occurrences of *read my lips* and *kinder, gentler* as well as variations of Lloyd Bentsen's 1988 remark to Dan Quayle: 'Senator, *you are no Jack Kennedy.*' Not all slogans were topical, though; earlier ones were remembered from the 18th century (*all men are created equal*), the first and second world wars (*they shall not pass; loose lips sink ships*), the 1950s (*the family that prays together stays together*) and so on.

Commercial product slogans are another group of allusions easily missed by a compiler who lives abroad. Only a few were perceived in the corpus (for example *go to work on an egg; an ace caff with quite a nice museum attached*) – but note Nash's (1985: 45) remark on advertising slogans as the 'new wit-object', playing on and responding to other texts of the same genre.

Various catch-phrases, clichés and proverbs (often authenticated as such by inclusion in anthologies) are recognised as preformed linguistic material in the public domain, as it were. Some can be traced back to a literary source: for instance Partridge (1977: 107) remarks on *I wasn't born yesterday* 'I'm not a fool' that it is to be found in the first half of the 19th century, in Marriott. Still, a printed record need not mean that a phrase was coined by that writer, who may well have used a phrase already in currency. Many phrases enjoy a long life: *There's gold in them thar hills* dates back to the 19th century gold rushes in the United States, but became popular in the 1930s and 1940s through its use in films about the West (Rees, 1989: 93). According to Partridge (1977: 219), it only became fairly general in Britain after the Second World War and in the 1950s. Oliver Cromwell's (1599–1658) instructions to his portraitist have come down to us in the form of *warts and all*, found as an idiom in contemporary dictionaries.

Various popular beliefs, assumptions and stories may be alluded to in more or less specific wording. *Death by a thousand cuts* used to be popularly linked to adventure stories featuring sinister Orientals; it may now have a financial application. *Coat hangers* are linked to abortion as a 'grisly symbol of back-street butchery' (Carlson, 1989: 32); pro-choice activists in the abortion debate have brought stacks of them to demonstrations in the United States. *Beads for the natives* refers to the practice of early Western traders in Africa and other faraway places of trading worthless goods for valuables in transactions with local people. It may now have an ironic application in less material contexts.

A writer's own experiences may function as sources of private allusions. Lodge (1985: 280) has a minor character remark in his single scene: 'People are surprisingly ignorant about twins. Why, Angelica gave me a novel to read once, that had identical twins of different sexes. I didn't have the patience to go on with it.' This reads like an allusion to a passage in Lodge's (1979: 171) earlier work where a sister and brother are indeed described as identical twins. Such a private allusion to a printed text is recognisable by a reader who happens to read the texts in quick succession, but there are also allusions to experiences that do not get into print. A reference to 'a policeman behind every bush' (Weldon, 1988: 239) is such a private allusion to Fay Weldon's being stopped by a traffic policeman in the middle of a desert.[24]

This chapter has focused on allusions in STs, where their function on the macro- or micro-level cannot be determined without a fairly clear idea of the connotations of the name or phrase used. Optimally, a culturally competent translator will recognise allusions, in whichever form they occur, and be familiar both with their sources and with the connotations they have for those contemporary native speakers who are competent readers (of that type of text) in order to analyse the text in which the allusion occurs. Recognition and analysis are a prerequisite for a conscious consideration of translation strategies for allusions. This chapter has presented the challenge to the translator at some length; Chapter 4 will address the choice of translation strategies.

The sources of the allusions in Chapter 3

lovely, dark and deep: Robert Frost, 'Stopping by Woods on a Snowy Evening'.

Though every prospect pleases, / And only man is vile: Reginald Heber, a hymn.

the madwoman in the attic: Charlotte Brontë, *Jane Eyre* (the first Mrs Rochester).

Ain't I a woman? asked by Sojourner Truth, an early American feminist, at a women's rights convention in 1851 (Tanner, 1971).

Oh! withered is the garland of war!/The soldier's pole is fallen: Antony and Cleopatra, Act IV, Scene 15.

and the Philistines slew Jonathan: 1 Samuel 31: 2.

How are the mighty fallen and the weapons of war perished! 2 Samuel 1: 27.

Adam and Eve being ejected from the Garden: Gen. 3: 23.

swift or strong: Eccl. 9: 11.

Sir Lancelot: one of the knights of the Round Table of Arthurian romance.

(Southern Trees Bear) Strange Fruit: sung by Billie Holliday (1939 and later recordings).

Neville Chamberlain: former prime minister of Britain (1869–1940).

Munich 1938: Chamberlain's meeting with Hitler in Munich is remembered as an example of misguided appeasement ('Peace in our time').

falling on barren ground: Matt. 13: 5–6.

If gold rusts, what shall iron do? Chaucer, *The Canterbury Tales,* 'Prologue', line 500.

Rude forefathers: Thomas Gray, 'Elegy Written in a Country Church-Yard' (1751).

Stoke Poges: where Gray's country church-yard was.

No coward soul is mine: Emily Brontë, 'Last Lines'.

Richard Nixon / Checkers / a dog: Nixon's defensive so-called Checkers speech on television ended with the appearance of the Nixons' dog, Checkers.

Valley Forge: George Washington and his army spent a long, hard winter at Valley Forge in 1777–78.

Read my lips. No new taxes: one of George Bush's soundbites during the 1988 presidential campaign.

kinder, gentler: Bush called for a *kinder, gentler America* in one of his speeches in 1988.

I'm not a crook: from a televised speech by Richard Nixon during the Watergate affair.

The voice of the turtle is heard in the land: Song of Sol 2: 12.

That there's some corner of a foreign field / That is for ever England: Rupert Brooke, 'The Soldier'.

Steve Carella: a detective in Ed McBain's crime novels about police work in a fictional precinct.

Tarzan of the Apes: the main character of a series of adventure stories by Edgar Rice Burroughs.

Sir Gawain, Sir Galahad, Sir Lancelot: knights of the Round Table in Arthurian romance.

Sam Spade: Dashiel Hammett's fictional detective (in, for example, *The Maltese Falcon*).

The Fairy Queen: Edmund Spenser, *The Faerie Queene*. Note the slang meanings of *fairy* and *queen* 'homosexual'.

Here's looking at you, kid: a line spoken by Humphrey Bogart ('Bogie') in the film *Casablanca* (1942).

Martha / chosen the better part: Cf. *Mary hath chosen that good part* Luke 10: 42.

But to be young was very heaven: Wordsworth, 'The Prelude'.

we owe a cock to Aesculapius: said to have been Socrates' last words.

The grave's a fine and private place,/ But none, I think, do there embrace: Andrew Marvell, 'To His Coy Mistress'.

turn into pumpkins at midnight: an allusion to the fairy-tale *Cinderella*.

the Dunmow flitch: a side of hog given traditionally in Dunmow to any couple who had lived in conjugal harmony for a year and a day (COD s.v. flitch).

asking for bread and being given a stone: Matt. 7: 9.

the Red Queen: a character in Lewis Carroll's *Through the Looking-Glass*.

Eternal vigilance is the price of liberty: Eisel and Reddig (1981: 49) attribute this to Barry Goldwater. Boller & George (1989: 56) note that it is often falsely attributed to Thomas Jefferson, but do not give an alternative source. Cf. 'The condition upon which God hath given liberty to man is eternal vigilance' (John Philpott Curran in 1790) (PDQ 129).

Let us possess one world, each hath one, and is one: John Donne, 'The Good Morrow'.

Separate but equal: a ruling dating back to the the case *Plessy v. Ferguson* in the United States Supreme Court, which decided to uphold segregation in public transport provided that the separate accommodation was equal. The same principle was approved for American public schools as well, and was not declared unconstitutional until the federal rights act of 1964 (*Encyclopedia Americana* 20: 70, 247; 24: 523; 27: 745g).

Pitti-Sing: a character in Gilbert and Sullivan's musical comedy *The Mikado.*

Irish Eyes are Smiling: a song.

Beauty and the Beast: a fairy-tale.

the most unkindest cut of all: Shakespeare, *Julius Caesar*, Act III, Scene 2.

at one fell swoop: Macbeth, Act IV, Scene 3.

What! All my pretty chickens and their dam: Macbeth, Act IV, Scene 3.

rise from the ashes: the mythical creature the phoenix is thought to burn and rise from its own ashes.

seek, and ye shall find: Matt. 7: 7.

forgive us our debts: Matt. 6: 12.

out, damn spot: Macbeth, Act V, Scene 1.

A Tale of Two Cities: a novel by Charles Dickens.

Oh, brave new world: originally *The Tempest*, Scene V, Act 1, but usually now evokes Aldous Huxley's novel (1932).

The only sure thing about luck is that it will change: attributed to Bret Harte in *Pocket Treasury* (1988: 35).

Nothing succeeds like success: proverb (PDP 228).

Fear of death is worse than death itself: proverb (PDP 39).

A woman has to be twice as good as a man to go half as far: attributed to Fannie Hurst in Spiegelman and Schneider (1973: 72).

Every decision you make is a mistake: attributed to Edward Dahlberg in Spiegelman and Schneider (1973: 93).

United we stand, divided we fall: proverb (PDP 198).

Blood is thicker than water: proverb (PDP 200).

ships that pass in the night: Longfellow, *Tales of a Wayside Inn*, 'The Theologian's Tale'.

everything's fair in love and war: proverb (ODP 36).

you can lead a horse to the water, but you can't make him drink: proverb (PDP 258)

waste not, want not: proverb (PDP 237).

Sam Spade: Dashiel Hammett's fictional detective (in, for example, *The Maltese Falcon*).

porlock: a person from Porlock is said to have interrupted Coleridge as he was writing 'Kubla Khan'.

the sear, the yellow leaf: Macbeth, Act V, Scene 3.

Cheshire: the Cheshire Cat in Lewis Carroll's *Alice in Wonderland*.

a very parfit gentil knight: Chaucer, *The Canterbury Tales*, Prologue.

this scepter'd isle: Shakespeare, *Richard II*, Act II, Scene 1.

there are more things in heaven and earth, Horatio, than are dreamt of in your philosophy:

Hamlet, Act I, Scene 5.

Stable doors: the proverb 'It's too late to shut the stable door after the horse has bolted' (PDP 198).

It was the best of times, it was the worst of times: Dickens, *A Tale of Two Cities*.

Onassis: a Greek shipbuilder and millionaire (1906?–1975) (PCE).

Rockefeller: a American family of millionaires.

Marshal Dillon: the main character of the film *Dodge City* (1939).

the Rubicon: the river crossed by Julius Caesar in defiance of the orders of the Senate ('Alea iacta est').

Oz: see p.11.

Cassandra: daughter of King Priam of Troy. She had the gift of prophecy, but no one would believe her prophecies.

Nelson: Horatio Nelson was famous for his indifference to danger.

Maurice Chevalier: French singer (1888–1972).

Anne Frank: young Jewish girl who died in a concentration camp and left a diary.

Darth Vader: an ominous character in the film *Star Wars*.

Maigret, Sherlock Holmes, Poirot: fictional detectives.

Nancy Drew: main character in a series of mystery stories for girls by Carolyn Keene.

Sarah Bernhardt: famous French actress (1844–1923).

Pollyanna: the main character in a series of books for girls by Eleanor H. Porter; she always tries to look on the bright side.

eyeless in Gaza: Milton, *Samson Agonistes*.

to out-Herod Herod: Hamlet, Act III, Scene 2.

O Liberty, what crimes are committed in thy name: cry of Madame Roland at the time of the French Revolution.

days of wine and roses: Ernest Dowson, 'Vitae Summa Brevis'.

a storm in a teacup: 'great excitement over small matter' (COD).

one small step for a man, one giant leap for mankind: said by Neil Armstrong when stepping onto the moon in 1969.

perfect love casteth out fear: 1 John 4: 18.

I have married a wife and therefore I cannot come: Luke 14: 20.

a man works from sun to sun, a woman's work is never done: proverb (ODP 32).

men seldom make passes at girls who wear glasses: attributed to Dorothy Parker (TDQ 21).

where are the snows of yesteryear? A translation of Villon's line *Où sont les neiges d'antan?* by Dante Gabriel Rossetti.

in the graveyards, every one: a line from Pete Seeger's song 'Where Have All the Flowers Gone?'

standing amid the alien corn: In Keats' poem 'Ode to a Nightingale', [Ruth] 'stood in tears amid the alien corn'.

tender is the knight: Cf. F. Scott Fitzgerald, *Tender is the Night.*

Faust /Mephistopheles: cf. *the fast lane* (in traffic, or metaphorically). *Faust(us)* sold his soul to the devil *(Mephistopheles)* in exchange for 'youth, knowledge, and magical power' (PCE 284).

Wigan peer: peer 'equal'. Cf. Orwell, *The Road to Wigan Pier* (1937).

beauty is in the eye of the beholder: attributed to both Margaret Wolfe Hungerford, c.1855–97, and Lew Wallace, 1827–1905 (TDQ 31).

biting the hand that feeds you: Edmund Burke, in *Thoughts and Details of Scarcity,* wrote: '... they will turn and bite the hand that fed them' (PDQ 81).

flaming from th' ethereal sky: Milton, *Paradise Lost,* Book I.

a chiel's among ye, taking notes: Robert Burns, 'On Captain Grose's Peregrinations'.

fatted calves: Luke 15: 11–32.

blessed is he that sitteth not in the seat of the scornful: Psalms 1: 1.

go thou and do likewise: Luke 10: 37.

twin compasses /like gold to airy thinness beat: John Donne, 'A Valediction: forbidding mourning'.

Though every prospect pleases / And only man is vile: see p.71.

tangled are the webs we weave / When first we practise to deceive: Sir Walter Scott, *Marmion.* ('Oh what a tangled web we weave/When first we practise to deceive')

her voice was ever soft, / Gentle and low, an excellent thing in woman: King Lear, Act V, Scene 3.

more joy in heaven: cf. Mark 15: 7.

hell hath no fury like a woman scorned: Cf. Congreve, *The Mourning Bride.*

Hastings, El Alamein: great battles.

Dixon of Dock Green: BBC television serial, 1955–1976.

Educating Rita: film by director Lewis Gilbert, 1983.

She Who Must Be Obeyed: Best known through the *Rumpole of the Bailey* series by John Mortimer. The phrase was originally an allusion to H. Rider Haggard's novel *She;* the character Rumpole used it of his 'formidable wife', and it was also applied to Margaret Thatcher (Rees, 1989: 185).

a knife hanging: the sword of Damocles.

a huntress and the moon: Artemis / Diana.

Oh, my prophetic soul: Hamlet, Act I, Scene 5.

That way madness lies: King Lear, Act III, Scene 5.

this scepter'd isle: Richard II, Act II, Scene 1.

only connect: E.M. Forster, *Howards End.*

miles to go before I sleep: Robert Frost, 'Stopping By Woods on a Snowy Evening'.

to die of a surfeit of lampreys: Henry I (1068–1135) is said to have died of this (Williamson, 1991: 48).

never was so much owed by so many to so few: Winston Churchill about the Battle of Britain (1940).

all men are created equal: Thomas Jefferson in the American Declaration of Independence.

they shall not pass: probably General R.-G. Nivelle's order of the day in June 1916 (TDQ 92: 13). It is often also attributed to Marshal Pétain (1856–1951) and to Dolores Ibarruri, known as 'La Pasionaria' (1895–1989); the latter because in its Spanish form *no pasarán* it became a Republican slogan of the Spanish civil war (1936–39).

loose lips sink ships: a warning against careless speech in the possible presence of spies.

the family that prays together stays together: this slogan of the campaign of McCalls magazine for family togetherness (1954) has given rise to modifications for several decades.

go to work on an egg: a slogan invented by Fay Weldon for the British Egg Marketing Board's campaign to sell more eggs (DMQ 10; Davison, 1989: 46).

an ace caff with quite a nice museum attached: television commercial and poster advertisement for the Victoria and Albert Museum in London (Simon, 1989: 36).

Notes

1. On the preceding page in her text, Weldon has used the words 'the riches of the years', thus alluding to Francis Thompson, 'The Hound of Heaven'.
2. Ruskin, however, in reality directed his attack at another of Whistler's paintings, 'Nocturne in Black and Gold: The Falling Rocket' (1877) (*Encyclopaedia Britannica* 19: 815).
3. 'Wings like bits of umbrella. / Bats! / Creatures that hang themselves up like an old rag, to sleep... ' (Lawrence, 1957).
4. Examples of Wilss's aggressive allusions (1989: 68): *Johannes der Täuscher,* used of a German politician with the first name of Johann (cf. *Johannes der Täufer* 'John the Baptist'; *Täuscher* 'traitor'); *Doping, Doping über alles* (title of an article on sports). A recent (1995) British example is *Rapid Reaction Farce* (for 'Force') in connection with the war in Bosnia.
5. The wording in Matthew (the King James version) as given in the Bible edition used in this study is actually *they that take the sword shall perish with the sword.*
6. Though some students have told me of a music video containing images of a king and the sea which is apparently based on the story of Canute.
7. These references appear to pay no attention to the differences between the characters of the various Arthurian knights. It is likely that Parker's American general readers today are not au courant with the distinctions.
8. A term suggested to me by Andrew Chesterman.
9. Wordsworth (1770–1850) used the phrase with reference to the early years of the French Revolution.
10. In this particular context, however, the responding character has not been accepted as a member of the in-group, though he would like to be. Emphasis on *all* original.
11. For example: 'US firm puts a smile in Irish workers' eyes' (Fernand, 1988) and 'Smiling Irish Eyes: Mulroney...wins a resounding victory' (Russell, 1988).
12. For example *Pünklichkeit ist die Höflichkeit der Könige, aber auch die Diebe kommen selten zu spät.* 'Punctuality is the politeness of kings, but thieves do not often come late, either.'

13. Cf. a Finnish example: the New Year's speech given by the prime minister (not the president, thus breaking a 60-year-old tradition) of Finland in 1993 ended with a proverb corresponding to the English one which says 'The darkest hour comes before the dawn'. Such use of a proverb was commented on unfavourably in the Finnish press, where it was seen as a too predictable and non-individual way of ending a speech.
14. Some of Newmark's 'cultural metaphors' (1988: 106–12) would fit among the examples discussed.
15. As in: 'Do you mind?' 'No, now that you've *porlocked* me already... ' (Seth, 1993: 1099) (The poet Coleridge was interrupted by 'a person from Porlock' when writing his 'Kubla Khan'.)
16. The cited lines occur at the beginning of the novel. There are further links between the alluding text and the evoked text, for example the epigraph on the title page and the chapter headings come from *A Tale of Two Cities*, as well as other allusions and references.
17. I owe this remark to Susan Bassnett (personal communication, 1993).
18. This example is invented; Iyer's (which follows) is authentic.
19. Both of these writers discuss literary allusion generally, but what they say is particularly true of modified allusions.
20. For Florence Nightingale, as in Moody (1985: 187).
21. True, the word *prospect* in the allusion does not have its common contemporary meaning of 'vision of the future, expectation', but means 'view of landscape'.
22. '*Lute, harp, and lyre, Muse, Muses, and inspirations, Pegasus, Parnassus, and Hippocreme* were all an abomination to him. In fancy I can almost hear him now, exclaiming "Harp? Harp? Lyre? Pen and ink, boy, you mean! Muse, boy, muse? Your nurse's daughter, you mean! Pierian spring? Oh aye, the cloister-pump, I suppose!"' (Coleridge, 1906: 4; emphasis in the original)
23. Cf. for example '...these "painted mists" that occasionally rise from the marshes at the foot of Parnassus' (Coleridge, 1906: 9); 'our language might be compared to the wilderness of vocal reeds, from which the favourites only of Pan or Apollo could construct even the rude syrinx' (p.20); 'he who serves at the altar of the Muses' (p.24).
24. Weldon, personal interview, Espoo, Finland, 17 March 1989.

4 Problem-solving: Theory and Practice

Eventually, a competent and responsible translator, after noticing an allusion in a passage of the ST and after analysing its function in the micro- and macrocontext, must decide how to deal with it. Whether or not the allusion is perceived as an actual problem, one of a number of possible strategies is going to be applied. In this chapter attention is focused on the problem-solving aspect of translatorial behaviour.

To begin with, we will consider the range of potential strategies for translating allusions. Then, questions of translation practice will be addressed: first as six Finnish translators are invited to discuss their work and their principles; and then as some of their work is examined to see what strategies they actually chose for allusions. This leads to a discussion of possible reasons for the decisions taken. A separate section illustrates problem-solving in practice; the examples used may also provide material for a teacher of translation wishing to discuss the translation of allusions in the classroom. All in all, the argument in this chapter is that considering a wide range of strategies is more likely to lead to successful translations than routine use of one strategy only.

Potential Strategies for Allusions

A distinction has been made earlier (Chapter 1) between proper-name (PN) allusions and key-phrase (KP) allusions. Potential translation strategies for these two groups are somewhat different. This is because it is often possible to retain a PN unchanged, while a KP as a rule requires a change in wording: *Pollyanna* goes in both English and Finnish, but *vanity of vanities* (Eccl. 1: 2) needs to be changed, for example, to *turhuuksien turhuus*. Also, in the case of unfamiliar KP allusions, there is commonly no single standard translation[1] for a KP.

The translation strategies for PNs are basically:

- to keep the name unaltered,

78

- to change it,
- to omit it.

These basic strategies for the translation of allusive PNs have the following variations:

(1) Retention of name (either unchanged or in its conventional TL form, see later); with three subcategories:

    (1a) use the name as such;

    (1b) use the name, adding some guidance (see later);

    (1c) use the name, adding a detailed explanation, for example a footnote.

(2) Replacement of name by another (beyond the changes required by convention); with two subcategories:

    (2a) replace the name by another SL name;

    (2b) replace the name by a TL name.

(3) Omission of name; with two subcategories:

    (3a) omit the name but transfer the sense by other means, for example by a common noun;

    (3b) omit the name and the allusion altogether.

Regarding the conventional TL forms or required changes of PNs (as in strategies 1 and 2), Newmark (1988: 214) remarks that while personal names are normally retained unaltered there are a number of well-known types of exceptions to this rule. Changes are required, for instance, for the names of rulers, many biblical, classical and literary persons, etc. The changes from *Charles II* to Finnish *Kaarle II*, from *John Paul* to *Johannes Paavali*, from *Adam and Eve* to *Aatami ja Eeva*, from *Plato* to *Platon*, from *Cinderella* to *Tuhkimo* and so on are required changes where a competent translator usually has no alternative. The same goes for certain place names (Newmark, 1988: 35), like *Florence/Firenze*, and many names of books, films etc. which have their 'official', sometimes very different translated forms. For instance *Jane Eyre* is known in Finnish as *Kotiopettajattaren romaani* 'The Governess's Novel' and *Howards End* as *Talo jalavan varjossa* 'The House in the Shadow of the Elm'.

To the question why strategies other than (1a) should even need to be considered, we may answer that while in intracultural communication (1a) would no doubt suffice, the demands of intercultural transfer are such that it is often not an optimal strategy for every name. The translation of allusions involves not just names as such, but most importantly, the problem of transferring connotations evoked by a name in one language culture into another, where these connotations are much weaker or non-existent. The familiarity or lack of it of a name for receivers in the target culture is therefore a factor of vital importance in decision-making. The empirical data in Chapter 5 will be presented in support of my argument that responsible translators need to be aware of and prepared to use the whole range of strategies where appropriate; but some observations on the question of familiarity are first in order here.

As this study involves translation between two Western language cultures with only relatively recent bilateral contacts of any great frequency, the familiarity of allusive names could be roughly illustrated as in Figure 1:

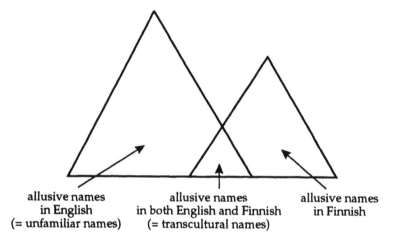

| allusive names   allusive names   allusive names |
| in English   in both English and Finnish   in Finnish |
| (= unfamiliar names)   (= transcultural names) |

Figure 1   The overlap of allusive names in English and Finnish

This figure is intended to show that both English and Finnish have a number of familiar names which have allusive potential in that language culture; Finnish, with a much shorter history of written documents and literature, no doubt has a comparatively smaller number. To some extent these names overlap. The larger triangle contains mostly English-specific names (for example *John Donne, Benedict Arnold, Mr Rochester, the White Rabbit*); the smaller one Finnish-specific names (for example *Koskelan Akseli, Seunalan Anna, Kalle Päätalo, Pertsa and Kilu*).[2] The tiny triangle where the two larger ones overlap contains names that are known in any Western culture (though frequently in somewhat differing forms, with 'required' changes or translations). Such names may be biblical (*John the Baptist/Johannes Kastaja*) or classical names (*Helen of Troy/Troijan Helena*), or names known through other literature, the media, and various phenomena of popular culture: *Romeo and Juliet/Romeo ja Julia, Uncle Tom/Tuomo-setä,*

Winnie-the-Pooh/Nalle Puh, the Beatles/Beatlesit, Star Wars/Tähtien sota, Madonna.

There is, to my knowledge, no data available on how familiar the names in English-language texts are for readers in other cultures. A small-scale experiment conducted for this study in 1991 tested the familiarity of a few names for a group of 51 Finnish university students and teachers. As familiarity appears to be an important criterion for the choice of an appropriate strategy, the results of the experiment are presented here.[3]

The names, all used allusively in the corpus, were chosen to provide variety in sources, but of course very different selections could have been made: *Agag* (biblical name), *Boadicea (Boudicca)* (British historical name), *Daisy Buchanan* (American literary name), *Thomas Gradgrind* (British literary name), *Carry Nation* (American historical name), *Pollyanna* (children's literature), *Nero Wolfe* (crime fiction), *the geese of the Capitol* (classical phrase containing a name). It was assumed that only *Pollyanna* and *Nero Wolfe* would be familiar to a sizable section of the respondents; translations of the first having been popular reading among young Finns, especially girls, for decades, and the second supported by a serial seen on Finnish television. This assumption was verified.

Scores were calculated as follows:

- Three points for a full recognition (for example: *Pollyanna* = 'always tried to be happy, looked for the bright side against all odds (children's book)'.[4] (Each example of answers given is my translation of an identification given in Finnish by a respondent in the test.)
- Two points for an answer showing some recognition but lacking some essential ingredient (for instance: *Pollyanna* = 'little girl in the care of a strict aunt').[5]
- One point for an even vaguer or more incomplete answer (for instance: *Pollyanna* = 'girl in children's book').
- No points for an incorrect identification (for instance: *Pollyanna* = 'parrot').

For the scores for each name, see Table 1. The overall distribution of scores is presented in Table 2.

The higher scores were as a rule achieved by those students or teachers who worked with the English language.[6] In contrast, all but one of the zeros were scored by those who did not work with English. This indicates that general Finnish readers would probably score on the low side. The average score in the test was 3.6 points for those working with English and 2.6 points for those who did not. This would roughly translate as a general

Table 1 Familiarity of English-language names for 51
Finnish respondents. (Sums of points scored by each name.)

Name	Total number of points
Agag	0
Boadicea (Boudicca)	16
Daisy Buchanan	3
Thomas Gradgrind	6
Carry Nation	4
Pollyanna	45
Nero Wolfe	55
the geese of the Capitol	4

Table 2 Distribution of scores among the respondents

Scores (Sums of points scored by each respondent)	Number of respondents with that score
0	16
1	7
2	5
3	7
4	3
5	5
6	4
7	1
8	2
9	1
10	0

reader recognising one of the names, and the translators(-to-be) with English as one of their working languages being fairly familiar with two. (But see Chapter 5 for a discussion of problems with reader response tests.)

The test, small as it is, would seem to support my view that translators need to assume that English-specific names in STs may well be unfamiliar to TT readers. This has obvious implications for the choice of translation strategies. Despite the lack of statistical data on the matter, the degree of familiarity is one criterion in assessing the usefulness of alternative strategies for allusions, and it will be made use of later. It is also of importance for the translation of KP allusions.

There is no criterion comparable to the treatment of a PN for the translation of KPs. The 'retention' (literally) of a KP makes no sense as a criterion as KPs are extremely seldom retained untranslated. Nor is there in most cases a single standard translation (see Note 1) available, the use of which could be labelled a retentive strategy; rather, KPs can mostly be translated in a variety of ways due to synonyms, variations of word order, etc. Standard translations for KPs exist only in the case of transcultural allusions: *brave new world/uljas uusi maailma*. These are, however, in a minority.

Therefore the list of strategies for the translation of KP allusions cannot be identical with the PN strategies list though the general approach is similar. A retentive strategy with regard to KPs can mean either a standard translation or a minimum change (see the definition later); the first concerns transcultural allusions, while in the second the allusiveness disappears, so that what is retained is the surface meaning only. The effect of the latter is so different from that of a standard translation that the two cannot properly be seen as one strategy. For the sake of clarity, then, a distinction is made here between use of a standard translation, where recognition can be expected of a competent reader *(go thou and do likewise/mene ja tee sinä samoin)* (Luke 10: 37) and minimum change, where recognition is unlikely, and possible only through backtranslation into the SL *(that not impossible she/tuo ei mahdoton hän).*[7] In the latter case recognition can be achieved only by those TT readers who are both bilingual and bicultural, while the effect for many general readers may well be a culture bump.

As the PN and KP lists of strategies do not quite match each other because of this intrinsic difference, they are labelled differently below, even where some of the strategies are identical. However, in more general discussion of strategies in this and the next chapter, where no distinction is made between PNs and KPs, the term minimum change is sometimes used as a synonym for literal translation, to refer to both minimum change of KP and retention of PN as such.

The potential strategies for KP allusions, then, are as follows.

A   use of a standard translation;
B   minimum change, that is, a literal translation, without regard to conno-
    tative or contextual meaning — there is thus no change that would aim
    specifically at the transfer of connotations;
C   extra-allusive guidance added in the text, where the translator follows
    his/her assessment of the needs of TT readers by adding information
    (on sources etc.) which the author, with his/her SL viewpoint, did not
    think necessary; including the use of typographical means to signal
    that the material is preformed;
D   the use of footnotes, endnotes, translator's prefaces and other explicit
    explanations not slipped into the text but overtly given as additional
    information;
E   simulated familiarity or internal marking, that is, the addition of intra-
    allusive allusion-signalling features (marked wording or syntax) that
    depart from the style of the context, thus signalling the presence of bor-
    rowed words;
F   replacement by a preformed TL item;[8]
G   reduction of the allusion to sense by rephrasal, in other words, making
    its meaning overt and dispensing with the allusive KP itself;
H   re-creation, using a fusion of techniques: creative construction of a pass-
    age which hints at the connotations of the allusion or other special
    effects created by it;
I   omission of the allusion.

Additionally, there are two seldom used possibilities: one is the throwing up of one's hands in desperation, stating that there are allusive
meanings involved which are beyond translation (with no attempt to explain what they are). This has occasionally been seen in Finnish television
subtitles, for instance when the comedy show *Benny Hill*, which relies on
many types of wordplay and play on allusions, defeats the translator, who
cannot, however, resort to simple silence as the actors go on talking. This
strategy is omitted from the list because it can hardly be used in the
translations of books or newspaper articles. The second is leaving the allusion untranslated, that is, leaving SL words in the TT. There is an example
of this rare strategy in one of the published TTs on p.101.

A further comment may be in order here. I claim that the translator from
English into Finnish mostly cannot count on KP allusions being familiar;
but in the absence of statistically reliable data on what percentage of Finnish readers are familiar with particular allusions, all further discussion on

familiarity is bound to be impressionistic rather than exact. However, my experiments in the classroom (see Chapter 6) indicate that allusions of the type discussed in this study often cannot even be recognised as allusions let alone identified as regards their source by Finnish university students of English, who, after all, should be more familiar with the sources providing allusions for the English language than other Finns. Hence I argue that the general public in Finland would be even less competent to identify them. (Most of the allusions in Finnish texts that are known to Finnish readers through translation other than biblical are probably allusions to texts by Finnish writers who wrote in Swedish, for example J.L. Runeberg.) Widely familiar (i.e. transcultural) translated KP allusions of English origin are rare in Finnish: occasional quizzing of friends suggests that the best-known Shakespearean allusion in Finnish is *ollako vai eikö olla* ('to be or not to be'); it proved difficult to elicit even one other example from these Finnish readers. Some empirical data on Finnish general reader responses are presented in Chapter 5.

Translator Attitudes and Comments on Strategies

The text corpus which provided the material for this study (see Chapter 1) contains both fiction and journalism. Seven of the works of fiction exist also in Finnish translations. While translation assessment is not the purpose of this study, it is nevertheless useful to examine how the translators of those texts had chosen to deal with allusions, and how they themselves see the role of the translator.

The translators of the seven texts were approached in writing. The project was outlined and their assistance requested.[10] The six translators who were reached all kindly agreed to be interviewed, Kalevi Nyytäjä (KN), Eila Salminen (ES) and Anna-Laura Talvio 'Elone (ALT) in person and Elsa Carroll (EC), Liisa Hakola (LH) and Erkki Jukarainen (EJ), owing to work pressures or geographical distance, in writing. The oral interviews lasted for from an hour to an hour and a half each; the written answers varied in length between 1 and 24 pages. The interviews were conducted between January and May 1992. A questionnaire (see Appendix 1) was used to give the framework for the oral interviews, which were tape-recorded. For the written interviews, the questionnaire was mailed to the translators. A definition of the term allusion was included in the introductory letter to enable the translators to think about the problem in advance. The following is a synthesis of the translators' opinions and observations.

None of the translators was represented in this study by their first published translation. On the contrary, they were all experienced translators, some with dozens of published translations of fiction to their credit. Three had started translating in the late 1950s or the early or mid 1960s, two in the late 1970s, and the youngest (with ten books translated so far) in 1988. All had academic degrees in languages, literature or linguistics (incl. one PhD); some had also worked in journalism, publishing or a translation bureau. Two mentioned that they had taught courses in languages or translation.

The translators mostly emphasised that they were not very familiar with translation theory and had little interest in the theoretical aspect of translation studies.[11] However, none thought that academic translation studies were worthless, only that they seemed to be of little practical relevance. One did express a wish for a more linguistic approach to translation studies in translator training. Living outside Finland as she was, though, she admitted she was out of touch with present curricula. She also thought that in her own case at least, theory was always present to some extent while she worked. Another looked with favour on recent developments, familiar to him through the professional journal *Kääntäjä*. Several had found that problems were most fruitfully addressed in discussions among colleagues.

The translators (with one exception) thought it important to keep the potential TT readership in mind while translating. The need for clarity came through strongly from their opinions: 'translators do not translate for themselves' (LH. All answers were given in Finnish; my translations). Consideration of the reader was seen to lead to better results and more books to translate. It was thought impossible to communicate with a faceless mass, without considering the receiver. The dissenter (ALT) pointed out that as all readers receive texts differently, depending on their own life experiences, she preferred to concentrate on the text rather than on the readers.

The translators generally thought of TT readers as readers of the ST author, or of the ST itself (in some of the oral interviews, there was confused laughter and surprise when it was pointed out to the translators that in fact, every word of the text the readers read is written, not by the ST authors but by the translators themselves). They thought of themselves mainly as interpreters or mediators of the ST. One (EJ) cited Kurt Vonnegut's view that the translator should be a more gifted writer than the ST author.[12] Opinions varied as to whether they translated for a particular type of reader. Some said they definitely did not, or that it depended on the genre in question. Two did have a visualisation of a reader in mind, which varied from text to text and could be quite specific (an authority figure, like a critical friend, or a relative or neighbour) or more generic (well-educated women for ES, the translator of Lodge).

The majority had first-hand experience of culture-bound differences in life through living abroad. They all said they often or occasionally realised in the course of their work that Finnish readers would not understand a particular concept, word or name in the ST. Everyday life was one source of such problems, and trademarks were frequently mentioned in this connection. In principle, they were prepared to resort to a number of active strategies to overcome such problems where possible. KN noted that culture-bound problems are fewer now than some decades ago, as the Anglo-American culture has become more familiar to Finns, and warned against 'writing down to the reader', that is, unnecessary explaining of sociocultural differences. Nevertheless, he thought it important that TTs should not contain 'question marks', passages which would puzzle the reader. Some of the translators considered the problem of sociocultural differences unavoidable and thought it best to accept a degree of loss in translation.

The majority recognised themselves in the description 'cultural mediator', but their emphases differed. For one, it was a question of the translator learning more and more about the source culture (KN); for another, of finding a way of conveying a different way of thinking (ALT); for a third, of exposing readers to what may be strange and exciting (ES). A dissenter saw the translator as a technician who serves the needs of the reader, working creatively along the boundaries of two cultures (EC). Other translators also stressed the creative writing aspect of translation as opposed to the more mechanical work of a scribe (LH, ALT).

These translators had not specifically recognised allusions as a problem area. Rather, they conceded that some allusions were difficult and dealing with them took both time and trouble. The translators mostly dealt with allusions on a case-by-case basis. Two pointed out that decisions on details always had to be subordinate to the whole, and that allusions were a problem of secondary importance from that point of view.

When asked what made them spot an allusion, the answers varied. One spoke of a need to be alert to the possibility, and thought it was often being puzzled by certain passages that made her suspect allusion (ES). The need to be well read was stressed (ALT); it is the familiar phrases that are recognised (EJ). It was believed that there is a learning process, similar to that of an art lover who learns to recognise the style of particular artists (KN). Clues ('invisible quotation marks', Lurie 1986: 158) had been noticed in STs (EC), taking the form of, for instance, comments on facial expressions, but internal clues like rhyme and rhythm were also found to occur. All accepted that they may occasionally miss allusions, one translator pointing out that it would be useful to verify them with the ST author (EC).[13]

Generally the tracking down of allusions was seen as time-consuming but necessary; the higher the literary quality of the text or the thematic importance of the allusion, the more necessary it was to make sure of the source. Every effort was made to accomplish this, though at least one (ES) suspected that the results were not always evident to casual readers. Both written sources and human informants were cited, and occasional examples were given of field trips undertaken to make sure of culture-bound details (to Fortnum and Mason to find out what exactly their trifle [Lurie, 1988: 91–3] was like [EC]; to a shoe store to discover in detail what type of shoe Hush Puppies are [ES]). One translator spoke of hours spent with a Shakespeare concordance to ascertain that a Shakespearean allusion in Chandler was correctly attributed by the author, and discovering that it was, in fact, constructed of two separate phrases in *Richard III* (KN).

As to their reactions to allusions in STs as a rule, some answers were practical, noting the need to trace the source and to decide why the allusion is used in the ST (ALT). The final decision on what to keep or omit could be made quite late in the process (EC). On an emotional level, translators recognised both dismay when faced with an unfamiliar allusion and satisfaction when they recognised one or were able to trace it to its source. These emotional reactions they doubtless share with other ST readers, but the practical aspect is part of the specific task of the translator.

In their interviews, the six translators were also asked about their views on translation strategies, not with regard to specific examples but to shed light on their general principles and attitudes concerning the translation of allusions. The views expressed can be summarised as follows.

Questions focused on alternatives to literal translation. When asked about adding guidance, the translators all agreed that they would add explanations where necessary as long as this could be done unobtrusively. Additions should not be pedantic or sound like explanations. Explanations are feasible 'when they are necessary for the understanding of the whole text, and the explanation itself is short, can be slipped into the text for example as an apposition or in the form of a dependent clause which is both logically and rhythmically appropriate' (EJ). There was, however, some fear expressed that explanations might detract from the pleasure a competent reader feels when making connections on his/her own. The use of overt explanations in footnotes was ruled out completely for fiction 'these days' (though sometimes there is no alternative and one has to use them [LH]).[14]

Omission was seen as a last resort; in the experience of one, it is more difficult to decide to omit than to retain (ALT). Current practice in Finland was said to require that the translator should make every effort to retain 'everything' – comparing translations, a translator had found that translatorial practice in Sweden differs in that omissions are more common there (KN).[15] This translator found omission of language-bound (homonymic) wordplay often justified. Another criterion for omission was utter unfamiliarity requiring long explanations (LH). The related point was made that it is likewise an ethical problem whether a translator should or should not include in the TT passages s/he has not understood (ES). For EC, there were many possible reasons for omission: 'Lack of resources? Lack of time? Lack of knowledge? Lack of space... Desire to make the text more fluent, more Finnish. Laziness? [Perceived] insignificance [of the allusion]? Boldness. Cowardice. During the shaman phase,[16] an arrogant feeling that had it been a Finnish writer writing for Finns she would not have used an allusion here/at this time/in this place.'

The translators did not speak of different editors or publishers having different views on omission or footnotes, perhaps because the TTs in the corpus were all intended for a largely similar general audience (see also Chapter 5 on Finnish readers).

Replacement by TL culture-specific material was thought a more possible strategy in general, though some translators were careful here, suggesting that it should be used mainly with such things as 'standard phrases, clichés, nursery rhymes' (EJ). When asked whether source-language poetry could be replaced by lines of a target culture poet, a translator rejected the idea, preferring to make use of even obscure existing translations of the poet alluded to, or to write a translation of his own (KN). Replacements were thought feasible 'if they are not inimical to the spirit of the text' (EC); this translator felt freer to use replacements now than when she was a beginner.

Only one specifically addressed the question of the minimum change strategy, where the translator simply translates the linguistic component without regard to connotative and contextual meaning. Hakola stated: 'Mostly it is possible to make sense of allusions both to oneself and then to the reader, if one will pay attention, take some trouble, and not make do with the word-for-word method of translation so common in Finland.' The generally expressed concern with the needs of the reader, however, shows that the translators were aware that some renderings are less than satisfactory from the point of view of TT readers.

The translators were not asked to comment on any particular examples of their own work or to explain why a particular strategy had been chosen in a given example. Asking a translator to explain or justify a particular

translation decision made several years earlier appeared unlikely to provide useful information. It seemed obvious that a finished translation had
inevitably been superseded in the translator's memory by subsequent
work, and so inquiries as to what had possibly gone on in their heads years
earlier could hardly elicit reliable data.[17] Still, some of the translators spontaneously offered comments on particular problems encountered, and
these are sometimes included in the following sections in the discussion of
particular examples.

Reverbalisation: Realisations of Strategies

Seven published translations of novels written in English were studied
for indications of what actual translatorial practice in Finland is currently
like with regard to allusions. This section describes the findings.

To summarise the findings, there were altogether approximately 160
perceived allusions (including a number of SACs) in the seven STs: c.70
PNs and c.90 KPs.[18] Two-thirds of the allusions were translated by the low-
effort, time-saving strategies of retention of PN as such (1a), standard
translation (A) (rarely) and minimum change (B) of KPs; hence all other potential strategies were represented by the remaining one-third of examples.
The proportion of least-change strategies and those involving more translatorial intervention may not be surprising, but it will be worth seeing, first,
what kind of examples the two types of strategies were used for, and later
(Chapter 5), the responses of Finnish readers to some verbalisations in
which the strategies resulted.

Strategies used for proper-name allusions

For PNs, the quick solution of retention of the name as such (1a) was
adopted in close to 70% of the instances ($N = 47$). Most of the names were
naturally unchanged (for example *Joseph E. McCarthy, Bruce Lee*); but where
appropriate, both lexical (for example *Swan Lake/Joutsenlampi; the Pied
Piper/Hamelnin pillipiipari*) and orthographical required changes had been
made:[19] the latter involving Greek names whose Latinised forms used in
English were replaced by forms closer to Greek, according to Finnish practice (for example *Scylla and Charybdis/Skylla ja Kharybdis; Oedipus/Oidipus*).

It was argued earlier in the chapter that the appropriateness of a strategy
in a given instance depends at least partly on the familiarity or otherwise of
the name. However, in the TTs, the retention of the PN was applied not just
to transcultural names but also to names very likely to be unfamiliar. This
tends to reduce a TT reader's chances of fully comprehending such passages; indeed, it will be seen later that general reader respondents had

difficulty understanding passages where names they did not know had been translated word-for-word, as if these were familiar names with standard translations (*the Walrus and the Carpenter/Mursu ja kirvesmies; the White Rabbit/Valkoinen jänis*). Responses to minimum change translations of KPs were similar.

It is impossible to assign the allusive names which occurred in the texts studied into the categories of familiar and unfamiliar names, as each individual reader's performance in recognising them would differ. It makes more sense to think of a supra-individual level, and of a continuum of names, where the existence of a Finnish form of a name outside the TT is evidence of overlapping (for example *Cinderella/Tuhkimo*); where people whose lives are discussed or whose names are mentioned in Finnish schoolbooks or the mass media are familiar to varying degrees (*Marie Antoinette, Bruce Lee*); where the familiarity of literary and other fictional characters depends partly on translation decisions made at different times in Finnish publishing houses and partly on the appearance of such characters in the theatre, on television and in films, cartoons etc. (often with international distribution: *Philip Marlowe, Bart Simpson*); and where contemporary British or American figures whose activities have won them national rather than international fame may be unfamiliar to the majority of Finnish readers (as indeed they may be on the other side of the Atlantic: *Anita Bryant, Phyllis Schlafly*). It is reasonable to retain the more familiar names unchanged and to make changes where required by convention. Still, the retention of an unfamiliar name as such may be a valid choice if the context can be thought to offer sufficient clues, or if the loss caused by the unfamiliarity is deemed not serious (as when the allusion works mainly on the micro-level). Most of the examples where PNs likely to be unfamiliar were retained as such could be thought to belong to such categories.

While recreational readers may not stop to ponder every unfamiliar name, losses are inevitable. Descriptions become less vivid; humorous asides disappear:

> '... I've got wonderful news. *Pandora Box* has invited us to her tower in Wales for the last week of June... ' (Lurie, 1986: 180)

Retention of this name unchanged does not allow a non-English-speaking reader to enjoy the humour of the allusion.[20]

Use of guidance (1b), that is, small additions or alterations intended to supply some of the implicit background knowledge in the allusion unobtrusively, occurred in under 10% of the cases considered ($N = 6$). Clarifying additions were mostly of a minimal nature: *Mr Agnew/Spiro Agnew;*

Lancelot/sir Lancelot. In one example an apposition was added to enable Finnish readers to understand the connotations of a name and therefore grasp the point of a conversation:

'I assume you think you were some kind of *Sir Galahad* protecting my good name when you punched that poor sexist fool at the library... ' (Parker, 1987a: 49)

'ja kun sinä mottasit sitä onnettoman typerää seksistiä siellä kirjastolla, taisit luulla olevasi jonkinmoinen *sir Galahad, ritareista puhtain,* jonka velvollisuutena on varjella mainettani... ' (Parker, 1988: 64) 'Sir Galahad, the purest of knights' (emphasis added, also on the apposition)

As a rule, the translators of these texts appear to have found little use for guidance in the texts studied, though their interviews showed that none thought that it should be, in principle, undesirable for translators to explain unfamiliar things to TT readers as long as such explanations were unobtrusive.

There were no examples of footnotes, giving extra information on PNs overtly (1c).

Replacement by another name (2), while very rare (*N* = 2), showed concern with the background knowledge of the reader. The pretended requirement that a bodyguard should:

'... look like *Winnie-the-Pooh* and act like *Rebecca of Sunnybrook Farm...* ' (Parker, 1987a: 11)

requires knowledge of an American series of adolescent girls' books with a sunny and well-meaning heroine. The translator chose to replace this name by that of *Pollyanna* (2a):

'... olla *Nalle Puhin* näköinen ja käyttäytyä kuin *Pollyanna...* ' (Parker, 1988: 15) 'to look like Winnie-the-Pooh and act like Pollyanna'

which conveys the desired tone. Both Rebecca and Pollyanna are fictional heroines who share an optimistic attitude to life, and both are equally incongruous models for gun-toting bodyguards. We may recall that approximately 50% of the respondents in the test on the familiarity of names had some idea of Pollyanna in a quiz of names without context, even though what precisely she stood for was vague for many. In a test of general readers (Chapter 5), most of the respondents who read a page of the Parker TT including this extract offered at least a partly coherent interpretation for the passage.

Even though recognition of Pollyanna, then, may be incomplete and miss some nuances, the replacement of the name has saved much of what might have been lost in translation. To retain Rebecca's English name would mean offering TT readers an unrecognisable allusion, and even the name given to her in the Finnish translation, *Hopeapuron Rebekka* ('Rebecca of Silver Brook') would puzzle most TT readers of Parker.[21]

The examples of replacement of a proper noun by a common noun (3a) ($N = 6$) mostly involved names which could indeed be deemed unfamiliar to Finnish readers. The common-noun replacements almost inevitably lack some of the nuances of the PNs, but their denotative meaning gets transferred, which it might not do if (1a) were the strategy chosen. Thus, *the Misses Eumenides* is rendered as *kaikki hornanhenget* 'all spirits of hell' (Allingham, 1986: 192; 1990: 200); the implications of the speaker's classical education (and of the fact that the Eumenides are referred to in this irreverent way) are lost, but at least there is no chance of the allusion being taken at face value (as referring to some old ladies in the neighbourhood, say) by TT readers.

Compare, however:

She did not *look like Carry Nation* (Parker, 1987a: 12)

hän ei näyttänyt *20-luvun suffragetilta* (Parker, 1988: 17) 'she did not look like a 1920s suffragette'

where the aim (presumably, and verifiably the effect – see Chapter 5) of the translation is to transfer connotations: contrary to the narrator's expectations, the radical feminist writer he meets is clean, well-dressed and wears make-up. Carry Nation (1846–1911), an unfamiliar figure to Finnish readers (as shown by the test earlier in this Chapter, where only one out of 51 recognised her name), fought against drink and is known to have been a formidable woman, tall and heavy, and dressed in 'stark black and white clothing of vaguely religious appearance' (*Encyclopedia Britannica* VII: 207). Retention of this unfamiliar name would have deprived the description of all content, while the replacement leads to an understanding of the surprise felt by the narrator when encountering the character in person. General readers (see Chapter 5, Example 12) described their image of 'a suffragette of the 1920s' with references to unattractive dress and/or hair, and aggressive behaviour. The connotations of the ST allusion and its common-noun replacement in the TT thus match quite well.

Among the few omissions (3b) noted, only one occurred outside Cross. The Cross translation was an abridged version for a women's magazine, and the translator in her interview (ALT) confirmed my assumption that the unfamiliarity of an allusion would be one criterion for the decision to delete a passage. Such decisions led to the loss of allusive references to *e.e.*

cummings, Humpty Dumpty (twice) and *Phyllis Schlafly* – all of them used on
the micro-level in Cross. In Lodge (1988: 241), an allusion to *Veronica's nap-
kin* was omitted because the translator could not discover its meaning (this
information was volunteered in her interview). The allusion (a comparison) occurred in the description of a picture of Bob Dylan on a T-shirt worn
by a minor character; as far as I can see, the religious connotations have no
thematic importance (though, on some level, the linking of Christ and Bob
Dylan may perhaps be regarded as an unspoken comment on a younger
generation of students in Lodge).

   Full comprehension of an allusive passage containing a PN is inevitably
limited to those who recognise the name and its connotations. In the following example, if *Daisy Buchanan* is taken to be the name of an extortionist
(a possible misreading based on the combination of money and implicit
threats of violence), the humorous nature of the description (and the
glimpse this gives of the character through whose eyes the situation is seen)
is missed. (Though *The Great Gatsby* has been translated into Finnish and
the 1974 film had a lengthy run in Finland at one time, the name Daisy Buchanan was unknown, out of context, to all but one of the respondents in
the test on p.82).

   'I thought I would knock this matinee idol on his kiester, and we
   could walk in over him.'
      'It might be a mistake to try, fellow,' he said. His *voice was full of
   money, like Daisy Buchanan.* (Parker, 1987a: 41)

      'Ajattelin että pudotan ensin tämän ompeluseuraidolin kannikat
   kanveesiin, minkä jälkeen me ylikäymme hänen matoisan majansa.'
      'Kaveri muuten erehdyt, jos yrität'; Kanttileuka sanoi. Hänen
   äänensä helisi rahaa, kuin Daisy Buchananin. (Parker, 1988: 55) 'His voice
   rang with money, like D.B.'s'

   However, by way of compensation, the translator has added colour (in
the form of alliteration and ludicrously archaic religious vocabulary) to the
lines preceding the allusion (*kannikat kanveesiin* 'drop his butt on the
ground in the ring', *ylikäymme hänen matoisan majansa* 'we shall walk over
his worm-infested body'). Though the unfamiliar name is retained unchanged, the passage therefore actually shows signs of re-creation, which
will be discussed further in connection with KPs.

Strategies used for key-phrase allusions

   Transcultural KP allusions have standard translations, that is, preformed TL wordings. The use of a standard translation can be seen as a

minimax strategy in Levý's (1967) terms, as it requires no new verbalisation from the translator and, being transcultural, helps to convey the full range of meaning, including connotations. Use of a standard translation (Strategy A) can therefore be thought a sign of translatorial competence.

In the texts studied, however, there were few examples of standard translations used for KPs (N = 4; three were biblical, one literary).[22] This supports my argument that there is, in fact, little overlap between allusive KPs in English and Finnish. It is therefore surprising that in two other instances, existing standard translations had not been made use of. This is unlikely to have happened for lack of recognition of the biblical nature of those allusions as there are clear enough clues provided in the STs:

'... And her advice to me would be, *go thou and do likewise.*' (Cross, 1985: 16)

But now, like a tardy bluebird of peace returning late to a deserted *ark after three times forty days and nights*, this blue airletter has flapped across the ocean to him. In its beak it holds, no question about that, a fresh *olive branch.* (Lurie, 1986: 133)

Nevertheless, the translators did not use the corresponding biblical expressions but translated along the lines of minimum change:

'... Patricen neuvo minulle olisi siis, *mene ja toimi samoin.*' (Cross, 1991: 30/45) 'go and act likewise'

The standard translation would be *mene ja tee sinä samoin* (Luke 10:37). In the other example, the biblical phrase *olive branch* (Gen. 8: 11) is not rendered with the corresponding Finnish biblical phrase *öljypuun lehti* 'leaf of an olive tree',[23] but literally as *oliivinoksa* 'olive branch'.

In view of the obvious clues to biblical language, it is likely that the translators did in fact, recognise the allusions but thought they were using the corresponding biblical phrases when they were not. Time and again, in teaching and in experiments conducted for this study (see Chapters 5 and 6), it was seen that Finnish respondents were unsure of precise biblical phraseology. It should be noted, too, that none of the 57 respondents who read a page of the Lurie TT containing the *olive branch* example (Chapter 5, Example 4) commented on *oliivinoksa*, though most of them recognised the biblical source of the allusion. This was thus acceptable to them as the appropriate phrase to be used with reference to the story of Noah and the dove.

The paucity of perceived examples of standard translations used suggests that this minimax strategy is, in practice, seldom available to the translator from English into Finnish.[24]

Minimum change (B) was by far the most common strategy for KPs in the texts studied. With over 60 examples, it accounts for two-thirds of the KP allusions in the seven TTs.

Instead of minimum change, the term 'literal' translation could be used, but with the use of the term 'minimum change' the emphasis is not on whether particular words, phrases etc. are semantic equivalents, but on the adoption of a strategy: whether or not the passage is translated with regard to more than the lexical meaning, that is, whether connotations or contextual and pragmatic considerations are taken into account or not.

A literal/minimum change translation can of course on occasion be a standard translation:

ST		*brave new world*
TT	Literal/minimum change:	*uljas uusi maailma*
	Standard translation:	*uljas uusi maailma*

but more often in this study, the two are different:

ST		*a man's house is his castle*
TT	Literal/minimum change:	*miehen talo on hänen linnansa*
		'a man's house is his castle'
	Standard translation:	*kotini on linnani*
		'my home is my castle'

or there is no standard translation at all:

ST		*a woman scorned*
TT	Literal/minimum change:	*hylätty/torjuttu nainen*
Standard translation:		none

As evidence of the lack of a standard translation of this last example, see Aaltonen (1989), who found that two published Finnish translations of one of Dorothy L. Sayers's novels both mistranslate this Congreve phrase in a similar way but with different words for *scorned*, thinking it active rather than passive ('a scornful woman').

A minimum change translation can work well if (1) the allusion is transcultural, so that the literal translation is also the standard translation, with the same connotations (*to be or not to be = ollako vai eikö olla*); or (2) a literal rendering is transparent enough on a metaphorical level (*there is no such thing as a free lunch = ilmaisia lounaita ei ole*; even a reader who meets this for the first time may well guess that it involves more than just the question of who pays for lunches). The meaning can then be perceived without recourse to the original source. If neither of these conditions is met, a minimum change translation will often mean a loss of culture-specific connotations so that the translation falls flat if compared to the ST. Even if not compared, it may be impenetrable or inadequate, a culture bump. Monocultural readers cannot grasp its full meaning on the basis of the translation offered, though as noted earlier, readers who are both bilingual and bicultural can uncover the meaning by back-translation.

In the following example, a minimum change translation would make the passage difficult to understand:

'... he's brought up to believe quite falsely that he's *inherited the blessed earth*. Money, position, background, servants, prospects ... ' (Allingham, 1986: 127)

If the words in italics were translated as *perinyt siunatun maan* 'inherited the blessed earth', without taking into account that *blessed* is used in the context as a mild expletive while *siunattu* does not normally have this sense (as a premodifier), the literal translation would obscure the Sermon on the Mount (Matt. 5: 5) connotations of the rest of the phrase, making the Finnish reader wonder in what sense the land the character is said to have inherited is blessed. The translators of the TT, however, chose to avoid this, preferring to rephrase with a commonly used TL metaphor to describe the young man's situation and omitting the biblical allusion:

'... Hänet on saatu väärin perustein uskomaan, että hänellä on *kaikki hyvä valmiina kuin tarjottimella*: rahaa, asema, vanha sukupuu, palvelijoita ja loistava tulevaisuus ... ' (Allingham, 1990: 134) 'he has been led to believe on false grounds that he has everything good set as if on a tray for him: money, position, an old family tree, servants and a brilliant future'

More often, however, the translators of the TTs studied were content with minimum change translations:

'So where are all the people in this town who used to stand around chanting *never* and throwing rocks at children?'
Cosgrove said, 'Most of them are saying, "Well, *hardly ever"*...' (Parker, 1987a: 109; first italics original)

Few TT readers would realise that this is a humorous allusion; from a receiver-oriented point of view, the Finnish phrase used (*tuskinpa koskaan*) is unmotivated.

In the following, the thematic importance of an allusion is less clear in the translation than in the ST:

> There is a knock on the door and Marion Russell appears on the thresh-
> old, wearing an oversized tee-shirt with ONLY CONNECT printed on
> it in big letters. (Lodge, 1988: 275)

This happens just as the two main characters, a university lecturer and
an industrial manager, have reconciled their differences, which are the central theme of the text. If only academia and industry would *connect*, Lodge
seems to be saying, it would be beneficent for society. The literary allusion
helps to reinforce this point; the TT version OTA VAIN YHTEYTTÄ
(Lodge, 1990: 383) 'Just get in touch' may even distract from it, as for
Finnish readers it is not a recognisable literary allusion.

Of the other possible strategies, extra-allusive guidance (C) was very
rarely added in the translations examined (N = 4). In one instance the
source of a phrase was added to the text – what Arnott (1971: 93) calls writing the footnote into the translation.[25] In another instance, borrowing was
indicated, not by naming the source but by slipping in a clue:

> 'In this country – *the land of the free* and all that shit – I need a man with a
> gun to protect me... ' (Parker, 1987a: 35)

> 'Että tässä maassa – *vapaiden maassa, vai miten se* paskaviisu taas meni –
> minä tarvitsen suojakseni aseistautuneen miehen... ' (Parker, 1988: 47)
> 'That in this country – the land of the free, or however that shitty song
> went – I need an armed man to protect me'

A third example had a proverb prefaced with *niinhän sitä sanotaan* 'it is
said'. Such additions, question tags and various pragmatic particles (Östman, 1982) serve to indicate that a saying is not created for the occasion but
is preformed. The use of typographical means (quotation marks, italics)
can be seen as a reduced version of pragmatic particles (cf. Lakoff, 1982:
245–7); there was one example where quotation marks around what would
otherwise have been a minimum change translation of a line of poetry
served to signal an allusion.

No examples were found of strategy (D), that is, the use of footnotes,
endnotes or the like.

There were some examples of internal marking (E) or more subtle attempts than (C) or (D) to suggest borrowing. The examples are too few (N =
6) to allow for much categorisation, but there were one or two examples
each of deliberately poetic vocabulary, word order, metaphor or sound effects, which set the expression apart from the context; this was noted in
Chapter 3 to be a factor in recognising the presence of allusions.

For instance, the translator faced with two lines of rhyming poetry embedded in the ST:

> The three cops investigating the case knew very little about high-level business transactions involving astronomical figures. They knew only that *tangled are the webs we weave when first we practise to deceive...* (McBain, 1984: 175)

compressed the image of tangled webs, kept the inverted, 'poetic' word order, but deleted the rhyme:

> ... He tiesivät vain, että *sotkuisia ovat petoksen verkot* ... (McBain, 1981: 198) 'They knew only that tangled are the webs of deceit'

In another example, the translator, realising that *the slings and arrows of outrageous fortune* is not a transcultural allusion and thus not recognisable in Finnish as a literary borrowing, achieves a comic effect comparable to that of the piling up of *slings and arrows and screws and nails and needles* with the combination of three TL words phonetically alike. She dispenses with *ruuvit* 'screws' which does not fit in phonetically:

> She believes that talking about what's gone wrong in one's life is dangerous: that it sets up a magnetic force field which repels good luck and attracts bad. If she persists in her complaints, all the *slings and arrows* and screws and nails and needles *of outrageous fortune* that are lurking about will home in on her. (Lurie, 1986: 237)

> ... Jos hän itsepintaisesti jatkaa valittelujaan, kaikki hänen ympärillään väijyskelevän viheliäisen onnen *stritsat ja nuolet ja naulat ja neulat* suuntaavat häntä kohti. (Lurie, 1988: 306) 'all the slings and arrows and nails and needles of the miserably bad luck lurking around her will home in on her'

Replacement by preformed TL item (F) occurred only once or twice; I prefer to cite an example which could be placed in this category as an example of (H), which it can also illustrate (see later).

There were up to a dozen examples of reduction to sense, that is, allusions rephrased to clarify their meaning (G). This strategy prioritises the informative function of the allusion, in a way seeing the allusion as an idiom whose meaning can be transferred without necessarily using any of its composite parts in translation. Rephrasal thus focuses on and tries to convey the meaning, but the actual words forming the allusion are dispensed with:

> He had seen *the writing on the wall...* (Lodge, 1988: 25)

Hän näki jo selvästi *tuhon enteet*. (Lodge, 1990: 43) 'he saw clearly the in-
timations of disaster'

A minimum-change translation, by contrast, would be uninformative
('what writing on which wall?') and might even misleadingly suggest
graffiti!

Examples of this strategy are mostly found in the Lodge and Allingham
translations. The Allingham translators could not be reached (Note 10), but
the translator of Lodge (ES) stated that the texts she translates are mostly
non-fiction. Emphasis on the informative function is characteristic of such
translation, and experience with such texts may have encouraged her to
make use of this strategy when translating fiction as well, thereby decreasing the risk of culture bumps.

Re-creation (H) is not a definable strategy in the same sense as for instance replacement by preformed TL item (F) or omission (I). Rather, it
empowers the translator to be creative, freeing him/her from the limi-
tations of the ST, and emphasises the necessity of considering the TT reader's needs. Any strategy which leads to the crossing of a cultural barrier is,
in a sense, re-creation. No rules or guidelines on how to achieve this can be
given, and re-creation can perhaps best be thought of as a fusion of strategies which is realised in context. Creativity requires freedom to act, but it
is noteworthy that one translator (Levine, 1975) who writes about the translation of allusions as re-creation worked closely with the author of her STs,
thereby securing herself the mandate to make considerable changes. Technically, re-creation is often likely to involve internal marking and various
replacements. Some examples of creative solutions have already been discussed under other strategies, but the best illustration of (H) in the TTs
studied is probably the following, which is technically a modified (F). In the
example there is a need for associations of bliss and thankfulness after the
birth of a child. The child's mother, who quotes St Julian of Norwich
(though it is suggested that she does not know the source) in the ST, is made
to express her feelings in religious phrases more familiar to Finns in the TT:

> '*All be well*,' she shut her eyes and said, quoting something she had
> read, but not quite sure what '– *and all will be well, and all manner of thing
> will be well*,' and Clifford did not even snub her by asking for the source
> of the quotation. (Weldon, 1988: 72)

> 'Ja kaikki on hyvin', Helen sanoi sulkien silmänsä ja siteeraten jotakin,
> jonka hän oli lukenut, olematta aivan varma, '*niin taivaassa kuin maan
> päällä*', eikä Clifford edes nolannut häntä kysymällä, mistä sitaatti oli.
> (Weldon, 1989: 103) 'all is well, in heaven as it is on earth'

This does away with the repetition of *all... well*, which might prove awkward in translation in the absence of recognition of its preformed nature. *Niin taivaassa kuin maan päällä* echoes the Lord's Prayer (Matt. 6: 10) (*myös maan päällä niin kuin taivaassa* 'in earth, as it is in heaven'). In a classroom discussion it was suggested that this makes it less plausible for Helen to be uncertain of the source, but this is hardly a serious problem, particularly because of the modification in word order. General readers tested (see Chapter 5) as a rule perceived the desired religious associations and the feeling of forgiveness and happiness after strain. Respondents commonly said they half-recognised the allusion, without being able to pinpoint its source.[26]

Omission (I) of KPs was hardly ever used in the TTs (cf. translator attitudes to it referred to earlier). One example of an omitted wisecrack shows, however, that omission had a place among strategies for at least one of the translators, even if it was used sparingly:

The breechblock. That's the whatchamacallit on top of the gun, where the cartridge sits just before you pull the trigger to send the bullet zooming on its way. The breechblock has little ridges and scratches left by tools at the factory (*tools, tools, capitalist tools!*) and these in turn leave impressions on the cartridge. (McBain, 1984: 96)

The translator omitted the reference to *tools of capitalism* evoked by the word *tools* in the description of the breechblock of a gun. Certainly the Finnish technical term used, *työstökone*, is not associated with political abuse, so the inclusion of *capitalist tools* would be unmotivated.[27]

SL phrases are sometimes retained in their foreign-language form to give local colour or for reasons of delicacy (as with expletives). In the texts studied, only a couple of instances were found of this strategy (which is not part of the earlier list). In one, the private eye Spenser is comparing his self-image to Humphrey Bogart in *Casablanca*:

If I weren't so tough, I would have thought about reading glasses. I wonder how Bogie would have looked with specs. *Here's looking at you, four-eyes.* (Parker, 1987a: 128)

The translator retains the English text but normalises the allusion:

Ellen olisi kova kundi, olisin alkanut harkita lukulasien hankintaa. Yritin kuvitella Bogien narisemaan kakkulat päässä: *Here's looking at you, kid.* (Parker, 1988: 169)

Later in the text (175) Spenser repeats his Bogart impersonation, this time with the line unmodified (*kid*). The translator follows suit.

The examination of the TTs shows that the most common strategies for the translation of allusions in these texts are those that involve the least amount of change: retention of the name as such for PNs and minimum change for KPs. The predominance of this leads to questions of translatorial principles, which the translator interviews were designed to clarify.[28] The TTs were translated by experienced translators, who were aware of allusions sometimes being difficult to translate and requiring a great deal of time and effort. The translators expressly said that they had not developed a systematised way of dealing with allusions but preferred to deal with them on a case-by-case basis; their main interest was how solutions would fit in with the text as a whole. In principle they recognised that various sociocultural items could be inadequately translated if TT readers' lack of familiarity with the source culture was not considered, and were willing to make efforts to overcome this difficulty; but they also felt that it was not realistic to aim at conveying all the elements in the ST. They were willing to provide subtle explanations rather than footnotes; to use replacements if suitable ones could be found; thought of omission as a last resort. On the other hand, in practice the translators did not attempt to serve as cultural mediators between author and reader in the sense of clarifying SL-specific allusions to TL readers, but tended to leave unfamiliar names and KPs in the text for readers to skip or puzzle over. There were few signs of attempts to create solutions 'that would have a familiar association for the reader' (Levine, 1975: 271). This means that TT readers were given less chance of participating in the literary process and deriving pleasure out of it.

The observed preponderance of least-change strategies deserves some reflection in the next section.

Possible reasons for the predominant strategy

The production of minimum change translations in preference to realisations of other strategies can be given various theoretical explanations; it is not possible to prove which is the reason for a given example in the corpus:

(1) The translator considered minimum change first, as a low-effort strategy (requiring minimum effort but perhaps not always leading to maximum effect, hence 'mini-' but not always '-max' [Levý, 1967]), and decided it would do (would not be impenetrable) because s/he thought the allusion familiar enough for potential TT readers.
(2) The translator searched for other ways to translate the allusion but found nothing satisfactory and decided to offer the allusion to bicultural TT readers and accept that others would miss it.

Both of these explanations are legitimate. The familiarity or otherwise of an allusion, while of vital importance for the choice of translation strategy, is difficult to determine; and loss in translation is known to be inevitable at times.

A further possible explanation suggests gaps in a translator's cultural or reading competence. A minimum change translation may be the result (in this case obviously not a conscious choice in the same sense as earlier) if

(3) The translator missed the allusion, thinking the words not preformed but the ST author's own, in other words, not noticing the intertextuality.

The translators who were interviewed accepted that this can happen, though it was thought to be more often an inexperienced translator's problem. Experiments with students (Chapter 6) suggest that the skill of recognising allusions and particularly of understanding their meaning develops quite late in the process of learning advanced English.

Dejean Le Féal (1987: 210) suggests that if translators do not understand what the author is 'trying to get at' it may be that they have missed what is implicit in the ST. She also remarks that readers tend to skip over problems, may perhaps not even always be aware that they have not fully grasped the author's meaning, and that this may be a reason why translators (as readers of the ST) are sometimes satisfied with less than crystal-clear comprehension. (This may also be thought by some to excuse the presence of culture bumps in translation.) A translator will not be motivated to consider different strategies if s/he is content to leave obscurities in the text, thinking that readers will either not notice or not care. Lack of time and/or of financial incentive could perhaps also sometimes be a factor.

It is also possible that minimum change is a result of translating with a certain view of the translator's task in mind. A translator does not stop to consider culture-bound differences in readers' background knowledge nor the range of available strategies if

(4) S/he is convinced that a translator is doing his/her work properly if s/he does not make changes, omit or explain because in his/her view it is the ST author who is responsible for the words in 'the text', which the translator simply renders into the TL.

(Cf. the 163 Finnish literary translators polled by Ratinen [1992], half of whom said they aimed at providing an 'accurate' or 'correct' translation.) This loss could perhaps be avoided by rethinking the translator's role and mandate. One more explanation is that

(5) The translator has not recognised that many allusions are not superfluous elements in the text but interwoven in its texture and structure to
such an extent that their loss, through undertranslation, may be a severe one. This loss could perhaps be avoided by rethinking the
translator's role and mandate.

The extent to which a translator is consciously aware of any of these
reasons for his/her own behaviour no doubt varies (cf. Jääskeläinen, 1993:
110).

All of these reasons are likely to have played a part in the choice of
strategies for the TTs studied. A competent, responsible translator may be
sensitive to allusions, notice them, trace their sources (not grudging the
time and effort this takes) and consider how best to render each one in context. This was the view the translators had of themselves. It is therefore
interesting that the translators said they had not recognised allusions as a
specific translation problem. In one sense, then, it can be said that their behaviour follows that outlined for instance by Hönig and Kussmaul (1984:
40): if allusions are thought of as of slight importance for the text as a whole,
they do not need special strategic consideration. Solutions can be arrived at
'locally', case by case.

In certain cases, however, such behaviour can be criticised if (1) the importance of an allusion in the larger context was missed because the
translator was unaware of its connotations, thus the analysis of the ST was
incomplete (= insufficient cultural or reading competence); or (2) the translator did not consider the likelihood of the minimum change translation
not communicating its meaning to TT readers (the risk of its being a culture
bump) (= insufficient metacultural or strategic competence). Apart from
this criticism the frequency of minimum change translations also suggests
that there is perhaps in practice a fear of intruding, of 'writing down to the
reader' (Nyytäjä interview, 1992), which explains the apparent unwilling-
ness to use other strategies. Comments on these lines, phrased for instance
as opposition to 'patronising the reader' (Loponen, 1993: 6; my translation)
are evident when translators discuss their work, especially in response to
criticism. It is indeed very difficult in practice to draw a line between unnecessary patronising on the one hand, and necessary mediating activity
on the other.

Still, it appears that the present general attitude to the translation of allusions may need rethinking in the light of the current emphasis on the
reader's part in the creative process. The problem with minimum change
translations – sometimes avoidable, sometimes not – is not just that they do
not always do justice to the ST author's skill. This aspect is somewhat out of

fashion at present, as work in translation studies has passed beyond mere comparison of ST and TT. The true problem, from my point of view, is that minimum change does not always enable the TT reader to participate in the creative process, picking up associations and interpreting in his/her own way what was only half-said in the text at hand. The chance to do this is denied the TT reader because s/he is not given the materials for such participation.

For an illustration, consider

> When was the last time we were supposed to have a world-beating aluminium engine? The Hillman Imp, right? *Where are they now, the Hillman Imps of yesteryear? In the scrapyards, every one,* or nearly. And the Linwood plant a graveyard, grass growing between the assembly lines, corrugated-iron roofs flapping in the wind. (Lodge, 1988: 11; emphasis added.)

A minimum change translation will convey only the denotation. Conversely, a translator who recognises the sources and wants to allow readers to participate could re-create the passage with allusive overtones recognisable to TT readers. S/he could play on the translation of the popular song *Where Have All the Flowers Gone?/ Minne kukat kadonneet?* A proposed re-creative translation would then be, *Minne Impit kadonneet?* 'Where have all the Imps gone?'. This would evoke the song, with the added advantage that the name *Imp* resembles an archaic Finnish word, *impi* 'virgin' (though the plural form is different). The double wordplay, reminiscent of the theme of *Where are the snows of yesteryear*, would be likely to make many Finnish readers smile in recognition and to note in passing the touch of ironic nostalgia. The effect would be similar to that registered by the NS informants who read the passage (Chapter 5; see also the responses of Finnish general readers reported in Chapter 5, Example 10).

Problem-Solving in Practice: Choosing from a Wide Range of Strategies

If not minimum change, then what? This section outlines a possible method of dealing with allusions, with the emphasis on using the full range of strategies instead of routinely opting for minimum change/retention of PN as such. The method is based on Levý's (1967) minimax idea: minimum of effort, maximum of effect. Still, no quantification of increasing effort or diminishing returns was attempted to justify the ordering of the strategies; the strategies are ordered in the way presented in flow-chart form (Figures 2 and 3) on the general (self-evident) principle that a quick way of

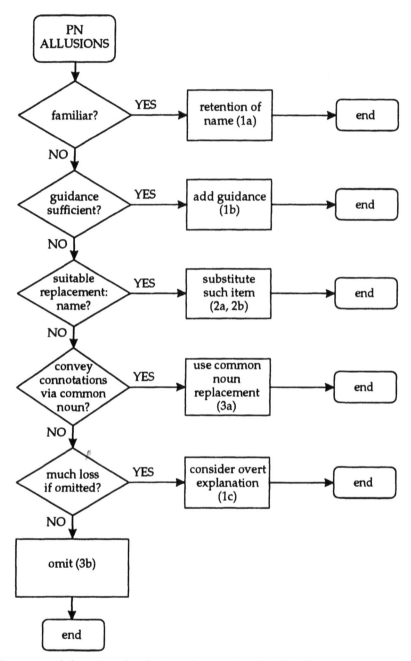

Figure 2   A 'minimax' ordering of strategies for PN allusions

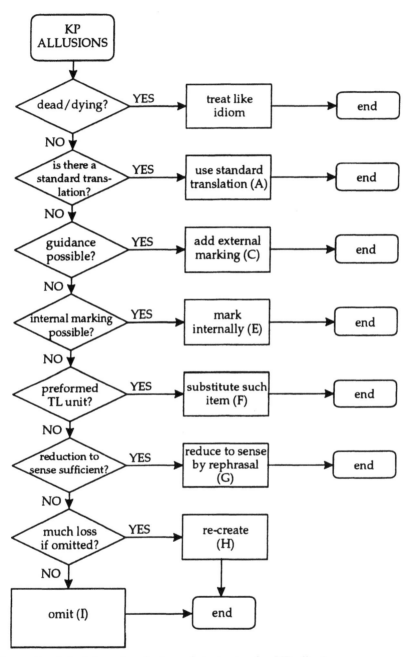

Figure 3   A 'minimax' ordering of strategies for KP allusions

achieving a satisfying solution is better than a time-consuming way and a good result better than a poor one. How to combine the two aims is often a problem. The flow-charts start with the strategies presumed to be the most effortless,[29] but encourage the translator to consider other possibilities if those high up on the charts do not lead to satisfactory solutions. (See, however, the cautions at the end of this section.)[30]

The function of the allusion in each example is taken into account, as it often shows why minimum change would not provide an effective translation for that example. For lack of space, however, it is not possible to show the context at length. (Cf. also actual reader responses to published translations in Chapter 5.)

This section may offer materials for language and translation classes focusing attention on allusions as one type of ST feature worth separate scrutiny. Where translations are proposed the TL is Finnish, but teachers and students working into other languages could no doubt suggest their own translations into other languages. The examples are mostly taken from the untranslated fiction in the corpus, and the translations are mine (though in two instances, duly marked, lines from published translations of Shakespeare by Paavo Cajander and Yrjö Jylhä have been incorporated in the translations). 'Proposed translation' means a translation constructed to illustrate a strategy which might work for the example in question. 'Rejected translation' means an illustration of a strategy leading to a translation thought inappropriate for that example for a reason stated in the discussion.

Retention of PN as such (1a) or with guidance (1b)

In the first example (previously cited in Chapter 3), the biblical name, being transcultural, can easily be retained. A translator of:

> 'Mother, lunch is ready,' said Monica...
> 'Ah, our good *Martha*,' said Father Benger (Pym, 1979: 144; emphasis added here and in the following examples and translations)

only needs to check the spelling of the biblical name in the TL. Where a required change is needed (*Martha* → *Martta* for Finnish readers), failure to make the change would obscure the biblical allusion and make Father Benger's remark puzzling. The function of the allusive PN is to subtly characterise the alluder, a clergyman conscious of 'having chosen the better part' (see also the continuation of this passage among the following KP examples).

Retention of a less familiar name, however, would not work as well. The function of the following allusion is again to characterise the alluder, by indicating some degree of sexism in his attitude to the addressee, an adult female investigator:

'Oh, all right... What do you propose doing, *Nancy Drew*?' (Paretsky, 1987: 275)

The character alluded to ('Nancy Drew, Girl Detective') is known as Paula Drew in Finnish translations, but both names would be likely to leave the reference opaque for most adult readers. Recognising this difficulty, a translator can decide to step in and guide the reader. A way of offering guidance is to use the 'title' given to this character in TL translations, for instance in Finnish *Neiti Etsivä* ('Miss Detective'). This will convey the putdown and is also likely to enable many TL readers to identify the source of the allusive remark.[31]

Added guidance may also be helpful with unknown names:

'... I'm telling you now, it's a powder keg. Whatever you do, *remember Agag*.' (Ashford, 1986: 147)

This is another biblical name like *Martha*, but rather less well known (it proved to be totally unfamiliar in the KLA test on names, see Chapter 4). In the Authorised Version, the captured king Agag comes *delicately* into the presence of Samuel and is put to death (1 Sam. 15: 18–33). The OED glosses the adverb as 'softly, lightly, ... gently... Opposed to roughly'. In allusions to this story in English texts, the meaning of the adverb appears to shade into 'cautiously, aware of danger':

... hearing only the discreet tippety-tip of *Agag-feet* along the padded floor... (Sayers, 1987: 213)

... as I would have had the press, the police, and public opinion all balefully against me if I'd ever been caught, *Agag on eggs* would have been clumsy in comparison. (Francis, 1971: 172)

'[Agag] was the one who had to *step warily*, wasn't he?' said Dungey. (Aird, 1990: 90)

In the 1933 Finnish translation of the Bible, the king enters *iloisesti* ('gaily, light-heartedly'),[32] hence unsuspectingly, and is cruelly cut to pieces. The unfamiliarity of the name in Finnish, though (it does not, for instance, occur in the Finnish dictionaries of quotations consulted), means that the name would not convey the clear warning required in the context. (The question of the translation of the metaphor *powder keg* is bypassed here.) A literal translation, therefore, would be incomprehensible. The translators

interviewed stressed the need for translatorial additions to be as unobtrusive as possible; guidance, therefore, needs to be minimal, a brief remark to
add some essential information. A covert clue:

> '... Muista *miten Agagin kävi'*. [proposed translation] 'Remember what
> happened to Agag'

would convey a warning whether or not the name itself is recognised. It
must be admitted, though, that the degree of familiarity with obscure
passages in the Old Testament suggested by the warning is, in itself,
implausible in Finnish.

Note that superfluous explanatory additions can be received as condescending as they can be thought to suggest that the information is too
esoteric for the audience to have. An example of this effect was the reaction
to an unnecessary, clumsy explanation given not by a translator but by an
author, which, when read out at a conference (Leppihalme, 1989), caused
spontaneous groans in the audience:

> 'Lordy,' Kate said. 'I'm with Archer. How I hate saints.'
> 'That,' Herbert said, 'is because you imagine them *like Mother Teresa,*
> *she of the child-care project in India and the Nobel prize.'* (Cross, 1985: 13)

Replacement by another name (2a, 2b)

Replacement by a more familiar SL or TL name may seem an attractive
solution in principle as they set the TT reader a similar task of working out
connections as that set by the ST author for the ST reader. In practice,
though, replacements with appropriate associations may be difficult to
find. A search for examples in the corpus that might illustrate problems re-
solvable by realisations of these strategies in Finnish unearthed only a few
(in addition to the Rebecca/Pollyanna example discussed earlier in this
chapter and in Chapter 5, Example 11), and even these are tentative:

> Dukakis depicted his opponent as a 'Santa Claus to the rich and *Ebe-*
> *nezer Scrooge* to the rest of us.' (Barrett, 1988)

Ebenezer Scrooge in Dickens's *Christmas Carol* has not become a familiar
character in Finland, so that neither his name nor a source reference added
as guidance, for instance *Dickensin Joulukertomuksen Ebenezer Scrooge* 'E.S.
in Dickens's *A Christmas Carol'*, will convey the meaning. Yet Uncle
Scrooge in the Disney comics, whose name alludes to Dickens's Scrooge, is
familiar enough to be used as a replacement. There is a problem with connotations, though, as *Roope Ankka* ('Uncle Scrooge') connotes above all
wealth. A translator might therefore construct a translation around the

name of Disney's Scrooge, but ironically emphasise the aspect of tightfist-edness, on the lines of:

Dukakisin mukaan Bush on rikkaille joulupukki ja 'meille muille *yhtä avokätinen kuin Roope Ankka*'. [proposed translation] '... and as generous as Uncle Scrooge to the rest of us'

This translation is nevertheless weaker than the ST as the Christmas link between the two ST names is lost.

There is a need for caution when assessing whether target cultural re-placements[33] can be used for names in fiction, as such names are implausible if uttered by characters who are presented as living in the source culture. Even substituting a TL name that has won some fame inter-nationally for an unfamiliar SL name used by the author needs to be weighed with great care:

She set off running. The tractor rumbled after her. Not fast. *Fangio* might have chafed a bit. But certainly fast enough... (Moody, 1985: 153)

At this tense moment in the narrative, the comparison of the speed of the pursuer to that of a racing car driver both makes the menace more concrete and allows the reader to see the presence of mind indicated by the ironic de-tachment of the pursued woman. If the source of the comparison is unknown, the reader may flounder. On the other hand, the following re-placement, while instantly recognisable to a Finnish target audience, might well destroy the illusion basic to the translation of fiction: that the language barrier is invisible:[34]

Hän lähti juoksemaan. Traktori tuli jyristen perässä. Ei kovin nopeasti. *Keke Rosberg* olisi varmaan pitänyt vauhtia hiljaisena. Mutta aika nopeasti kyllä... [? rejected translation]

Replacement by common noun (3a)

An interpretive version of the preceding example may dispense with the name itself but transfer the connotative meaning by a common noun phrase. Thus 'Fangio', if thought unfamiliar, could be replaced by 'a racing car driver' or 'Formula driver'. Along these lines:

We don't want teachers to turn into *Gradgrinds* (Hadfield, 1988)

could be rendered, using the reduction-to-sense strategy, as

ei opettajien pidäkään muuttua *opetuskoneiksi* [proposed translation] 'teachers are not supposed to turn into teaching machines'

or, at greater length,

ei opettajien pidäkään muuttua *vain faktatietoa suoltaviksi opetuskoneiksi* [proposed translation] 'teachers are not supposed to turn into teaching machines which just spout facts'

These would be more informative than retention of name as such and less intrusive than retention of name with guidance:

muuttua *Dickensin romaanihenkilön herra Gradgrindin kaltaisiksi* [rejected translation] 'turn into people like Mr G. in Dickens's novel'

The reduction-to-sense translations try to convey what kind of teacher is not desired, without actual reference to the little-known (to TT receivers) Mr Gradgrind, 'the founder of a school where only scientific fact is taught and where the warmth and imagination of human character are stifled' (Lass *et al.*, 1987: 89).[35]

In another example from fiction, reduction to sense is proposed for another Dickensian PN:

'I daresay you're not picking up more than twentyfive a week, are you, at *Dotheboys Hall* or whatever it calls itself?' (Rendell, 1984: 142)

TL readers may well not recognise the name of the school in Dickens's *Nicholas Nickleby*, but the coherence of the interpersonal relationship of the two characters in the scene requires recognition of the attitude of the speaker. A wealthy but uncultured industrialist, he despises his educated son-in-law's ill-paid work as a teacher. If the name were retained it would in all likelihood be taken by TT readers as the actual name of the school where he works. Reduction to sense could be realised for instance by:

'vai miten paljon *siellä koulurähjässä* sinulle maksetaan?' [proposed translation] 'how much do they pay you at that lousy school?'

where the alluder is overtly shown to despise the school, or:

'vai mitä sinulle oikein maksetaan siitä *luokan edessä seisomisesta*?' [proposed translation] 'how much are you actually paid for standing in front of a class'

where the focus of the putdown is the speaker's conception of the work of a teacher.

Footnotes (1c)

The remaining strategies are appropriate alternatives only rarely. Overt explanation in the form of for example a footnote may be contrary to reader expectations and often to present practice in translations of fiction: in Finland, explanatory footnotes are currently said to suggest academic writing to readers and publishers. As an example, we might consider the following rejected translation of the previous *Agag* example:

'Muista miten Agagin kävi.'†

---

† *Ks. I Samuelin kirja 15: 18–33.* [rejected translation]
'See 1 Sam. 15: 18–33'

This strategy emphasises the allusion like a searchlight, in effect ruining it. In a crime novel, a biblical source reference attached to a warning uttered by a shady character might be regarded as a singularly inappropriate deviation from the norms of the genre.

In other genres, footnotes have their defenders. Oksala (1990: 94), a translator of classical poetry, argues that the present fashion of no footnotes is 'against democracy of knowledge' (my translation). Thinking of scholarly translation, he sees it as the duty of scholarship to provide readers with 'weapons' (his term) which they can use if so inclined, without a lessening of their pleasure in reading. A different view is held by Dagut (1987: 80), who fears that heavy annotation will 'turn a work of literature into an ethnographic source-book'. I believe that the value of footnotes is strongly dependent on global strategies and such considerations as the genre and function of the TT.

Attitudes to notes depend at least partly on the function of the translation in the cultural context of the TL. Masnerová (1989) describes a changing approach among translators and publishers to the use of explanatory notes in translations of fiction into Czech in the post Second World War era: at first commentaries were thought 'a democratic means to assist readers in becoming acquainted with vast cultural treasures of world literature' (p.72), but this sometimes led to extremes, and was followed by a radical decrease in notes. She links this with the changing cultural standards of the reading public and an increase in international cultural contacts. In Finland, too, there has been a development on similar lines: the pre-war desire to educate a largely uncultured readership declined as secondary-level educational services began to be provided for a larger section of each age-class. A complementary reason is that most readers today are doubtless looking for entertainment rather than instruction when reading general fiction.

Omission of name (3b)

We have seen that omission of the PN allusion with no attempt to convey its meaning appears to be contrary to present ethical norms among translators. Some semi-allusive descriptions involving names generally unfamiliar to TT readers could perhaps be omitted with little loss; however, even such descriptions may partly work. A TT reader may be unaware of the connotations of the name, but the description may still convey a basic point: for instance that a character looked like somebody famous (often an actor or actress). There may be initial problems of inference if a new character is introduced with such a description, but in the texts of the corpus, such descriptions usually include fairly detailed authorial clarification, as in the following (where the name, though, cannot be thought unfamiliar):

> Between the cigarettes that dangle from his lips like a second tongue, his long dour *Buster Keaton-like* face, and the thatch of greasy black hair on the top of his head, he does not make a good first impression. (Valin, 1987: 19)

The rest of this section illustrates how the suggested method would work with KP allusions.

Dead and dying allusions: like idioms

If the allusion does not appear to have much connection with its source, it may be wiser to treat it like an idiom. It is not appropriate (as a rule) to try to evoke the connotations *unkindest cut* has in *Julius Caesar* if the alluding context concerns lamb chops. As previously noted in Chapter 3, a given allusion may quite often occur in contexts where it must be deemed dead, but may be reanimated in a particular instance. Whether an example is used as an idiom or not can therefore only be established with regard to each context – and even then, not always conclusively. In the following, we can no doubt assume that the KP is not meant to evoke the scene in *Macbeth*:

> But it is not a matter of imposing the whole apparatus to mental concepts *in one fell swoop*, then judging the result, as a whole, on the basis of how charitable it is overall. (Wallace, 1988: 214)

Generally speaking, the same might be said of:

> 'have to buy a whole wardrobe *at one fell swoop...* ' (Cross, 1985: 99)

It is possible, though, that if a SL reader is particularly sensitive to allusive connotations, s/he might read this example as suggesting that the character who uses the phrase does not quite appreciate its connotations. In other words, the allusion would not be dead for that reader. This kind of interpretation would not be open to a TT reader if the phrase were rendered by a TL idiom like *kertaheitolla*, which would otherwise seem appropriate enough.

Some dead or dying allusions (for instance those that are biblical) may be transcultural and hence have standard translations.

Standard translation (A) and minimum change (B)

The minimax strategy for transcultural KP allusions is standard translation. The transcultural allusion has connotations in the target culture as well, so that even in translation the allusion offers competent readers the pleasure of recognition and the chance to participate in the literary process, comparable to a ST reader's participation. There may be slight changes required which are due to factors outside the translator's control. The Pym example quoted above (*Ah, our good Martha*) continues:

> He and Mrs Beltane moved slowly into the house, as if conscious of being the ones who had *chosen the better part.* (Pym, 1979: 144)

To convey the irony and to evoke the biblical source (Luke 10: 42), the translator needs to use the wording of the gospel. Similarly, *loaves and fishes*[36] may need the appropriate numerals added: Finn. *viisi leipää ja kaksi kalaa* 'five loaves and two fishes' (Matt. 14: 13–31).

A standard translation may fuse with minimum change:

> Few have even investigated the great child abuse hoax. However, someone has got to stand up and say *the emperor has no clothes.* It is just plain common sense that child abuse is not as frequent as 1-in-10, as some zealots suggest. (*The Sunday Times,* 1988)[37]

> Jonkun täytyy sanoa ääneen, että *keisarilla ei ole vaatteita.* [proposed translation] 'Someone has to say aloud that the emperor has no clothes'

It was found earlier, however, that standard translations were far from common in the TTs studied (four instances out of c. 90 KP allusions), undoubtedly because each language culture tends to allude to its own sources. While I have not looked into alluding by Finnish authors, it appears likely that alluding, especially to literary sources, meets with difficulties in Finland because of a lack of shared sources. The writer Jouko Tyyri (cited in Kahila, 1990: 59) comments: 'It is no longer possible simply to allude to a passage in the Bible... It no longer raises any kind of response in the reader. If the reader does not know the Bible, it is no use alluding to it. We no longer have enough shared texts to allude to' (59; my translation).

He cites also *The Kalevala* and Kivi's *Seven Brothers* (once major works for Finnish national consciousness) as no longer well enough known for allusive purposes. A present-day British writer who likewise feels that his/her readers do not know the Bible can perhaps still expect that the biblical phrases s/he wants to use will nevertheless have an effect through their 'free semantic energy' (Schaar, 1991) and the centuries-long influence they have had on the English language. This possible intercultural difference in frequency of alluding could be investigated in future research. If translators feel that alluding is less common in Finnish, it may well make them opt for reduction to sense as a strategy.

If a minimum change or literal translation is not a recognised standard translation, much of the meaning is inevitably lost:

> 'The present computer is so slow that it can take up to ten days to go through its database of three hundred and fifty thousand prints. But some genius is working on a new computer that'll cut the time down to one day.'
>
> '*Always jam tomorrow,*' said McMahon. (Ashford, 1986: 90)

It is clear enough that a literal translation of McMahon's line would be incomprehensible to readers unfamiliar with the White Queen's rule 'jam to-morrow and jam yesterday – but never jam to-day' (Carroll, *Through the Looking Glass*, Chapter 5). A translator would need to look for alternatives to avoid the culture bump.

Guidance, external marking (C)

Extra-allusive additions resemble the ways ST authors sometimes signal allusion to call attention to the fact that a phrase is borrowed rather than original. This can take, for instance, the typographical form of inverted commas or italics. The following is an example where italics were used by the author. To a newly widowed character, a friend's mention of 'tomorrow' calls up the bleak non-future of Macbeth:

> 'Not now... ' She sighed with exasperation. 'I mean, tomorrow, next week, from now on.... ?'
>
> *Tomorrow and tomorrow and tomorrow* ... I hadn't thought that far ahead yet. (Babson, 1988: 10; emphasis in the original)

The italics emphasise that the words have been used before with special meaning, in case potential readers of the passage might think that the repetition of the word indicated for example the character's annoyance at being asked to make decisions. Italics or inverted commas could be used in

translation, too, for this example and for many other KPs that TT readers
are unable to recognise as allusions without some such translatorial
assistance.

The signal may also take the form of an introductory phrase; in this way
a TT reader could infer that a puzzling expression in the text was preformed – information that competent ST readers would possess as part of
their cultural literacy. A source reference can also be slipped into the
dialogue:

> 'I don't think I've ever met a bodyguard before.'
> 'We're just regular folks,' I said. *'If you cut us, do we not bleed?'*
> 'Literary, too,' Linda Smith said. (Parker, 1987a: 38)

> 'En ole tainnutkaan ennen tavata henkivartijaa.'
> 'Ihan tavallista väkeä,' vakuutin. *'– Jos meitä pistätte, emmekö vuoda verta?'*
> *'Ja Shakespearet luettu,'* totesi Linda Smith. [proposed translation incor-
> porates the translation of the Shakespearean line by Yrjö Jylhä] 'If you
> cut us, do we not bleed?' 'You've read your Shakespeare'

This proposed translation deals with the allusion by citing the line in the
form used in Jylhä's translation of *The Merchant of Venice* (Act III, Scene 1),
but adds guidance, in the form of a translatorial alteration in Linda Smith's
comment, which serves to identify the line as a quotation.

In the following, if the name of the source of comparison is added, it
helps to identify him:

> He had the furrowed look of someone whom the Almighty Power had
> just hurled *flaming from th' ethereal sky.* Penny liked them like that.
> (Moody, 1985: 116)

> Hänellä oli *Luciferin* uurteet kasvot, ikään kuin Kaikkivaltias olisi
> juuri singonnut hänet *liekeissä alas korkeuksista.* [proposed translation]
> 'He had the furrowed face of Lucifer, as if the Almighty had just hurled
> him down in flames from the heavens'

There is no way of evoking Milton for general Finnish readers by any
translation of *th' ethereal sky,* but *alas korkeuksista* has a religious flavour. The
translation suggests not the details but some of the essential elements of the
story of *Paradise Lost.*

Internal marking (E)

Internal marking or what might be called simulated familiarity (signal-
ling an allusion by using stylistic contrast, found to be an element in the

recognisability of allusions, cf. Chapter 3) can sometimes be achieved by using lines from an existing translation of a classic to translate an allusion (in the Shylock example above, though, the Jylhä translation shows little stylistic contrast and could be thought simply to state a biological fact). The metaphors in the following, however:

> 'He was a husband in a million, a good kind man, a wonderful man to his friends. You ask anyone, ask Jack... He was one in a million!'
> *Oh! withered is the garland of war! The soldier's poll is fallen...* Strange, Wexford thought, that when you considered Charlie Hatton you thought of war and soldiers and battles. (Rendell, 1981: 89)

are clearly poetry. The allusion to *Antony and Cleopatra* (Act IV, Scene 15) (discussed in Chapter 3) is thematic: it is offered as a significant aid to interpretation. If a translator makes use of the Cajander translation:

> ' ... Hän oli niin harvinainen mies!'
> *Oi, kuihtunut on sodan voittoseppel, sen lippupuu nyt kaatui...* Aika outoa, Wexford tuumi, että Charlie Hattonista tuli aina mieleen sota ja sotilaat ja taistelut. (My proposed translation contains Paavo Cajander's translation of the Shakespearean line in italics.)

the sentence will be marked as an allusion by the metaphors, the poetic vocabulary (*voittoseppel* 'garland of victory', *lippupuu* 'flag pole, standard'[38] – not *lipputanko*, the everyday term) and inverted word order. The words themselves are unlikely to suggest any particular text to Finnish readers, so that the example, because of its unrecognisability, is not comparable to standard translations of the *to be or not to be/ ollako vai eikö olla* variety; but the line of poetry would heighten the atmosphere in both ST and TT, bringing in a comparison with a more literary way of expressing one's loss than that used by the young widow speaking, as well as echoes of a different way of viewing 'soldiers and battles'. The allusion can also be made more visible by using italics.[39]

Replacement by preformed TL item (F)

The replacement of a SL allusion by a TL-specific allusion is seldom an effective alternative. As pointed out earlier, TL-specific allusions disturb the desired illusion in translation that TL readers are able to experience a foreign world despite the language barrier; in most cases, rendering *haggis* as *kalakukko* (an East-Finnish speciality made of rye flour and fish) will shatter the illusion, nor will a Finnish poet's verse be plausible instead of a quoted passage of English poetry. Also, texts with matching associations are not readily available. It would seem that TL material usable for this strategy is preferably anonymous – that this will work best with proverbs and similar instances of folk wisdom:

'*Sticks and stones,*' she said lightly. 'You know how it goes on.' (Rendell, 1984: 32)

'*Ei haukku haavaa tee,*' hän hymähti. [proposed translation] '[A dog's] bark does not cause a wound' (Finnish proverb)

This is not a standard translation, which term implies a greater degree of lexical similarity between SL and TL versions (as in for instance *a man's house is his castle/ kotini on linnani* 'my home is my castle'); rather, here an idea acknowledged in both cultures (that a verbal attack will not cause physical harm) is couched in different images in the two languages.

A subtle use of TL-specific material is to modify it, in this way allowing readers to wonder whether or not an allusion is intended:

Underfoot there were leaves which crackled like cornflakes as they walked. The air was warm with residual heat. Beneath the trees were shadows. *Lovely, dark and deep.* (Moody, 1985: 36)

Instead of looking up translations of Frost's line, a Finnish translator might perhaps modify a line of a Finnish popular song. Thus *Metsässä ei liikahda lehtikään* 'Not a leaf is stirring in the woods' could turn into *Lehtikään ei liikahtanut* 'Not a leaf stirred'. This can be taken as a non-allusive detail in the description of the wood, but a sensitive reader might also be reminded of the atmosphere of the song. As TT readers will not be comparing TT and ST they will not consider whether the line of Frost is rendered appropriately, but the modified TL allusion could add depth to the description of the woodland scene. The use of poetry identifiable as the work of an individual TL writer, even if modified, might disturb the illusion: thus *Kaukana kavala maailma* (Aleksis Kivi) 'Far away the wicked world' modified as *Kavala maailma tuntui olevan kaukana* 'The wicked world seemed far away', while in many ways apt, might distract some readers and set them to wonder if and why the Finnish poet was being cited.

Modified allusions whose function is humorous may profit from replacement by TL-specific material – the briefer, the better:

'And you heard nothing?'
'I said. Besides, who'd hang around when they'd just killed someone?'
'Someone out for sport might. Who hadn't realised there'd been a fatal accident.'
Mulberry-bush time again. 'It wasn't an accident.' (Moody, 1985: 76)

As the author has made alterations to the familiar in the expectation that the primary audience will be able to follow, the translator can try to first devise something familiar and then modify that, if necessary, for humorous effect. The reference in this example to a children's rhyme has the meaning of 'here we go again', and could be rendered for instance with a line from a TL nursery rhyme: *piiri pieni pyörii*. (This translation needs no verbal modification because it is modified situationally.) Reader responses (Chapter 5) suggest that the humour of modified allusions is not easily conveyed if the allusion is to an unfamiliar source.[40]

Reduction to sense by rephrasal (G)

The reduction of the allusion to sense lends itself particularly to often-repeated and hence not especially creative allusions. This strategy could be considered for instance for brief allusions to slogans in domestic politics, local advertising campaigns and the like, which would mean little or nothing to the TL audience:

> Betty and Raymond Heitger invited about a dozen of their friends and neighbours over to watch the *heartbeat-away sweepstakes*. (Shapiro, 1988)

The colourful image, which suggests that the debate could go either way and is a reminder of the saying that a vice president is only a heartbeat away from the presidency, cannot be rendered as economically in a language where the political cliché is unfamiliar. A translator might therefore decide to use the purely denotational: 'to watch the vice-presidential debate on television'. Further emphasis can be added with the help of an adjectival attribute (for example 'exciting', 'crucial' or the like).

The answer *always jam tomorrow* (see the example under standard translation) can be effectively translated using this strategy, that is, finding an informal TL expression corresponding to the speaker's meaning, such as the Finnish *näkis vaan* or *paljonhan sitä puhutaan*.

A literal translation of some unfamiliar allusions in a way reduces them to sense, but without the rephrasal:

> Kirk's turn to scream. It was a nice noise. '*I know I have the body of a weak and feeble woman*', she said humbly. She caught him under the chin with both fists. His head snapped back with a noise loud enough to start a fifty-yard sprint. '*But I have the heart and stomach of a king.*' She brought the edge of her hand down on his nose. Blood spurted. He fell to his knees. (Moody, 1985: 183)

TL readers in general are unlikely to think the first half of the allusion preformed: Penny's words sound like a modest disclaimer even as she is proving that she is not physically weak. The comparison to a king in the second half, on the other hand, may well set bells ringing because of the unlikelihood of such a comparison in today's world. But as its source cannot be recognised in the target language culture, and as a literal translation of the second sentence would be a clear culture bump in some languages (Finn. *Minulla on kuninkaan sydän ja maha*), rephrasal is needed:

> ' Tiedän, että minulla on *heikon naisen ruumis,*' Penny sanoi nöyrästi... 'Mutta minulla on *kuninkaan sydän ja rohkeus.*' [proposed translation] 'I know I have the body of a weak woman. But I have the heart and courage of a king.'

To Elizabeth I, whom Penny is quoting,[41] *heart and stomach* meant courage. Alternatively, some allusive wordplay could be used by having Penny say: *minulla on leijonan mieli* [proposed translation] 'I have the heart of a lion'. This has associations with the name of a king, Richard Lion-Heart being known as *Rikhard Leijonamieli* in Finnish history books.

Omission (I)

Omission, as noted earlier under PN allusions, is not one of the strategies Finnish translators are eager to use. In their interviews, they thought of it as a last resort, but acknowledged that there are instances, for instance homonymic wordplay, where no other strategy may be appropriate. Still, if the loss caused by an omission is considered negligible in the context and if the alternative is a culture bump, there would seem to be no real reason to go to extremes to avoid omission. As an example, consider:

> 'I've as much right in this house as you have. Probably more.'
> 'How come?'
> 'For one thing, I've known the family all my life.'
> 'Ain't known *my* family all your life,' Oliver said. He folded his arms. *If he'd been green, he could have sold a lot of peas.* Except he didn't look particularly *jolly.* (Moody, 1985: 84)

If there is no recognition of the Jolly Green Giant food products in the target culture, to force the comparison would not be consistent with the tone of the passage. Oliver has already been established as an imposing figure, and his refusal to allow the other man access would be definite enough even if the last two sentences of the passage were omitted.

Re-creation (H)

Re-creation is (usually) a time-consuming strategy. In a wide sense, of course, all translation is re-creation: a change of language means re-creating a situation. In a narrower sense, Holmes (1988: 48), when discussing verse translation, opposes re-creation to retention, seeing these as the two basic alternatives. My adoption of the term re-creation was, to some extent, influenced by Levine (1975). Describing her own close collaboration as translator with the author, she refers to inventions and changes when translating into English problematic elements such as Cuban Spanish puns and invented words: '[W]e took the liberty of creating them in places where there weren't any, or in places where they did exist but where we couldn't find near equivalents' (Levine, 1975: 270). Her illustrations of English-language jokes substituted for Spanish ones include 'famous books' such as '*Under the Lorry* by Malcolm Volcano' (p.271).[42]

> Our basic aim was to re-create the system of the original text, and therefore we had to invent jokes that would have a familiar association for the reader... But again, this translation is a version or recreation, not only in the metaphorical sense that all translations are, but also in the concrete sense that many textual changes were made. (Levine, 1975: 271–2)

Re-creation indeed seems an appropriate description for the search for a translation that would convey as much of the meaning and 'feeling-tone' (to repeat Weldon's quote of Freud, see Chapter 3) of the allusion in context as possible. It is also a creative process, not just re-creation but creation, resembling the work of an author, hard to describe and harder to implement.

(Re-)creation means freedom from constraints, freedom to consider a hierarchy of factors and to construct a TL version that may dispense with the allusion itself yet not just reduce it to sense but attempt to give it some *Mehrwert* (Dittgen, 1989: 19). Something no doubt is lost in the process, a lot may be changed, something (perhaps nothing lexical, but the meaning or effect) needs to be retained. It has been suggested (Frank, 1988: 146) that one possible approach to translating wordplay, where re-creation is often needed, would be to give more attention to 'the imitation of the word-play as process'. Kussmaul (1991) quotes translators engaged in this kind of imitation, with their dialogue leading to unexpected but funny results. (See Kussmaul [1991] also for an overview of work done on creativity in translation.)

The following two examples where re-creation is attempted are not humorous but emotionally charged; some of that emotion, conveyed through allusions, needs to be transferred to TT receivers directly, without intellectual analysis, so that it hits them as it does (receptive) readers of the STs.

In the first example, the allusions are understated but have a strong effect if spotted. An elderly policeman addresses a young woman terrorist, whom he has met off-duty as it were, and grown fond of:

'I like you. But I can't imagine a situation in which your kind of random violence is morally justified. I'm sorry. I'll have to let them know you're coming... '
'You would, too. I'll tell you something about your kind – you think you've got a monopoly of duty. When *we* die, when we are tortured, when we stick out life-sentences in the pen – that's not duty.'
She spoke seriously, without contempt, *her voice gentle and low – an excellent thing in woman*. But Pibble felt as though he had been *scythed down by her bladed wheels*. (Dickinson, 1985: 146–7; emphasis on *we* in the original)

The two contradictory allusions, to Cordelia and to Boadicea, describing Pibble's feelings for Tony, the young woman, indicate the turmoil in his mind: as an older man, he feels tenderness (not wholly paternal) for Tony; as a policeman responsible for law enforcement, he must condemn the terrorist. The line of *Lear* echoing in his mind occurs in the scene where Lear is grieving for the death of his daughter; the image of a warrior queen 'scything down' people associates with the destruction caused by terrorist acts. Still, Boadicea lost her war; Tony is in danger of death or a life-sentence; and Pibble will grieve for the loss and the waste like Lear.

It is clear that no translation can make all of this evident in a culture where the sources of the allusions are little known or unfamiliar. On the other hand, this is perhaps a particularly sophisticated example of the use of allusion (in this corpus), with the allusion to Cordelia easily missed by ST readers as well. Compromise is unavoidable, but some of the elements may be transferred. My tentative proposal brings in a 'dear daughter', 'a chariot of war', adds Boadicea's name as a source reference to be looked up if desired, and specifies by way of compensation that what Pibble felt was 'a sharp pain in his chest':[43]

... Hän puhui vakavasti, halveksimatta, ja hänen äänensä oli lempeä ja hiljainen, *kuin rakkaan tyttären ääni*. Kuitenkin Pibblen rintaa *vihlaisi, ikään kuin hän olisi jäänyt Boadicean sotavaunujen alle*. [proposed translation]
'She spoke seriously, without contempt, and her voice was gentle and low like the voice of a dear daughter. And yet Pibble felt a sharp pain in his chest, as if he had been run over by Boadicea's chariot of war.'

Losses include the aspect of the death of the daughter, and Boadicea's eventual defeat. The Jylhä translation of *Lear* renders the lines as: *Äänes oli vieno,/Sävyisä, hellä: naisess' oiva merkki* 'Your voice was soft, gentle and tender: a fine sign in a woman' (Act V, Scene 3). None of the adjectives used would by themselves or in combination evoke this scene for Finnish readers. Nor would the metaphor of *bladed wheels* evoke anything specific, unlike in English. Still, the proposed translation does contain the elements of war, ancient times and a woman warrior.[44]

In another example, re-creation is used for a picture caption on the cover of the Christmas 1988 issue of *The New Statesman and Society: The Ghosts of Christmas Present*, which was attached to a picture of starving children in the Sudan. This was a seasonal allusion to Dickens's *A Christmas Carol* (a text largely unknown in Finland). The Finnish words for *ghosts* have no link to Christmas, but as the purpose of the caption was to shock the reader by linking affluent Western ways of celebrating Christmas to the starvation of children in Africa, a phrase associated with Christmas was needed. Re-creation could for instance result in turning a line of a well-known Finnish Christmas carol (*Koska meillä on joulu* 'Because it's Christmas') into a poignant question:

> *Koska meillä on joulu?* [proposed translation] 'When will we have a Christmas?'

as *koska* is both a subordinator ('because') and an interrogative ('when').

To sum up, if the translation of allusions is seen as a decision-making process where the translator makes a series of 'moves, as in a game' (Levý, 1967: 1171),[45] this suggests that the moves can be charted and put into a priority order. Such a priority ordering could be based simply on observations on how translators deal with allusions. However, as reader response tests suggest (see Chapter 5) that in some individual cases at least current practice was not entirely successful (generalisations on the basis of a small number of examples only are always problematic), a more balanced use of the different strategies than that found described earlier in this Chapter might make for better reader satisfaction.

Assuming that a responsible translator will not want unnecessarily to impoverish or obscure the author's text nor to leave the reader puzzled or unable to follow it, it is clear that receivers must be taken into account. If TT readers (of texts of the type and function under consideration in this study) are entitled to TTs which are coherent, offering elements needed for responses and interpretations, just as ST readers can respond to and interpret implicit messages in texts in their own language – a basic assumption in this study – translators need to consider what strategies will lead to such a TT, as their goal. If they suspect that a given strategy is ineffective in a translation situation characterised by a certain combination of factors, they would be well advised to look for more effective alternatives.

Will the application of a given strategy result in a translation which conveys the function and meaning of the allusion, meets reader expectations and allows for reader participation? Such qualititative criteria are, to some degree, inevitably speculative, but it would serve little purpose to try to construct a quantifiable set of parameters instead. If a translation is to conform to Levý's idea of a 'minimax' strategy, criteria would need to be both translator-oriented ('mini-') and product-oriented ('-max'). A translator will then choose 'that one of the possible solutions which promises a maximum of effect with a minimum of effort' (Levý, 1967: 1179). S/he will not be content with a translation that is not going to work, but neither will s/he wish to spend time trying to construct ever better translations if one s/he is content with has already been found. In teaching translation, accordingly, a priority ordering of strategies can give us a possible method of dealing with allusions, as outlined earlier. Starting with easy and effortless strategies (cf. the flow-charts, Figures 2 and 3) will save translators time, but consideration of less common strategies where the more common ones are not deemed effective will help ensure that the full range of potential alternatives is noted in individual cases.

Several cautions are in order here, to clarify the position taken. Perhaps most importantly, it needs to be remembered that all decisions ultimately depend on factors (including genre, text type, function of TT, intended audience, context etc.) which are considered earlier in the translation process than are ST allusions. Thus it is recognised that the 'global strategies' (Séguinot, 1989) which the translator makes initially, regarding the translation task as a whole, will clearly affect 'local strategies' too: for example reduction to sense may be more often acceptable in informative than in literary texts, and target cultural replacements in film and television than in print. The present discussion concerns local strategies only, or ways of dealing with a ST allusion once it has been spotted. (Clearly, the identification of an allusive problem, which sparks off the problem-solving and decision-making, is by no means automatic: if a translator's SL skills and/or cultural competence are insufficient s/he may well not diagnose the problem when it occurs.)

It should be noted, too, that this presentation of a priority ordering of strategies is not offered as a fool-proof method of arriving at an optimal solution (a criticism made by Toury [1992: 67] of the series-of-steps technique). For instance, an overly eye-catching translation of an allusion, however apt, may be detrimental to the coherence of the translation. Omission with no compensation will avoid a culture bump but mostly result in some degree of loss.[46] The acceptance of each strategy also depends on target cultural norms, which are not immutable.

There may be a need for better metacultural awareness of crucial differences between ST and TT audiences. The neglect of readers' requirements and expectations are doubtless partly due to a lack of available data. Hlebec (1989) sees a need for research on readers' expectations to be undertaken in order to guide future translators working on similar texts; the reader-response tests reported in Chapter 5 may shed some light on Finnish reader expectations and reactions with regard to the translation of allusions.

The sources of the allusions in Chapter 4

brave new world: Shakespeare, *The Tempest,* Act V, Scene 1. Aldous Huxley's novel (1932). 'Current usage is generally ironic' (Lass *et al.,* 1987: 32).

that not impossible she: Richard Crashaw, 'Wishes to his Supposed Mistress' (1646).

Joseph (Joe) McCarthy: United States senator (1908–57), known for his anti-Communist stance.

Bruce Lee: film actor and martial arts performer.

Swan Lake: ballet; music composed by Tchaikovsky (1876).

the Pied Piper of Hamelin: medieval legend: a figure who rid a town of its rats by 'charming them away with his flute-playing' (PCE 667). Retold in verse by Robert Browning.

Scylla and Charybdis: Greek myth: two sea monsters preying on ships and sailors in the Strait of Messina.

Oedipus: Greek myth.

the Walrus and the Carpenter: characters in a poem in Lewis Carroll's *Through the Looking-Glass* (Chapter 4).

the White Rabbit: see p.29.

Marie Antoinette: queen of France at the time of the revolution of 1789.

Philip Marlowe: Raymond Chandler's fictional detective.

Bart Simpson: boy character in the animated cartoon *The Simpsons.*

Anita Bryant: American former beauty queen known for her anti-homosexual stance.

Phyllis Schlafly: American anti-feminist.

Pandora's box: Greek myth: Pandora, against all advice, opened her box and allowed all kinds of troubles to escape to plague humankind.

Spiro Agnew: Richard Nixon's vice-president 1969–73.

Sir Lancelot, Sir Galahad: knights of the Round Table.

Winnie-the-Pooh: eponymous hero of A. A. Milne's children's classic.

Rebecca of Sunnybrook Farm: main character in Kate Douglas Wiggin's stories for young readers.

the Eumenides: Greek myth: the furies. See for instance Aeschylus' *Oresteia.*

e.e. cummings: American poet (1894–1962).

Humpty Dumpty: egg-shaped character in nursery rhyme.

Daisy Buchanan: heroine of F. Scott Fitzgerald's novel *The Great Gatsby.*

there's no such thing as a free lunch: attributed by Alistair Cooke to an Italian immigrant who was asked what 40 years of living in America had taught him (DMQ 18).

What, never? Hardly ever: W.S. Gilbert, *H.M.S. Pinafore.*

only connect: E.M. Forster, *Howards End.*

the land of the free: Francis Scott Key, 'The Star Spangled Banner'.

tangled are the webs we weave: see p.75.

the slings and arrows of outrageous fortune: Hamlet, Act III, Scene 1.

the writing on the wall: Dan. 5: 25.

tools of capitalism: socialist or communist phrase of derision.

the snows of yesteryear: Dante Gabriel Rossetti's translation of Francois Villon's phrase *les neiges d'antan.*

in the graveyards, every one: see p.74.

Martha: sister of Mary and Lazarus (John 11: 1–44).

Nancy Drew: main character in Carolyn Keene's adventure stories for young readers.

Fangio: Juan Manuel Fangio, Argentinan racing car driver (active in the 1950s).

Keke Rosberg: Finnish racing car driver (active in the 1980s).

Gradgrind: family in Dickens's *Hard Times.*

Dotheboys Hall: school in Dickens's *Nicholas Nickleby.*

Buster Keaton: American film actor.

the emperor has no clothes: see p.11.

tomorrow and tomorrow and tomorrow: Macbeth, Act V, Scene 5.

lovely, dark and deep: see p.71.

mulberry bush: nursery rhyme ('Here we go round a mulberry bush').

Notes

1. By standard translation I mean a preformed TL version. English and Finnish biblical phrases are a typical example. They are originally translations from a common ST.
2. The first two of the Finnish names are those of fictional characters in novels by Väinö Linna and Aleksis Kivi respectively; Kalle Päätalo is a prolific writer much read in Finland; the last two names are those of the main characters of a series of adventure stories for young readers by Väinö Riikkilä.

3. In this test (conducted as part of the test designated as KLA in Chapter 5), the respondents were 47 students and 4 teachers at the Kouvola department of translation (University of Helsinki). They were asked to underline any familiar names among eight names listed (without context), and to give a brief note of identification. (For the second part, see Chapter 5; for details on the respondents, see Appendix 2.)

4. Cf. Lass *et al.* (1987: 178): 'The child heroine of a series of novels by Eleanor H. Porter; she always looks on the brighter side of things. A "Pollyanna attitude" now denotes a rather foolish, saccharine optimism.' The respondents did not express awareness of the 'degeneration' of the name Lass *et al.* allude to, but presented Pollyanna's attitude at face value.

5. This could apply to other characters in texts of the same genre, such as Emily in *Emily of New Moon* by L.M. Montgomery.

6. Three of the five respondents with five points; two of the four with six points; the one with seven points; one of the two with eight points and the one with nine points were all people who worked with English.

7. An allusion to Richard Crashaw, 'Wishes to his Supposed Mistress', as in the example: '…tell you if our *not impossible she* is serious about killing herself?…' (Hill, 1991: 129, my emphasis)

8. Replacement of the allusion by better-known source-culture specific material (strategy 2a on the PN list) is not noted on the KP list as it seems to be of no practical value with KPs.

9. Interestingly, students' reactions to such a strategy have been quite positive: 'It was just too much for them to cope with and they said so' — a student's comment in my translation class, 1990. I have no information on the reactions of monolingual viewers.

10. The two translators of one of the texts (Allingham) could not be reached. Although the paperback edition used gave the TT the publication date of 1990, it turned out that the text was a reprint, and had actually been translated in 1960–1 (letter from the publisher, WSOY, 1992). Because of the time lag, the publisher no longer had the translators' addresses on file and could not put me in touch with them.

11. The translator with the PhD (Hakola) did not answer this question.

12. 'All I require of a translator is that he or she be a more gifted writer than I am, and in at least two languages, one of them mine.' (Kurt Vonnegut, *Fates Worse Than Death*, p. 181, cited by EJ in his written answers to the questionnaire.)

13. In the course of the study I spoke to one of the authors of the corpus, who verified, among other points, that the description of the character Annabel Lee (whose name, of course, is allusive) as someone who was: 'more than a little *mad*, and very *bad*, and hated Nell' (Weldon, 1988: 193) was indeed intended as an allusion to the description of Lord Byron as *mad, bad, and dangerous to know* (Weldon, personal interview, Espoo, Finland, 17 March 1989). However, the usefulness of author interviews is limited as some use of allusions may be unconscious, so that an author does not necessarily always know whether s/he is alluding, let alone what s/he is alluding to.

14. The translator Kersti Juva (1993), when discussing her experiences in translating Sayers's *Gaudy Night*, explains that after considerable thought and consultations with the Finnish publisher she came to the conclusion that a number of culture-specific terms (for example *Bodleian, bursar, don*) should be

left untranslated while a glossary explaining the terms was to be appended at the back of the book. This decision is unusual.

15. A similar observation was made by the translator Risto Raitio (personal communication, April 1992), who had made some comparisons between his own translations of fiction and Swedish translations of the same texts.

16. EC's term for the first, fast rendering of the translation.

17. Explanations may be difficult even without a time gap. EC cited Jean Cocteau: 'An artist cannot speak about his art any more than a plant can discuss horticulture.'

18. In a few instances, it is difficult to assign allusions to one or the other category as they may contain elements of both PNs and KPs.

19. While some critical remarks could be made on a few of these, I shall simply note that the Finnish renderings of the *White Rabbit* as *Valkoinen jänis* and the *Cheshire Cat* as *Virnukissa* (for instance in Lurie, 1988: 77) are not those used in the two full-length translations of *Alice* (*Irvikissa* in Swan [1906] and *Mörökölli* in Kunnas and Manner [1972]). (There is now a third full-length Finnish translation of *Alice*, [Martin, 1995], but that was not available to the translators of the texts examined.) In her interview, the translator of Lurie (EC) said that she had used her children as informants on children's literature, without specifying in which particular form they had met *Alice*. Other names than those used in the full-length literary translations have been used in translations of picture book or film and TV versions. For example a video cassette of Disney's film *Alice in Wonderland* (1951) on sale to Finns in the early 1990s refers to the Cheshire Cat as *Veijarikissa*, another name not used by Swan or Kunnas and Manner.

20. The phrase *Pandoran lipas* 'Pandora's box' itself is used in Finnish often enough for a journalist to have drawn attention to a misunderstanding of its meaning (Nortamo, 1992). Hence, rendering the name as *Pandora Lipas* might work quite well.

21. *Pollyanna*, by Eleanor H. Porter, was first published in Finnish translation in 1916, under the title *Iloinen tyttö*, 'The Happy Girl'. *Rebecca of Sunnybrook Farm* by Kate Douglas Wiggin was translated as *Villiruusu*, 'Wild Rose', and first published in 1919. My students (in the 1990s) have expressed no recognition of the latter.

22. My comments on biblical phrases in Finnish are based on the Bible translations of 1933 (The Old Testament) and 1938 (The New Testament), which were in official use in the Finnish Lutheran church when the TTs were published. These biblical translations have since been replaced by a more modern version (1992), which has not had much time yet to affect the Finnish language.

23. Literally, *öljypuu* translates as 'oil tree'. In non-biblical connections, the tree is known as *oliivipuu* 'olive tree'. *Oliivi* 'olive' is hardly ever used of the tree, it usually means the fruit, as in *oliiviöljy* 'olive oil'.

24. See also the discussion of dead allusions earlier in the chapter.

25. The appropriateness of Arnott's description was made clear in an experience in class: a student spontaneously brought up an example of a footnote she claimed to have noted in a TT. When she checked, she found that the translator had not in fact used an actual footnote but appeared to have slipped the information needed by the TT reader into the text itself. A check of the ST (Francis, 1990: 148) next showed that the 'extra' information (on the Wars of the Roses connotations of York and Lancaster) had actually been given by the ST author himself, and there was no translatorial intervention.

26. The most common source named was indeed the Lord's Prayer, but mostly the source was given vaguely as 'biblical'.

27. Whether the allusion should be seen as something more than a wisecrack (for instance as a straight or ironical reference to policemen enforcing law and order in a capitalistic society) is difficult to determine.

28. The attitudes of a larger number of literary translators to their role were recently the subject of an inquiry by Ratinen (1992), who reports (after my interviews had been conducted) that of the 163 literary translators who returned her questionnaire, the following percentages saw as a major task of theirs:
    — acting as mediator: 53.4%
    — providing an accurate interpretation, a good and correct translation: 49.7%
    — making a good book or writer better known: 15.3%
    — maintaining and developing language and culture: 9.8%
    — furthering international understanding: 6.1%
    — other: 6.1% (my translation).

29. But omission, clearly effortless, comes late on the flow-chart because it does not maximise effect and because of the current translatorial norm against it (in Finland).

30. The flow-charts do not represent a complete model of a translation process from beginning to end. Such models have been devised in greater or lesser detail, ranging from the simplicity of Nida and Taber's (1969) to more complex models as in Lörscher (1991: 118). Holmes (1988) argues convincingly that it is simplistic to think of translation as a serial process only (p.102); there is also a 'structural plane, on which one abstracts a "mental conception"' of the ST, which then serves as a 'general criterion against which to test each sentence during the formulation' of the TT (pp.82–3). Holmes then develops this into another quite complex model (pp.83–5).

31. *Paula* is easier for young Finnish readers to pronounce than *Nancy*. The presence of other allusions to Nancy Drew in the corpus suggest that the name and 'title' are well known among American readers. Cf.
    'Well, you had good reason to be frightened,' she said.
    'While you, Kate Davis, *girl detective*, don't?' (Valin, 1987: 170; emphasis added.)
    In this example the real name of the character addressed is used, but the apposition *girl detective* has a similar effect as *Nancy Drew* in the Paretsky example. The Nancy Drew mystery stories are known as *Neiti Etsivä-kirjat* ('Miss Detective books') to Finnish readers. Many of them have been available in Finnish translation for the past 30 years at least.

32. Cf. the Coverdale translation 'tenderly' and the Geneva Bible 'pleasantly'. (QED s.v. delicately)

33. This strategy is used more often in film and TV translation; discussions with students suggest that it often works, but that some receivers have reservations concerning the strategy. An example recalled by a student was an American film where mention was made in dialogue of the Oprah Winfrey Show; this was replaced by mention of a controversial Finnish series of TV interviews, Hermunen.

    A related but global strategy, the use of TL names for 'localising' the text in the target culture is little used today outside of children's books. It used to be more common: Masnerová (1989: 68) notes that Czech translators were inclined towards localising the text in their own country in the late 18th and early 19th centuries. In Finland likewise, there was for example an early adaptation of *Robinson Crusoe* (1911), where the protagonist was made into a Finn with the Finnish name of 'Risto Roopenpoika' (Hämäläinen, 1988: 132–3). This was an adaptation for children.

34. In addition to Keke Rosberg not being the name chosen by the author, there is also a difference in time between the names considered, as Juan Manuel Fangio was active as a racing car driver in the 1950s, Keke Rosberg in the 1980s.

35. The KLA test indicated that this character in Dickens's *Hard Times* is not a familiar name in Finland.

36. As in:
    She went to the bank and cashed the check he had given her, bought her panty hose and a fresh supply of *loaves and fishes*, and went back to feed the multitudes. (MacLeod, 1980: 160) In this example *multitudes* reinforces the biblical allusion.

37. The originally Danish Andersenian allusion is transcultural: it is listed also in a Finnish dictionary of quotations (Sinnemäki, 1989).

38. Rendell uses the word *poll* 'head', but the Tudor edition of Shakespeare's *Complete Works* and the New Swan and Arden editions of the play have *pole* 'standard'.

39. A minimum change translation would be close to the proposed translation for the first part of the allusion, but would be a stylistic mismatch for the second part: the literal *sotilaan pää on kaatunut* 'the soldier's head has fallen' resembles the Finnish expression *sitten kun minun pääni kaatuu* 'after my head falls' in other words, 'when I'm no longer alive', which is dated and has overtones of old age.

40. Transcultural allusions have connotations in both languages, and monocultural TL readers may well think of some of them as TL-specific: for example *John Brown's body lies a-mouldering in the grave/Kalle-Kustaan muori makaa hiljaa haudassaan* (a popular song); *Go to work on an egg/Mene munalla töihin* (an advertising slogan).

41. This line occurred in the speech the queen gave at Tilbury on 9 August, 1588 at the approach of the Spanish Armada (Fraser, 1989: 223).

42. Cf. Malcolm Lowry, *Under the Volcano* (1947).

43. Other translators are likely to come up with very different versions. In Kussmaul's (1991) empirical investigation of creative translation, 'highly original' translations were produced 'quite often' (p.98).

44. The statue of Boadicea and her daughters in London shows them in a scythe-wheeled chariot, 'and it is in fact those murderous knives which stamp our perception of her indelibly' (Fraser, 1989: 3). Fraser points out that historically this depiction is false.

45. Levý's metaphor implies a conscious weighing of options, while recent research suggests that experienced translators have automatised their problem-solving behaviour to a greater or lesser degree.

46. Hönig (1993: 121) argues that terms like loss and compensation 'cannot successfully be integrated into any functional approach to translation'. It would seem, however, that if for instance a humorous allusion is omitted, there will as a result, mathematically speaking, be a little less humour in the TT than if a suitable humorous translation were found for the allusion, or if the translator compensated for the loss by adding a touch of humour elsewhere in the text.

5 Empirical Data on Reader Responses

Translators seldom have access to the way their readers respond to the solutions chosen and the strategies adopted. After all, general readers rarely approach translators to offer congratulations or criticism, and reviewers often disregard the translator's work entirely unless they want to call attention to some language error. Translation studies grants TT readers importance in theory but can offer little practical help (cf. Chapter 2). In literary studies receivers tend to be seen in the abstract and the singular – the 'implied', 'informed' or 'ideal' reader is a fictional construct, 'in no way to be identified with any real reader' (Iser, 1978: 34). Are real readers then negligible? Should there not also be some interest in the responses of individuals, actual real-life people whose reactions can be tested to provide empirical data?[1] If texts need to reach not just their primary addressees, the readers of the ST, but also, when translated, their secondary readers, what both groups of receivers make of the text – how they read it – is an essential part of the communicative process.

Reader-response criticism argues that what goes on between the text and the reader is not passive reception but creative interaction. Iser (1974, 1978) is one who sees the meaning of a text as the result of a process of interaction between author and reader, meaning emerging not from the text alone but also from the reader's processing of the text. He speaks of gaps left in the text for the reader to fill in. This idea of an implied reader filling in gaps in the text to produce meaning cannot be tested empirically. If instead we think of actual readers engaged in the same gap-filling activity – and allusions can indeed be seen as one sort of gap or blank to be filled in – we can doubtless foresee that because of their individuality, readers may well actualise a range of different meanings for a given text. A relativist embracing the idea of a multiplicity of meanings might accept *all* the responses to allusions offered by the respondents as equally legitimate; however, I prefer to adopt the more controversial but surely common-sense position that some of the TT reader responses given here show that the reader in question has

132

either missed the point or is expressing an interpretation that clearly differs from one suggested by a textual analysis of the corresponding ST passage. Such responses are due to the reader failing to note the presence of intertextual elements, but it is the translator's choice of strategy that largely determines whether the meaning suggested by the intertextuality *can* be received by monocultural TT readers.

I do not suggest, however, that TTs should be valued only to the extent that they correspond to STs in all detail; TT readers are unlikely to compare TT to ST and to judge their satisfaction by the results of such comparison. Still, a TT reader him/herself can be conscious of not having been given the necessary materials to work with, while a different solution might have enabled him/her to make better sense of an allusive passage.

This chapter looks into the responses of real readers to allusions in target texts in order to verify the assumption that minimum-change (literal) translations of unfamiliar allusions may well be culture bumps for receivers who do not share the cultural background of the primary (SL) audience, unless the translator takes steps to prevent this. There are naturally numerous problems connected with this kind of inquiry, which I do not try to minimise; but to bypass the viewpoint of real readers altogether seemed the weaker alternative.

Notes on the Finnish Target Culture

As there is 'a direct correlation between a culture's distance from our own and the number of reculturings the translator must make' (Frank, 1988: 27), a brief description of some aspects of the Finnish target culture is in order, to put the empirical data given here into a social context. Finland has long had a very high literacy rate due to the influence of the Lutheran church, which from the 17th century on desired that adult parish members should be literate, and enforced this by requiring that engaged couples should have to know how to read before they could be married. What was required was not, of course, functional literacy; the goal was simply that parishioners should be able to decipher written religious instruction. The ability to write was thought unnecessary, 'nor did the parish schoolmasters themselves always possess this skill' (Paloposki, 1986: 52; my translation). There were a number of early types of religious and secular schools in the 18th and 19th centuries, and after the School Act of 1866 the school system began to provide basic schooling for an increasing number of children and secondary schools for a small élite. Compulsory education was established in 1921, but only a minority of each age class went to secondary school, learning languages other than their own. It was only after the Second

World War that German was ousted from its position as the foreign language most widely taught and replaced by English; the visibility of
Anglo-American culture has grown in Finland as in other Western European countries in each succeeding decade. Foreign language learning did
not become available to all school-goers until the 1970s with the arrival of
comprehensive education.

In the early 19th century most readers of literary texts in Finland had
been educated in Swedish, and there was little translation into Finnish of
other than religious or legal texts.[2] An increase in translation into Finnish
was linked to a rise of national consciousness from the 1840s on and a consequent desire to bring the native tongue closer to the standards set by
more established languages and cultures. This trend stimulated decades of
translation activity, and Finnish translations of famous Western and Russian writers have as a rule been available since the latter half of the 19th
century.[3] Translations have been influential in the education of many
self-taught writers and readers, but the cultural diffusion has been slow:
for example familiar allusions to Shakespeare are limited to a few examples
only. For a long time translations from English were quite rare: three books
were translated in 1885, five in 1895, 12 in 1905, 25 in 1915, etc. Only in the
1920s was there an explosion of literature translated from English, but
numbers fell again in the 1930s. Most of the books translated from English
were light entertainment, detective stories and the like (Kovala, 1989: 26),
and these were not infrequently translated via their Swedish or German
translations (p.28). All this changed after the Second World War, and currently English is the foreign language most often translated from. English
also dominates in film and television: Jalonen (1985) has examined the
period 1923–78 and found that 57% of imported films and 58% of translated
fiction in those years were of British or American origin. For imported television programmes in 1963–78, the corresponding figure was 61% (p.266).
English-language books, films and television programmes are also imported from other countries than Britain and the USA; if such sources were
included, they would further increase the figures. Jalonen summarises his
findings for the top six countries as follows: during the period 1923–78 41%
of cultural imports to Finland came from the United States, 18% from
Britain, 7% from France, West Germany and Sweden respectively, and 3%
from the then Soviet Union (p.266).

As a rule, Finns are keen readers: there is a widespread network of free
lending libraries provided by each municipality and regularly used by
nearly 50% of the population, and most families subscribe to a newspaper.[4]
This is in contrast to the United States, where c. 60% of the adult population
apparently never read a book, and most of the remaining 40% only read one

book a year on the average (Kernan 1989: 159) – a factor no doubt partly responsible for the perceived need for more 'cultural literacy' in that society (for the debate on this in educational circles in the late 1980s see for instance Franklin, 1988; there has been no comparable debate in Finland). An international report in 1992 stating that Finnish children and teenagers were the most accomplished readers among their contemporaries in many European countries was noted not only in Finnish educational circles but also in the national press.

Books by native-language writers are generally more popular than translations among the majority of readers.[5] Particularly popular in Finland have been realistic novels recounting national experiences in times of crisis (the civil war of 1918, the war years 1939–44, the change from a rural to an urban society in the post-war years) and written by writers who knew these from personal experience (for example Väinö Linna, Kalle Päätalo). Writing provided a possible way for the writer to achieve upward social mobility; and many Finnish writers have emerged from the rural or urban working class (in addition to Linna and Päätalo this group includes, for instance, Pentti Haanpää, Lauri Viita, Timo K. Mukka, Heikki Turunen, Alpo Ruuth and many others). Writers who depart from the realistic tradition tend to be read by a smaller number of readers.

Some 60% of fiction published in Finland since 1954 has been 'of foreign origin', that is, translations (Eskola, 1987: 136). In the major English-speaking countries, in contrast, the vast majority of published titles are domestic: only 2 or 3% are translations (Venuti, 1995b: 26). The figures are not directly comparable as Venuti's do not seem to refer to fiction only, but they do indicate that the work of translators is of considerable importance for Finnish readers.

Questions of Method

Designing the experiments

A comparative readership survey was not the method adopted, as a controlled experiment would have to take into account the countless variables which have an effect on a person's reading competence and skill at interpretation. Corcoran (1990: 143–4) lists 'aspects of the perspective and construction of the reader (sex, family and class background, race, age...)' which may help or hinder reading, and argues that not enough is known yet about the 'cultural framing of the reader'. Taking this into account, a controlled experiment would not only not compare 'Finnish farmers and American university teachers' (Mäkelä, 1990: 49, my translation) but would also refrain from making comparisons between ST and TT readers unless provision could be made for the fact that some of them doubtless are keen readers of fiction and others read only for information; some were raised on Greek mythology and others watched television instead of reading; some read and wrote poetry in their teens while others listened to pop music;[6] some had teachers who made literature come to life and stimulate self-discovery, while the teachers of others thought of literature as a canon of texts to be examined. Individual readers necessarily respond to texts differently because of non-quantifiable differences in their backgrounds. While obvious demographic variables could be matched, it was impossible to ensure that a group of Finnish readers and a control group of native-language readers would be sufficiently well matched with regard to their reading histories, personal life experiences, the influence of relatives and teachers at various ages, etc. So, apart from the practical and financial problems of an attempt to set up such a large-scale experiment, even the most laborious matching of subjects would in the end have resulted only in an illusion of all necessary variables having been controlled. It should be noted, for instance, that x years of education would not mean an equal amount of literature teaching received for ST and TT readers alike, as the national curriculum in the Finnish school system provides little grounding in literature and (as far as I know) no specialist literature courses corresponding to those in the English-speaking world.

Instead of an actual control group of native-language readers, then, a small group of experienced native-language readers[7] were asked to provide comments on their understanding of the allusive passages used in the experiments; where their responses coincided sufficiently, this was thought to indicate a response norm, an accepted 'meaning' for the allusion.[8] The native-language readers thus suggest how a particular allusion is understood in the 'interpretive community' (Fish, 1980), where interpretations are 'conventional and communal' and 'exist prior to the act of reading' (Freund, 1987: 107–8). Despite criticism of Fish's position, no doubt justifiable when 'the more recalcitrant features of texts' (Freund, 1987: 110) are concerned, this view of meaning being 'determinate and decidable' (p.109) has definite attractions with the particular problem under discussion in this study. The experiments described later focus not on the interpretation of entire texts but on the understanding of certain (allusive) phrases and passages in those texts. Granted, such passages may well function not just in their immediate contexts, but also for instance as aids to characterisation or the expression of a theme (cf. Chapter 3). The interpretation of such macro-level use of allusions probably requires experience in reading and would show more inter-individual variation, comparable for instance to the interpretation of metaphor. (Exploring macro-level effects would have presupposed respondents willing to read and contemplate not just extracts but full-length texts and to record their responses in detail; such respondents were not available.)

This chapter, however, addresses a more collective and culture-specific type of understanding. This might be related to the understanding of realia – illustrated, for instance, in Kelletat (1991), where he ponders the translation of such intracultural information as *Tampereella käänsivät junan tois-inpäin* 'in Tampere they turned the train the other way round'[9] and requires both a map of Finland and a street plan of Tampere to ensure a proper understanding of the sentence.[10] To repeat an example used earlier and soon to be examined for its effects on Finnish readers, in a collective or communal sense a reference to the '*White Rabbit*' is a reference to the white rabbit in *Alice's Adventures in Wonderland*. It can be assumed to be familiar to the primary readers, the collective native-language audience, though obviously not to every individual native-language reader. The existence of readers not sufficiently literate to identify the Rabbit does not invalidate the argument that a reference to the *White Rabbit* is a commonly recognised reference to *Alice*; and the inclusion of the name in dictionaries of quotation and allusion (as in Lass *et al.*, 1987, Rees, 1991, etc.) is further evidence of the collective or communal nature of this allusion. An allusion containing this name:

> Behind them was a warren of corridors down which eccentric looking persons hurried with *White Rabbit expressions* (Lurie, 1986: 191)

thus has a more or less definable, culture-specific meaning; it will be seen later that in translation this meaning was accessible only to a minority of the Finnish TT readers tested.

I would argue that it is commonsense to accept that many phrases used allusively in English have communally accepted meanings generally recognised by native-language readers. For instance, the phrases *a woman scorned* or *hell hath no fury* refer to a woman's anger and distress at being turned down by the man she desires; and authors, when they use such phrases, expect them to be largely transparent to the interpretive community of competent ST readers. Less widely used allusions work in the same way, only among a smaller audience of readers who belong to a particular subsection based on such variables as age, nationality or educational background.

While there may be a multiplicity of meanings in a text, then, the meaning of particular textual elements like many allusions is culturally conditioned, at least in part. This claim is not refuted by the obvious fact that not every native-language reader would read a given passage in the same way; this variation can be related to national and other demographic differences but also to personal differences in reading experience and reading competence and to differences in performance due to such factors as the degree of attention paid, not to mention the problem caused by reading extracts of texts in the experiments instead of full-length texts.[11] Enkvist and Leppiniemi (1989: 192) argue that understanding results from:

> an interplay between the text, the situational context, and the receptor (including his linguistic skills, his knowledge of the world, his purpose and his judgements of relevance, as well as his text-processing capacity at the relevant moment, which may vary with his alertness, sobriety and a number of other transient influences).

The translator needs to consider whether the communally accepted meaning of an allusive phrase can be conveyed by a minimum change (literal) translation, in other words, whether the phrase has become transcultural or part of the cultural milieu of the TL readers. In the absence of data on readers' responses – the general lack of feedback from reader to writer in print media is commented on in Wilss (1989: 7–8) – the translator can only rely on intuition. It is one of the purposes of this study to provide some data on the extent to which (certain) allusions in English-language texts are (currently) understood by Finnish readers. This is relevant for the choice of translation strategy – a choice which has to be made for every allusion perceived in every text to be translated.

To sum up, this study is not primarily concerned with responses to texts (novels, articles) as a whole, where a variety of individual responses and interpretations is inevitable, but to segments of text and understanding of particular words and phrases in them. To continue with one of the examples mentioned above, *hell hath no fury*, it is doubtless in most cases desirable that the rendering of those particular words (originally occurring in one of Congreve's plays) should make a TT reader reading a translated novel, for instance, realise that when the words are used in a fictional context, they mean that a character's acts are seen (rightly or wrongly) as motivated by anger at being rejected by a (potential or former) lover. The difference between the successful communication of the allusive meaning in the ST and a communicative breakdown or culture bump in the case of the TT if the allusion is inadequately translated (as it might be if the translator did not recognise the allusion or overlooked the cross-cultural nature of the translation problem), is shown in Aaltonen (1989), who notes that the phrase *a woman scorned* used in fictional conversation in a novel by Dorothy

L. Sayers was mistranslated by two Finnish translators of different generations who apparently did not know the meaning of the phrase. Troupp
(1987) mentions errors caused by misunderstandings of allusions in older
Finnish translations of Wodehouse. As we know, '"making sense" of a text
entails being able to place it within the cultural framework of the reader'
(O'Neill, 1990: 86).

Purpose of the experiments

The empirical data presented later were gathered in order to explore
how TT readers respond to allusions in translated texts. Do culture
bumps in fact occur? Are there baffled responses or responses deviating
from the response norm of ST readers? If so, this may be at least to some
extent due to the inadequacies of a translation which does not – for whatever motive – take cultural differences sufficiently into account. It is not
always necessary for the words, or sometimes even the sense,[12] of the TT
rendering to correspond closely to the ST allusion, but the translation
should make sense to TT readers. Admittedly, the problem is partly
inter-individual; but even competent TT readers can be baffled if the
translator assumes that readers are more bicultural than they in fact are.
By contrast, where allusive meanings are transferred to TT readers, either
a more effective translation strategy has been chosen,[13] or the problem has
not arisen because the allusion is familiar and there is therefore no cultural barrier to cross.

The question whether there are particular translation strategies which
are more successful than others in translating allusions could not be fully
dealt with in the experiments. Only a limited number of texts could be
given to the informants to consider. The main aim was to try to verify
whether literal translations of certain examples did, in fact, result in difficulties of comprehension, in other words, culture bumps. A few examples
of other strategies were included; but a comparative study of strategies
(which might have used published translations and other-strategy translations of the same passages constructed for experimental purposes; or
pairs of examples judged to be of similar difficulty but translated using different strategies) could not be undertaken.

The empirical data presented may well not be generalisable to any striking degree. Still, as the question of responses to allusions in translation has
not, to my knowledge, been the topic of reader-response inquiries before,
the tests conducted should shed some useful light on this particular translation problem, and perhaps encourage more research on how the work of
translators is received by TT readers.

Arranging the experiments

General reader test

All versions of the general reader test (GRT) had the same format. The selections of texts chosen for the three versions differ, as there were two conflicting wishes, one for comparatively large numbers of responses to individual texts, another for responses to a fair number of texts. Some texts were therefore used in all versions of the general reader test, others with only one or two groups of respondents.

The versions of the tests are designated as first and second general reader tests, GRT 1 and GRT 2 (the latter with versions 2a and 2b). In all of them, the general readers were given a selection of translated passages c. one page long from published TTs to read, and were asked what they understood a certain (underlined) allusive word or phrase to mean in each extract. The questions had to be open-ended and rather vague so that the readers would not be fed any lines but had to consider their own responses and answer the questions in their own words. In GRT 1, only allusions translated by minimum change/retention of name were chosen; this turned out to be a problem in that many GRT 1 respondents felt awkward about admitting that they did not know the 'correct' answers, even though it was emphasised in the instructions that the purpose of the test was to evaluate the translation strategies used, not the respondents themselves. Eventually 23 of 36 questionnaires were returned. The problem was solved by using student assistants for GRT 2, who were asked to hand three questionnaires each to general readers of their acquaintance as part of a study assignment. The questionnaire was modified to include texts which were assumed not to contain culture bumps, to give respondents a better chance of experiencing some success. Two slightly different selections of texts were used (GRT 2a and GRT 2b).

The general readers were Finnish adults without a background of academic studies in English (which might have led to a higher degree of biculturalism than is usual among general readers in Finland today). Many of the respondents did know English (and/or other foreign languages) and occasionally (some, frequently) read texts in those languages, but others were monolingual. Respondents numbered 80 in all (23 in GRT 1, 22 in GRT 2a and 35 in GRT 2b). Information on the age and sex of the respondents and their reading habits in foreign languages – the latter being undoubtedly a factor in biculturalisation – was requested (the ability to read a foreign language fairly fluently generally presupposes at least 12 years of education in Finland).[14] As Eskola (1987) notes that translated fiction is mostly read by upper- and middle-class readers in Finland, no attempt was made to reach only monolingual respondents. (See Appendix 2 for more detailed information on the respondents.)

The number of respondents (80 in all) is quite high; experimental work in translation studies often involves far smaller numbers. Toury (1991: 52) notes that 'samples of insufficient size seem to be a common weakness' in translation experiments. Krings (1986) used only eight students in his. An explanation is that the think-aloud protocol method produces so much material that its analysis soon becomes cumbersome (Toury, personal communication, Jan. 1993). Séguinot (1992) specifies that an hour-long videotape of one translator at work 'takes well over a year to transcribe and analyse' (p.41). My respondents, of course, were readers, not translators. A multiple-choice questionnaire would have facilitated the analysis of their responses, but was not adopted as it might have encouraged guesswork and obscured what the readers themselves thought.

The respondents were informed what the purpose of the study was, in other words that I was working on the translation of allusions and wanted to find out how translations of allusions were understood. To clarify my use of the concept, the instructions also included some examples of allusions to Finnish and foreign sources.

A check was also made of the associative skills of the respondents: they were given the additional task of underlining any unmarked allusions they found in the extracts and to name their sources if familiar; an extract taken from a Finnish novel was included which contained a line which can be taken as a modification of *to be or not to be* in a Finnish dialect:[15]

> Elämä päättyi aina samoin: se tappoi jokaisen. Ainoa tosi on epätoivo ja siksi vain parodia on mahdollista. *Oonks mie vain enks mie oo... Johan on pulma.* (Kilpi, 1983: 268) 'Life always ended the same way: it killed everyone. Despair is the only truth, and therefore nothing is possible but parody. *Am I or ain't I? Some problem.*' (My translation and emphases; the translation fails to show the sociocultural associations of the Finnish dialect.)

Most of the respondents reacted to the allusion either by naming *Hamlet* or by writing down the standard Finnish version of the line (*ollako vai eikö olla, siinä pulma*), or at least underlining it. The reading competence of individuals cannot be reliably estimated on the basis on one example only, but the result of this check (see Appendix 2) at least suggests that the respondents were capable of noting an allusion familiar to them, even if it occurred in a modified form; this would be an indication of some reading competence. Without some such check, the results of GRT could be thought to be on a much shakier basis.

GRT respondents filled in the questionnaires at home. There was obviously no way of ensuring that they did not consult reference works or other people, but they were requested not to do so.

The Finnish target texts are not reproduced in this volume for reasons of space; the source texts are reproduced in Appendix 6.

Kouvola test

More informants were provided for two of the texts used by a test (referred to as the Kouvola test or KLA) where the respondents were mostly students of translation working with various languages at the Kouvola department of translation (University of Helsinki). (A few of the respondents were teachers of these students.) This test (Appendix 4) was quickly carried out during a guest lecture to provide data on immediate reactions, which could then be contrasted with those written down by GRT respondents after due reflection. The audience returned 55 questionnaires with answers; c. ten questionnaires were returned untouched or not returned. Four of the answers were from non-native speakers of Finnish and were eliminated for that reason. (One part of the KLA test, on recognition of names, was presented in Chapter 4 as evidence of the claim that not all proper names used allusively in English are familiar to Finnish readers. The other part, discussed in this chapter, was similar to the GRT test but contained only two texts.)

The tests were conducted in 1991–92.

Culture Bumps? Reader Responses to Allusions in Target Texts

Responses to literal translations

The favourite strategy of the translators of the published texts examined was found to be literal translation where an allusive name was retained or a phrase was translated by minimum change. The hypothesis in the experiment reported here was that such translations would, when the allusion was unfamiliar, cause problems for TT readers – become culture bumps. Their interpretations would not always be the legitimately alternative interpretations of competent readers but would reveal real problems of understanding, caused by a lack of familiarity with the sources of allusions in the source culture, and hence with their meaning. This was borne out by the results: unfamiliar allusions did prove to be difficult to understand by the majority of the respondents. Such a result is in itself not unexpected, but is apparently not always considered in translation practice.

The following examples are shorter than the extracts given to the re-spondents. The STs of the passages used are to be found in Appendix 6.

Example 1. The White Rabbit

Respondents in GRT 1 and the KLA test were given a page of the pub-lished translation of Lurie (1988) to read (ST: Text A, Appendix 6,) and were asked to explain how they understood the meaning of the phrase *Valkoisen jäniksen ilme* 'White Rabbit expressions' and on what they based their interpretations.

Behind them was a warren of corridors down which eccentric looking persons hurried with *White Rabbit expressions*. The sound rooms were cosy burrows furnished with battered soft leather chairs and historical-looking microphones and switchboards... (Lurie, 1986: 191)

Hissien takana oli kanitarhamainen käytävien verkosto, missä ravasi omalaatuisia tyyppejä kasvoillaan *Valkoisen jäniksen ilme*. Äänitys-huoneet olivat kodikkaita pesäkoloja kalusteinaan pehmoisia nahka-tuoleja ja historiallisen näköisiä mikrofoneja ja kytkintauluja. (Lurie, 1988: 248)

In an article cited in *The Annotated Alice* (1970: 37 note 2) Lewis Carroll de-scribes the Rabbit as '"elderly", "timid", "feeble" and "nervously shilly-shallying"' and contrasts him with the vigorous and purposeful Alice. The paragraph on the Rabbit in Lass *et al.* (1987) calls him 'a self-important and vaguely ridiculous character, always very busy doing something that is not clear' (p.236). The five native-speakers consulted on this allusion more or less agreed with Lass's description, adding the dimension of anxiety (also men-tioned in Rees, 1991), one of them describing her idea of *White Rabbit expressions* as 'worried/anxious, even "important"'.[16] In Lurie's passage the employees of the BBC are thus running around, looking worried and anxious, or vaguely ridiculous in their self-importance. But a reader in whose child-hood reading *Alice* has not featured may not associate *White Rabbit expressions* with that text, but may be perplexed by the allusion when it occurs in a TT.

How did the Finnish readers read the translated passage, and did they base their readings on the context alone or a recollection of the White Rab-bit in *Alice*?

Far from clearly recognising the Rabbit as worried and anxious or self-important and vaguely ridiculous, the majority of the Finnish readers re-sponded differently. Some said the phrase could mean anything at all, others went by the standard characteristics of the hare in Finnish folktales, seeing a timid creature about to flee at the slightest danger. For one, white meant innocence; another associated rabbits with childbirth; a third remembered that the hare changes the colour of its coat in winter. For one, 'White Rabbit' was a possible name for a Red Indian. There was the occasional creative touch: one reader thought the expression was 'curious, expectant, unbiased, like a little child, but also suspicious and helpless';[17] this reader called the phrase 'an interesting, curiosity-evoking image'. This last response shows the reader participating with enjoyment in the creation of the text even though the result departs from the response norm of the native-speakers. However, linking the phrase with the unseeing eyes of a drug addict ('a pale sort of person with an unfocused look – a drug addict or the like'), as one reader did, while a creative reading in one sense, departs so far from the meaning of Lurie's description that it could even perhaps be called a misreading.

The allusion does not carry the full force of the description of the scene by itself. Many readers stated that their answers were based solely on context or guesswork. The context in the Lurie TT gives the reader *omalaatuisia* 'eccentric' and *ravasi* 'trotted, hurried' in the vicinity of the allusion, not to mention the various rabbit metaphors (*kanitarha* 'rabbit farm' for 'warren', *pesäkolo* 'burrow'). As *kanitarha* suggests a place where rabbits are kept in captivity, not where they abound in a natural state, this led some readers to think of cages and thus imprisonment or frustration. *Eccentric* appears to have given rise to idiosyncratic interpretations departing from the norm: readers' descriptions contained words translating as 'stupid, weird, strange, lifeless, resigned, distant, empty, rigid, mechanical, robot-like, indifferent, dead to the world'. *Hurried* may have contributed to the more appropriate descriptions of 'busy, bustling, impatient, running around'. Stereotypical Finnish views[18] of rabbits gave rise to frequent descriptions like 'frightened, scared, being pursued, timid, worried, anxious, under stress'. (This reasoning came out from the remarks added by some respondents, for example 'the hare is usually a timid animal', 'the hare is a symbol of timidity'.) On the other hand, among the readers who named the source, descriptions were fairly uniform, with the adjectives *kiireinen* 'hurried' and *pelokas, hätääntynyt* (and close synonyms) 'frightened, anxious, worried' predominating. One GRT 1 respondent, a woman in her forties who said she read foreign books and newspapers, also in English, every week, produced a description consistent in all detail with native-speaker and reference work descriptions: 'This of course reminds me of *Alice in Wonderland* and the <u>white rabbit</u> [the underlined words were written in English in an otherwise Finnish text]: worried, bustling, hurried; a feeling of importance and the final purposelessness of it all'.

Table 3 GRT 1 reader responses to Example 1: The White Rabbit

Those who named Alice (N = 3)	
Hurried, anxious	3

Those who did not name Alice (N = 20)	
Frightened, timid	4
Expressionless	3
Curious	2
Other responses[a]	7
No answer	4
	23

Table 4 KLA reader responses to Example 1: The White Rabbit

Those who named Alice (N = 16)	
Hurried, anxious	13
Bustling, impatient	1
No description, just source	2

Those who did not name Alice (N = 35)	
Frightened, timid	8
Blank, resigned, imprisoned	5
Rigid, mechanical	3
Hurried, bustling	2
Self-important	1
Other responses	10
No answer	6
	51

a This includes one reader who did name the source, but only among other potential sources, as a guess. Her description was *huolehtiva* 'caring'; this was the reader who spoke of childbirth associations.

All in all, only one in four of the respondents in the two tests named *Alice* as a source (see Tables 3 and 4). There was an intergenerational difference in the KLA test, where 15 of the younger age group (19 – 30) (N = 42) named the children's classic, as opposed to only one of the older group (of teachers, aged 35–53) (N = 9). This may reflect the presence of *Alice* among university set books in recent years, though students in the English section of the department of translation did not name the source more often than students in other sections. In this context it may be worth noting that Lurie (1990: 49–50) has found that many of her students at Cornell University 'know the classics of children's literature only in cheap cartoon versions, if at all' as children, but 'often, in late adolescence' discover them and eagerly embrace them.

Among the general readers (GRT 1), three out of 23 respondents confidently named *Alice*. These three were all women in their forties and fifties.

The translator of Lurie may have caused some difficulty by not using either of the versions of the White Rabbit's name found in the two full-length Finnish translations of *Alice*, which are *Valkoinen/Valkea kani(ini)*.[19] In her interview, the translator commented that an identifying addition would not have been out of place, and had second thoughts about the translation of the name. However, there have been many abridgements of *Alice* published in Finland, not to mention cartoons, where names may have been differently translated, and in fact none of the 19 readers who did link the name to *Alice* commented on the translation of the name.[20]

It is interesting that three of the readers who did not recognise the source added a note saying they did not mind not understanding it: 'it gives scope to the reader's imagination', 'ignorance does not matter'. There were none of the annoyed remarks to which certain other impenetrable allusions gave rise.

The responses to this culture-bound allusion with a descriptive function indicate that translators cannot count on *Alice*, a text frequently alluded to in English, being nearly as familiar to Finnish readers. In this context, however, it afforded a wide range of possible meanings to readers (only 10 of the 74 respondents did not offer an interpretation): that some of them were wide of the mark did not seem to cause reader dissatisfaction.

The allusions in Examples 2 and 3 are mainly used for micro-level humorous effect, and they show very well how responses to an unfamiliar allusion differ from those to a transcultural one. The unfamiliar allusion is impenetrable to many and easily leads the reader astray.

Example 2. The Walrus and the Carpenter

They don't offer forks at the raw bar. They just serve oysters or clams or shrimp, with beer in paper cups. There are bowls of oyster crackers and squeeze bottles of cocktail sauce. They named the place the Walrus and the Carpenter, but I like it anyway. (Parker, 1987a: 93)

Äyriäisbaarissa ei käytetä haarukoita. Tarjolla on vain ostereita ja simpukoita ja katkarapuja sekä olutta pahvimukeissa. Tiskillä on kulhoissa osterikeksejä ja pursotepulloissa dippikastiketta. Joku älypää oli ristinyt paikan Mursuksi ja Kirvesmieheksi, mutta minä pidän siitä siltikin. (Parker, 1988: 123–4)

A page including this extract (ST: Text B, Appendix 6) was given to general readers (GRT 2, version b). They were asked why the raw bar was named the Walrus and the Carpenter. The phrase was an obvious culture bump: only two readers linked this with Lewis Carroll,[21] and of these, only one had a clear understanding of the connection: 'The name is a reference to a passage in *Alice in Wonderland*, where the Walrus and the Carpenter[22] eat the oysters who had been lying on the seashore.'[23] A third of the respondents were unable to see a link between the raw bar and its name, so that they left the question unanswered, or answered with a question mark (or several: '????'), or wrote down versions of 'I don't understand'. Another third went by the context: a description of the place as offering no forks and serving beer in paper cups combined with images of the brute force of a walrus and the strength and blue-collar skills of a carpenter. All this suggested a rough place for working-class customers ('Walruses are not particularly neat eaters'). A *kirvesmies* (literally 'axe man', hence 'carpenter') meant mainly a construction worker to the respondents (in a country where most houses used to be built of wood until recently), so a mention of that trade made many readers imagine 'a rough and ready place,' one that is 'dingy, working class'. One respondent wrote: 'The walrus is a big strong animal, and a *kirvesmies* [this respondent underlined *kirves-* 'axe'] – the word itself is strong – is a valued trade (the sweaty and skilled work of a real man). The place was therefore a place for real men.' Another, after describing her idea of carpenters, concluded: 'All I can think of is that the bar is popular among carpenters. The walrus means nothing to me.' The walrus as a rule had no clear connotations. A few respondents tentatively pointed to its eating habits ('Perhaps walruses eat oysters and other seafood'), but only the one previously mentioned linked this with Carroll's poem.[24] (See Table 5.)

Table 5 GRT 2b reader responses to Example 2:
The Walrus and the Carpenter

Rough place, working-class customers	13
No answer or 'means nothing to me'	13
Seafood, fishing	4
Clear identification of *Alice*	1
Vague suspicion of literary allusion	3
Other	2
Total[a]	36

a The total number of respondents was 35. One answer was listed twice as it referred to the sea and fishing and also suspected literary allusion (among other possible explanations).

With this text, too, it was found that the translator did not make use of an existing standard translation: the Walrus and the Carpenter are rendered as *Mursu ja Nikkari* in Kunnas and Manner's (1972) translation of *Through the Looking Glass*. Readers were asked if this alternative translation would make any difference to their interpretation. Responses (*N* = 15) showed that both pairs of names were equally unfamiliar to the respondents, who commented at most that *nikkari* 'joiner' suggested a less macho-type worker or one more adept with his tools (like a cabinet-maker); consequently an impression of a somewhat higher class of place was received ('more money, thought and warmth spent on the furnishing of it'). Preferences for one form or another were thus based on personal associations ('*Nikkari* is considerably "tamer",' '*Nikkari* gives more scope for various associations,' '*Nikkari* would imply more use of different implements and more graceful habits,' '*Mursu ja nikkari* sounds stupid'). There was no recognition of this pair of names as a literary allusion other than by the sole respondent who identified the source; in fact, one respondent who suspected literary allusion wrote: 'If this is a literary quote, it would no longer be one if *Kirvesmies* were changed to *Nikkari*. At most it could then be a parody of its original.'

The translator had, in fact, added guidance, but this was not commented on in any way by the readers. His addition of *Joku älypää* ... ('Some smartass [had named the place ...]') was no doubt designed to suggest to the discerning reader that there was a subtle reason for the choice of name, but in absence of recognition of the source of the allusion, the clue was almost useless. Only three respondents even mentioned the possibility that the name might be a literary allusion they could not place.

One reader spontanously suggested that the name should have been retained in its SL form.

The test thus shows that the ST joke was not conveyed to more than one of the 35 readers, and even the link between a sea mammal and a seafood bar was obscured by the stronger connotations of the 'axe man'. A third of the respondents were so puzzled that they had no answer to suggest.

Example 3. A light-blue body stocking with a big red S on the front

The example (ST: Text C, Appendix 6) occurs in a conversation where the male private eye Spenser and his putative woman client meet for the first time and both try to gain the upper hand:

'Your appearance is good,' she said. '... Are you dressed up for the occasion or do you always look good?'
'I'm dressed up for the occasion. Normally I wear a light-blue body stocking with a big red S on the front.' (Parker, 1987a: 15–6)

'Ulkomuotosi on moitteeton', Rachel sanoi. '... Pukeuduitko tapaamistamme varten, vai oletko aina noin moitteeton?'
'Tätä varten vaan. Normaalioloissa käytän vaaleansinistä vartalosukkaa, jossa on edessä suuri punainen S-kirjain.' (Parker, 1988: 21–2)

The allusion is to the fictional figure Superman. This was recognised by at least[25] 40 of the 57 respondents (GRT 2), who thus had no problem with the minimum change translation given to this transcultural allusion.[26] Asked to explain Spenser's words, many pointed out, in more or less depth, that the claim made was a joke ('an example of a wry sense of humour'), with Spenser, who is being interviewed for a job as a bodyguard for a feminist,[27] comparing himself to Superman. The word 'ironical' was used repeatedly, as in 'An ironical comparison of his own abilities and resources and the "supernatural" survival skills of Superman'. A few readers analysed the relationship of the two speakers, one saying the answer shows ideological differences between Spenser and the feminist writer Rachel, and proving her competence as a reader by accurately forecasting the development of the relations between the two in the rest of the novel (which she said she had not read). Several saw this as Spenser's way of paying Rachel back for a tactless question or of testing Rachel's sense of humour.

Some did think that the statement was to be taken at face value, as a literal description of Spenser's leisure wear (one of these thinking that the S stood for 'sexy', as did another, who was less definite about what Spenser

usually wore), or as an example of the sort of garment he would never actually wear. A couple of respondents concentrated on the expression 'body
stocking' and described that. One was reminded of Batman. It was perhaps
to be expected that some of the oldest respondents were among those who
did not recognise the allusion. Most, however, were comfortable with it,
three even offering such extra information as Superman's real name (*Clark
Kent = Lauri Kenttä*). It is noteworthy that only one respondent refrained
from answering this question (one of 57 as opposed to 13 of 35 for Example
2). (See Table 6.)

Table 6   GRT 2 reader responses to Example 3:
A light-blue body stocking ...

Superman named	40
Other	16
No answer	1
Total	57

   Generally speaking the comments on this allusion suggest that most of
the respondents were quite competent receivers of implicit messages when
the sources of such messages were familiar to them.

   Other extracts used in the tests included both sources that proved to be
fairly familiar and those that were quite unfamiliar. For familiar allusions,
minimum change was mostly unproblematic, but unfamiliar ones translated by minimum change as a rule puzzled the general readers.

   Biblical sources can be expected to be transcultural to a considerable de-
gree. In the following example full of biblical expressions (ST: Text D,
Appendix 6), even a translation 'error' (see my comments on *olive branch* in
Chapter 4) did not disturb communication. (See Table 7.)

Example 4   An olive branch

   But now, like a tardy bluebird of peace returning late to a deserted ark
   after three times forty days and nights, this blue airletter has flapped
   across the ocean to him. In its beak it holds, no question about that, a
   fresh olive branch. (Lurie, 1986: 133)

   Mutta kuin vitkaslentoinen rauhan sinilintu, joka palaa myöhästy-
   neenä tyhjäksi jätettyyn arkkiin kolme kertaa neljänkymmenen päivän
   ja yön jälkeen, tämä sininen ilmakirje on nyt lepattanut hänen luokseen
   meren poikki. Nokassa sillä on, aivan epäilemättä, tuore oliivinoksa.
   (Lurie, 1988: 174)

Table 7   GRT 2 reader responses to Example 4: An olive branch

Mention of Noah and/or the flood	39
Peace, reconciliation, good news[a]	10
Source given simply as biblical	4
Other responses	2
No answer	2
Total	57

a Many of those who named Noah also spoke of hope, good news etc. The table separately lists those who gave the precise biblical source (the story of the flood), and those who made no such mention but spoke of peace, reconciliation, etc.

A non-biblical religious expression, however, caused difficulties, all the more as it was of some importance for a coherent representation of the main relationship in a text (ST: Text E, Appendix 6):

Example 5   With my body I thee worship.

For a little while he let the tide of relief and peace close over him but as the surge rose up in his blood he took hold of himself and pushed her away as he struggled to get up.

'No. Stop it,' he whispered fiercely. 'Not here I tell you. Not in this hole and corner. I won't let you. You're mine as well as your own. We've got something to lose. 'With my body I thee worship' and don't forget it, my – my *holy* one.' (Allingham, 1986: 120) (quotation marks and italics ST author)

Pojan valtasi helpottunut hyvänolontunne, mutta pian se vaihtui kiih- koksi, jota vastaan hänen oli ponnistettava kaikki voimansa. Hän yritti irrottaa tytön kädet kaulaltaan ja nousta ylös. 'Ei, jätä minut rauhaan', hän sanoi tukahtuneesti. 'Ei täällä, tässä loukossa'. Minä en salli sitä. Sinä olet minun enkä anna sinun särkeä kaikkea. Muista, että 'minä palvon sinua myös ruumiillani' ... *jumalattareni.*' (Allingham, 1990: 127) (quotation marks and italics in TT as in ST; the allusion is trans- lated as 'I worship you also with my body', 'my holy one' as 'my goddess')

In many of its love scenes, the novel has allusions to famous love poetry and more indefinable intertextuality to suggest that the main characters are deeply and romantically in love. The respondents of course were unaware of this macro-context. The young man's 'No' can be taken to mean 'not yet': he wants to marry his girl first, thinking anything else would cheapen their love (*we've got something to lose*). The authorial addition of quotation marks around the allusion (retained by the translators) emphasises that the words are borrowed. Four NS readers out of five stated that the grounds given by the young man for his refusal are religious.[28] The allusion is to the marriage ceremony (the Book of Common Prayer).

The majority of the general readers, however, did not recognise the source and missed the allusion to marriage. The allusion is a culture bump because the Finnish Lutheran marriage ceremony[29] does not contain a similarly worded phrase; instead, Finnish couples promise to love each other *myötä- ja vastoinkäymisessä* 'in good times and bad', and this is the phrase that is popularly recognised as shorthand for marriage vows. The translation cannot include the clue of the archaic *thee* of the ST as there is no Finnish pronoun similarly restricted in use; and the rendering of *my holy one* as 'my goddess' further obscures the interpretation of the passage in Christian terms.

Only three of the KLA respondents, all students working with English, named the source of the allusion. Another three were aware of the religious background but unsure of its precise nature: 'An allusion to the Bible? Some grounds for celibacy or something? Mary Magdalene?' Over half did not answer the question at all,[30] or just put a question mark, or wrote down versions of 'I don't understand this'. The answers given were sometimes fairly general comments: 'He finds love-making important', 'despite his refusal he is in love with her', but others clearly showed that many readers had followed the gist of the young man's argument: 'He is very much in love and desires this woman, but does not want to "touch" her because he respects her or for some reason they cannot be together'. A couple of the comments, however, seemed to misinterpret the situation: 'His body and soul are separate', 'He feels for her physically, too, though earlier perhaps he couldn't.' (See Table 8)

The general readers of GRT 1 perceived the motivation of the young man more easily, perhaps because of their more mature years (average age 42.3 years) or because in contrast to the KLA respondents, they received the questionnaires individually and could answer them at their convenience. Many heard the young man utter 'an elevated declaration of love': 'he doesn't want to use her, he feels for her deeply,' 'he wants to live with integrity and make the relationship public'. Only one, however, recognised the source as referring to the marriage ceremony; another knew she had heard it before but added: 'what is means is unclear to me'. One expressed her irritation in no uncertain terms: 'incomprehensible babble, especially the marked clause [with the allusion], no coherence'. There were some misunderstandings: 'A selfish thought: he thinks he could perform better under other circumstances.' (See Table 9.)

Table 8 KLA reader responses to Example 5:
With my body I thee worship

Recognition of source (marriage ceremony)	3
Vaguely religious	3
Respect for the girl, love-making a commitment	12
Other responses	3
No answer or 'Don't know'	<u>30</u>
Total	51

Table 9 GRT 1 reader responses to Example 5:
With my body I thee worship

Recognition of source (marriage ceremony)	1
Vaguely religious	3
Respect for the girl, love-making a commitment	12
Other responses	3
No answer or 'Don't know'	<u>4</u>
Total	23

The tests show that only a small minority of the readers realised the young man was alluding to the marriage ceremony. This made his argument harder to follow, and while general life experience perhaps helped the majority of GRT 1 readers on the right track, even in that group a third of the respondents were unclear of what the young man's lines implied. It must be admitted, though, that the brevity of the extract given made interpretation difficult. However, in the macro-context of the ST, the lines are surely meant to indicate honourable strength of character and commitment, and a translation which fails to convey this detracts from the coherence of characterisation and plot.

In the following example (ST: Text F, Appendix 6) the use of the allusion is an element in characterisation, emphasising the differences in cultural literacy between the literary scholar Vinnie and the retired businessman Mumpson.

Example 6   Pumpkins at midnight.

'I was just looking for a taxi.'
Mr Mumpson stares out across the empty, rain-sloshed, light-streaked pavement. 'Don't seem to be any here.'
'No.' She manages a brief defensive smile. 'Apparently they all turn into pumpkins at midnight.'
'Huh? Oh, ha-ha... ' (Lurie, 1986: 22)

'Haeskelen tässä vain taksia.'
Herra Mumpson tähyilee tyhjän, sateen pieksämän, valojen juovittaman asfaltin poikki. 'Ei niitä näytä olevan.'
'Ei.' Vinnie onnistuu väläyttämään torjuvan hymyntapaisen. 'Muuttuvat kai kurpitsoiksi keskiyön hetkellä.'
'Täh? Ai. Hah-hah... ' (Lurie, 1988: 32)

GRT 2b respondents were asked to explain what Vinnie meant by her reference to pumpkins at midnight and to comment on Mr Mumpson's reaction. As they were given only a small section of the scene to read, they could obviously not be aware of the macro-level function of the allusion, but those who commented on Mumpson's response saw that it was slower than appropriate and perhaps was meant to hide his puzzlement at the allusion.

As regards the source, the test revealed a clash between two occurrences of pumpkins in imported cultural texts: the traditional one in the story of Cinderella and the newer (to Finns) of pumpkins at Halloween, familiar through many channels (including films, exchange students, etc.) but in this test shown to be so especially through the *Peanuts* cartoons, where one of the characters spends much of his time waiting for the Great Pumpkin to appear at night. Some of the respondents who saw this as the source were doubtful as to precisely how the TT could be understood in that light. Three other respondents were vague about which children's story had vehicles changing into pumpkins, and two identified stories incorrectly: one thought this happened in *Snow White*, another in *Sleeping Beauty*. (See Table 10.)

The remaining examples of retention of name or minimum change all involved unfamiliar allusions, and all caused problems of understanding. It was noticeable that modified allusions in particular worked badly in literal translation. Modified allusions are often meant to raise a smile, but in the absence of recognition of the allusion, modifications are not spotted.

In the following example (ST: Text G, Appendix 6), there is a description of police work which includes (as a joke), a modification of the proverb *A man works from sun to sun, but a woman's work is never done* (ODP 32). Modifications often use transpositions for humorous effect, and the words *man* and *woman* are duly transposed in the ST:

Table 10   GRT 2b reader responses to Example 6: Pumpkins at midnight

Mention of Cinderella	15
Mention of Halloween / *Peanuts*	10
Mention of other children's fiction	5
Denotation only	4
No answer	1
Total	35

Example 7   *A woman works from sun to sun but a man's work is never done.*

Then you wash (yes, that's right, *wash)* all the shells in your favorite detergent (a woman works from sun to sun, but a man's work is never done) and you are now ready to compare them. (McBain, 1984: 97) (italics ST author)

Sitten kaikki luodit pestään (aivan niin, *pestään*) tutkijan mielipesuaineella (nainen tekee työtä vuorokauden ympäri, mutta mieheltä ei työ lopu koskaan) ja niin ollaan valmiita luotien vertailuun. (McBain, 1981: 108) (italics in TT as in ST)

The saying is true in agricultural societies where a man's working day begins at sunrise and ends at sunset, but a woman must work even longer days. As no similar saying appears to be familiar in Finnish, the general readers could only rely on their own perceptions of sex roles and work: 'Men's work is more important', 'Women do everyday routine and repetitious tasks. Men's work requires more creative thinking – is demanding in a different way', 'A woman works 24 hours a day, but she does finish some of her jobs. A man works continuously and it never stops. He may not achieve anything concrete.' Only one respondent noticed that there was a reversal of sex roles. Another wondered if the male chauvinism was seriously meant or ironical. Some respondents called the line offensive to women. There was no perception of humour in the extract: the transposition of words in an unknown saying is after all unlikely to be recognised as funny. The readers approached the saying from a serious point of view, interested in its truth value, and questioned its relevance in the context: 'A mildly chauvinist idea: women do routine work, which must always be done on time. Men's work is intellectual, and there is always plenty of that. Still, I don't understand how the sentence fits in with the text.' (See Table 11.)

Table 11   GRT 1 reader responses to Example 7:
A woman works from sun to sun

Comparison of men's and women's work	17
Expresses male chauvinism	6
Speaks of useless work	2
Reversal of roles	1
Other responses	2
No answer	1
Total[a]	29

a   The table includes alternative and complementary explanations given; the total of respondents was 23.

There was another joking modification of a saying which GRT 1 respondents also discussed seriously (as the type of problem and the results are the same as in example 7, it is not discussed in full detail). This wisecrack, used in conversation between two policemen in McBain, transposed the American political slogan *Separate but equal*[31] into *Not even equal but separate* (ST: Text H, Appendix 6), resulting in the policemen laughing and the addressee expressing his approbation. The Finnish readers wrote about attitudes to racism, but only one spoke of the line as a joke. None named the source. Question marks and 'Don't knows' were frequent, one reader commenting: 'I think the sentence is badly translated, for even if one reads it many times, it is still difficult to say what the writer had in mind.'[32]

In the absence of connotations, readers can only make use of the context or of general world knowledge. Context played a dominant role in the interpretation of a passage (ST: Text J, Appendix 6) where the anglophile Vinnie has named her deceased American lover's daughter Barbie 'the Barbarian', and when her attitude to the girl becomes less hostile, directs her aggression towards Barbie's mother, *that Visigoth realtor*, seeing Barbie, with her low self-esteem, as a victim of her mother. Respondents were unsure of the meaning of *länsigoottilainen* 'Visigoth', and tended to look for clues in such matters as the mother's way of making a living as a real estate agent and in psychological perceptions of mother–daughter relationships.

Example 8   That Visigoth realtor her mother.

Barbie's continual assertion of her lack of intelligence has begun to annoy Vinnie. Stop telling me how stupid you are, she wants to say. You graduated from the University of Oklahoma, you can't be all that stupid.

'That's all right,' she says instead. 'I think you've done very well, considering everything.' Almost against her will, she reclassifies The Barbarian as an innocent peasant – the victim rather than the accomplice of that Visigoth realtor her mother, who is no doubt responsible for Barbie's low opinion of her own intelligence. (Lurie, 1986: 266–7)

Barbien jatkuva älykkyytensä niukkuuden vakuutteleminen on alkanut käydä Vinnien hermoille. Lakkaisit jo selittelemästä, miten tohelo olet, hän haluaa sanoa. Olethan sinä suorittanut akateemisen tutkinnon Oklahoman yliopistossa: et sinä nyt niin hirveän tohelo voi olla.

'Ei se mitään', hän sanoo sen sijaan. 'Minusta sinä olet kaiken kaikkiaan pärjännyt oikein hyvin.' Melkein vastoin tahtoaan hän luokittelee Barbaarin uudestaan, nyt viattomaksi maalaistytöksi, joka on länsigoottilaisen kiinteistönvälittäjä-äitinsä uhri pikemminkin kuin tämän rikoskumppani. (Lurie, 1988: 343)

The NS readers also described the mother as 'dominant, interested in cash', 'sounds a real horror', 'a strong-minded, even aggressive – but successful – woman', 'a ruthless, uncultivated dealer in real estate'. Only two showed interest in the historical aspect, that is, in who the Visigoths were, and thus made it clear that they had seen the link between *Visigoth* and *Barbarian*.[33]

The Finnish respondents saw the mother as domineering, too strict, critical, unfeeling, aggressive, etc. Some respondents made it clear that they based such interpretations partly on her being a real estate agent: 'I don't understand "Visigoth" in any way at all. A realtor suggests a certain ruthlessness, aggressivity and efficiency. Not a positive evaluation of the mother', 'realtors are ruthless people who stomp on others.' Relatively few linked *Visigoth* with *Barbarian*.[34] The word *victim* in the context may also have contributed to the mother being seen in negative terms.

Several gave no answer; some thought the phrase meant the mother was a German (and negative connotations of *German* were made explicit). There were a few interpretations based on *Gothic* horror and *Gothic* architecture ('When Barbie was a child her mother had been interested in real estate business only, so that she seemed as distant as a Gothic church spire'). Two respondents spontaneously suggested that *hunni* 'Hun' or *vandaali* 'Vandal' might have made for a better translation. Those words might indeed have helped some of the respondents who complained of not understanding the passage to see the link between Vinnie's visualisations of the two American women. Some of the readers expressed annoyance at the impenetrable phrase: 'What on earth is this creature "Visigoth realtor mother"?'

The 'psychological' interpretations of the mother–daughter relationship (for example 'the mother has contributed to Barbie's low sense of self-esteem by emphasising her own intelligence, practicality and efficiency and perhaps comparing them with Barbie's') also tended to obscure the humour of the allusion.

Even though Vinnie feels grief and guilt, she is on another level observing her own reactions in a detached way, aware of her own foolishness and contradictions. (See Tables 12 and 13.)

Table 12   GRT 1 reader responses to Example 8:
That Visigoth realtor her mother

Visigoth linked with barbarian	1
Psychological comments only (mother/daughter)	7
Comments on realtor/business-woman only	6
A hard person (no grounds given)	2
Gothic architecture	3
German	2
Other responses	2
No answer or 'Don't know'	2
Total[a]	25

a   The total of answers listed exceeds the number of respondents ($N = 23$) as two answers are listed twice: in them, the suggestions that the mother was a German were subsidiary to her being a realtor.

Table 13 GRT 2 reader responses to Example 8:
That Visigoth realtor her mother

Visigoth linked with barbarian	12
Psychological comments only (mother/daughter)	6
Comments on realtor/business-woman only	3
Greedy for money	4
A hard person (no grounds given)	6
Gothic architecture	1
German/Western European	6
Other responses	11
No answer or 'Don't know'	9
Total[a]	59

a   The total exceeds the number of respondents ($N = 57$) because some of the responses contained elements of more than one answer.

Irony may be difficult to spot in an extract (but note that quite a few responses to the transcultural Superman example spoke of irony). In the following example (ST: Text K, Appendix 6), the minor character Edwin's attitude to Chuck Mumpson (*what's-his-name*), whether dead or alive, is one of snobbery, nor does he seem to notice that Vinnie is devastated by the loss of her secret lover. The modified allusion he uses is a subtle way of downgrading the dead man, a pinprick attack.

Example 9   Some corner of an English field .

'How is what's-his-name, by the way?... Is he still digging for ancestors down in Wiltshire?'
'Yes – no,' Vinnie replies uncomfortably...   [S]he hasn't dared mention Chuck. She knows it will be nearly impossible for her to tell the story without falling apart... But she plunges in [telling Edwin that Chuck is dead]. Several times she hears a tell-tale wobble in her voice, but Edwin seems to notice nothing.
'So there's some corner of an English field that is forever Tulsa,' he says finally, smiling.
'Yes.' Vinnie strangles the cry that rises in her. (Lurie, 1986: 275)

'Kuinkas Mikä-hänen-nimensä-nyt-olikaan muuten voi?... Vieläkö hän kaivelee esi-isiä Wiltshiressä?'

'Vielä – ei', Vinnie vastaa vaivaantuneesti... [H]än ei ole uskaltanut mainita Chuckia. Hän tietää, että olisi miltei mahdotonta kertoa tästä ratkeamatta itkuun... Mutta hän rohkaisee mielensä [ja kertoo Chuckin kuolleen]. Usean kerran hän kuulee paljastavaa värinää äänessään, mutta Edwin ei näytä huomaavan mitään.

'Niin että jollain englantilaisella niityllä on nurkkaus, joka on ikuisesti Tulsaa', mies lopulta sanoo hymyillen.

'Niin.' Vinnie kuristaa itsessään kohoavan itkun. (Lurie, 1988: 353)

The most striking phrase in the translated allusion is undoubtedly *Tulsa*, for Edwin, the British speaker, the epitome of unsophisticated Midwestern America. Rupert Brooke's original line glorified England ('That there's some corner of a foreign field/That is forever England'). (See other modifications of the line in Chapter 3). The modification shows Edwin heartlessly using Chuck's death as something to quip about, to show off his own ready wit and sophistication in contrast to Vinnie's *cowboy friend* (a description occurring earlier in the extract). Very little of this came through to the respondents, many of whom could not understand it at all: 'A reference to Chuck being an American. Tulsa = a city in the US. Still, I don't get the point of the sentence.' Another respondent said: 'I've no idea what Tulsa is. For that reason I can't follow the thought.'

Those who gave interpretations thought as a rule that Edwin was offering comfort sincerely:[35] 'A comforting idea, that death is part of life and it is immaterial where it takes place – on any field life is going on. His tone of voice is warm and convincing, which shows that he believes in what he is saying.' For another, Tulsa stood for 'the country of dreams, a good place to return to.' A few readers were more perspicacious and sensed irony or *Schadenfreude* in Edwin's words. None offered a source, though one called the line 'a fine saying', which suggests this reader had an inkling of its preformed nature. (See Table 14.)

Table 14 GRT 1 reader responses to Example 9: Some corner of an English field

Ironical, amused, *Schadenfreude*	4
Comfort	8
Denotation only	2
Other responses	3
No answer or 'Don't know'	6
Total	23

See also Chapter 6 for the responses of 33 students of English to the ST extract.

The final example of responses to minimum change translations involves a passage with two allusions, the effect of which was missed by practically all of the respondents, leaving the passage flat, with a denotative meaning only.

Example 10.   Where are the Imps of yesteryear?

In his musings on the achievements of the British motor-car industry, the protagonist of Lodge's novel wonders:

> When was the last time we were supposed to have a world-beating aluminium engine? The Hillman Imp, right? Where are they now, the Hillman Imps of yesteryear? In the scrapyards, every one, or nearly. And the Linwood plant a graveyard, grass growing between the assembly lines, corrugated-iron roofs flapping in the wind. (Lodge, 1988: 11)

> Milloin viimeksi meillä pitikään olla maailman markkinat valloittava alumiinimoottori? Oliko se Hillman Imp? Missä takavuosien Hillman Impit nyt ovat? Kaatopaikoilla, joka ikinen, tai ainakin lähestulkoon joka ikinen. Ja Linwoodin tehdas on hautuumaana, ruoho kasvaa kokoomalinjojen välissä, aaltolevykatot repsottavat tuulessa. (Lodge, 1990: 23)

The first of the two allusions in the ST passage (ST: Text L, Appendix 6) is a modification of Villon's *Où sont les neiges d'antan?*, whose English translation (by Dante Gabriel Rossetti)[36] is *Where are the snows of yesteryear?* The second modifies Pete Seeger's song of the 1960s, *Where Have All the Flowers Gone?* Lodge uses *scrapyards* for *graveyards*,[37] but the latter word is included in the sentence that follows the allusion in the ST. Consulted, the NS readers recognised the sources without trouble and thought the allusions conveyed 'conventional nostalgia for lost youth and its innocence and naiveté' – or, to those who couldn't 'feel too nostalgic about a grubby little Hillman Imp,' irony and wry humour. Again, these tones were not recognised by GRT 1 respondents (with one exception), nor did the TT make full use of existing translations of the allusions to allow TT readers to recognise and respond to preformed material. In the test, this extract differed from the rest in that nothing was underlined for the respondents to focus on; instead they were asked to underline and explain any allusions they noticed in the passage (the concept had been explained and examples given in the instructions). Most of them saw nothing to comment on. Only one response resembled that of the NS readers, stating that the passage meant 'destruction of dreams, or that good old times were past'. The TT wording, in other words, did not raise the desired connotations for these readers but was devoid of implicit meaning. The translator did not use one of the existing Villon translations (at least those by Aale Tynni or Veijo Meri have been published) or the Finnish version of Seeger's song to emphasise the *ubi sunt* theme. While the Villon translations are little known and seldom quoted in Finnish, such elements could have been used for re-creation (see a proposed translation for this example in Chapter 4). Instead, the minimum change translation had one reader wondering if the details of petrol consumption given earlier in the passage could possibly be true, and several underlined and explained the meaning of the Finnish idiom *yli hilseen* (occurring earlier in the extract), a rendering for 'gets on his tits'. Nearly 50% did not mark the passage in any way. (See Table 15.)

Table 15   GRT 1 reader responses to Example 10:
Where are the Imps of yesteryear?

Allusion marked: nostalgia	1
Allusion marked: no connotations	1
Other section(s) marked	11
No answer	<u>10</u>
Total	23

It appears, then, that instead of recognising the connotations and subtle ironies, TT readers (with one exception) read the text at the denotational level, as an inquiry into the present whereabouts of old Hillman Imp cars.

Responses to other strategies

The remaining examples all involve allusions which, judging by the previous examples, can be assumed to be unfamiliar. The responses suggest that the translations chosen have improved the TT readers' chances of understanding the meaning of allusive passages. As explained earlier, the experimental data in this study were not gathered to allow for a comparison between responses to various strategies but to show that in literal translation unfamiliar allusions may well be culture bumps; for that reason, there were only a few examples of other strategies in the questionnaires, but the responses to these examples show that much of the meaning of the allusions has indeed been received.

In the first example of more 'interventional' strategies (where the translator has visibly intervened and assumed the role of cultural mediator), an unfamiliar name has been replaced by a more familiar one.

Example 11   Rebecca of Sunnybrook Farm

'What you want, Mr. Ticknor, is someone feisty enough to get in the line of someone else's fire, and tough enough to get away with it. And you want him to look like Winnie-the-Pooh and act like Rebecca of Sunnybrook Farm. I'm not sure Rebecca's even got a gun permit.' (Parker, 1987a: 11)

'Herra Ticknor, te haluatte jonkun, joka on tarpeeksi rivakka astuakseen tuleen jonkun toisen puolesta ja tarpeeksi kova selvitäkseen siitä. Hänen vain pitäisi olla Nalle Puhin näköinen ja käyttäytyä kuin Pollyanna. Lieköhän Pollyannalla ollut aseenkantolupaa.' (Parker, 1988: 14–5)

Either the translator was unfamiliar with Kate Douglas Wiggin's story for pre-teenage readers, *Rebecca of Sunnybrook Farm*, or he assumed his readers would be, and therefore chose to replace that name by the name of another naively optimistic fictional girl. Indeed, KLA respondents (see Chapter 4) showed that the name of Pollyanna was reasonably well known; even though the precise connotations of the name were not always clear, it was recognised by approximately half the respondents as the name of a little girl in a book or film. The parallelism with the well-known Pooh helps in the context. The point in the ST passage (ST: Text M, Appendix 6) is that bodyguards must be physically tough (unlike Winnie-the-Pooh) and always be prepared for the worst (unlike Rebecca and Pollyanna) if they are to protect their clients successfully. As the conversation in the extract is part of a series of scenes where the world views of Rachel (represented here by Ticknor) and Spenser are shown to conflict, it needs to be intelligible, or the TT reader will be unable to see the contrast. GRT 2 respondents were asked: 'How do you understand the underlined requirement? What does the speaker pretend a bodyguard should be like and how should he act?' Only the parts of the responses that show reactions to the name Pollyanna (that is, mostly the answers to 'how should he act?') are listed here, as the name of Winnie-the-Pooh proved to be fully transcultural. (See Table 16.)

Table 16 GRT 2 reader responses to Example 11:
Rebecca/Pollyanna

Nice, well-behaved, correct	14
Active, self-assured	7
Joyful, positive, bubbly, innocent	5
Obedient, doll-like	4
Other responses	14
No answer or 'Don't know'	13
Total	57

Readers were not asked if they identified the source, and so only a few mentioned 'the girls' books I read 45 years ago' or the Disney film. Some readers were clearly familiar with both names though they gave no information on sources: 'You can't be a bodyguard, on guard and a killer, if you believe the best of everyone, and your I.Q. is 30. Forgive me, Pooh, forgive me, Pollyanna.' Another added that A.A. Milne was one of Raymond Chandler's favourite authors and that Parker emulates Chandler. Some respondents provided sophisticated analyses of Ticknor's requirements: 'The allusions to fictional characters in children's literature emphasise the impossibility of a bodyguard's task. Spenser thinks the duties of a bodyguard and the ideological world view of a feminist writer are irreconcilable. A bodyguard should be reflective and simple = Winnie-the-Pooh, and act in a conventional, nice and brisk way = Pollyanna – but if necessary, be prepared to kill.' One added the remark: 'The text is amusing.' Other responses were guesswork by readers who did not recognise the name: 'mean on the job', 'tough and direct'. Such readers doubtless thought (and in some cases stated that they thought) that there was meant to be some contrast between Pooh and Pollyanna.

The name was unfamiliar to half the respondents, who either refused to speculate or took it to imply that a bodyguard should be variously 'curious', 'tough', 'an intelligent gentleman', 'a tripping Barbie doll', 'a fussy old woman', etc. When evaluating the success of the strategy, it should be remembered that in all likelihood, the name of Rebecca would have been unfamiliar to most readers.

In the following example (ST: Text N, Appendix 6), an unfamiliar name[38] was replaced by a common noun. The translator appears to have recognised that the name would convey nothing to the majority of readers, and replaced the name by a noun phrase which, while inexact as a description of Carry Nation herself, could be expected to make inferencing possible.

Example 12   She did not look like Carry Nation.

I met Rachel Wallace on a bright October day ... She didn't look like Carry Nation. She looked like a pleasant woman about my own age with a Diane Von Furstenberg dress on and some lipstick, and her hair long and black and clean. (Parker, 1987a: 12)

Tapasin Rachel Wallacen eräänä kirkkaana lokakuun päivänä ... Hän ei näyttänyt 20-luvun suffragetilta, vaan suunnilleen ikäiseltäni miellyttävältä naiselta, jolla oli Diane Von Furstenbergin suunnittelema mekko ja huulissaan jonkin verran punaa. Hiukset olivat pitkät ja mustat ja puhtaat. (Parker, 1988: 17) ['She did not look like a 1920s suffragette']

The ST allusion is meant to convey Spenser's surprise at meeting the feminist writer. In popular source-cultural imagination, Carry Nation is a large, hatchet-wielding leader of the temperance movement, dressed in severe black and white (*Encyclopedia Britannica* VII: 207). Rachel turns out to be pleasant-looking: she is well-dressed and clean and wears discreet make-up. In other words, she looks neither militant, ugly nor frightening. At least some of these aspects were perceived by all the respondents. They were asked to describe what Rachel Wallace did not look like, that is, what the expression 'a 1920s suffragette' suggested to them.

The respondents made unfavourable comments on a 1920s suffragette's dress and hair (undoubtedly reinforced by the immediate context – however, there was only one remark on make-up which is likewise singled out in the passage)[39] but also on her behaviour and facial expression. It is notable that every respondent had something to offer: there were no 'Don't know's' and no one left the question unanswered. (See Table 17.)

Some of the respondents (both men and women) made it clear that they did not share the stereotype: 'a tough, masculine woman who does not use clothes or looks to emphasise her femininity. For a *man* undoubtedly a frightening and unappealing woman' (emphasis in the original), or (after a description): 'in other words, she did not look like a feminist in the negative sense of the word.'

One of the readers believed he had noted a discrepancy: 'Suffragette: a hard and masculine woman (probably, though, dating back to the turn of the century, not the 1920s, which makes one wonder how well-informed Spenser really is).' The translator's slip, if slip it is,[40] thus led this reader to read it as part of the characterisation of the protagonist (with an effect probably counter to the intentions of the author, a professor of English. Spenser is presented as 'unexpectedly literate' on the back cover of the paperback).

Table 17 GRT 2a reader responses to Example 12: Carry Nation/A 1920s suffragette

Dress	11
Hair	7
Behaviour	6
Untidiness	4
Facial expression	4
Voice	2
Other responses	6
No answer or 'Don't know'	0
Total[a]	40

a   The total of responses listed below exceeds the number of respondents ($N = 22$) as most answers contained more than one element, for instance 'short hair, untidy clothes, loud voice'.

In the following example, the ST (Text O, Appendix 6) has two rhyming lines of poetry containing a metaphor. Instead of a minimum change translation or a rhyming version, neither of which would be recognisable as an allusion in Finnish (though the latter would doubtless be recognised as poetry), the translator decided to retain the poetic metaphor but to compress it, dispensing with the rhyme. The translation thus sounds like a piece of folk wisdom:

Example 13   Tangled are the webs we weave

The three cops investigating the case knew very little about high-level business transactions involving astronomical figures. They knew only that tangled are the webs we weave when first we practise to deceive... (McBain, 1984: 175)

Juttua tutkivilla kolmella poliisilla oli perin vähän tietoa korkean tason kaupoista, joissa rahasummat liikkuivat tähtitieteellisissä lukemissa. He tiesivät vain, että sotkuisia ovat petoksen verkot... (McBain, 1981: 198) ['They knew only that tangled are the webs of deceit']

The respondents as a rule had no difficulty explaining this on the denotative level (though no one spoke of deceivers being caught in their own tangled webs). None expressed surprise at the wording – in other words, there were none of the annoyed remarks that accompanied responses to some of the culture bumps. Not surprisingly, there were no attempts to suggest a source either. (See Table 18.)

Table 18   GRT 2a reader responses to Example 13: Tangled webs

Complicated crimes, difficult to unravel	13
They smell a rat (illegal activity)	4
Other answers	3
No answer	2
Total	22

Two of the 'other answers' also spoke of fraud or crime in more general terms.

Another example with an allusive metaphor was changed to another metaphor from the same sphere of life in the TT. The ST allusion (ST: Text P, Appendix 6), *there's gold in them thar quarters*, a line occurring in many Westerns (usually in the form of *there's gold in them thar hills*) and meaning 'there are opportunities in the way indicated' (Rees, 1991: 315), was not given a minimum change translation (*noilla seuduilla/kukkuloilla on kultaa*). Instead, another metaphor dispensing with the potential reader puzzlement caused by *seuduilla* 'areas' (or another possible translation for *quarters*) but still suggesting the gold rush, and hence the chance of growing rich quickly, was used.

Example 14   There's gold in them thar quarters.

'... Who are you working for? The little lad himself?'
'No. I belong to the other side of the family. I am protecting the interests of the girl friend.'
'Are you indeed? Quite a client!' He was openly envious. 'There's gold in them thar quarters. Oh well, good luck to you ... ' (Allingham, 1986: 76)

'... Kenen laskuun te oikein työskentelette? Pojanko?'
'En. Minä suoritan tiedusteluja hänen tyttöystävänsä puolesta.'
'Niinkö! Siinä onkin asiakas!' Mies ei välittänyt peitellä kateuttaan. 'Todellinen kultakaivos! Onneksi olkoon! [...]' (Allingham, 1990: 82)
['A veritable gold mine!']

Most of the respondents understood the gold-digging metaphor to mean that the girl friend or her family was rich. Quite a few added that she might also be naive, and hence susceptible to inflated bills. Two respondents suspected irony: could she in fact be quite poor? (See Table 19.)

Table 19 GRT 2 reader responses to Example 14:
Gold in them thar quarters/Veritable gold mine

Rich	32
Rich and naive	16
Naive	1
Irony: poor in reality	2
No answer	6
Total	57

In the last example of this section (first presented in Chapter 4), there was a more extensive alteration: the words of a medieval mystic, St Julian of Norwich, who must be deemed totally unknown to Finnish readers, were replaced by a modified allusion echoing the Lord's Prayer. The alteration was successful in that all readers either were able to suggest a source or explained the meaning of the allusion (or both).

Example 15   All be well, and all will be well, and all manner of thing will be well

'All be well,' she shut her eyes and said, quoting something she had read, but not quite sure what '– and all will be well, and all manner of thing will be well,' and Clifford did not even snub her by asking for the source of the quotation. (Weldon, 1988: 72)

'Ja kaikki on hyvin', Helen sanoi sulkien silmänsä ja siteeraten jotakin, jonka hän oli lukenut, olematta aivan varma, 'niin taivaassa kuin maan päällä', eikä Clifford edes nolannut häntä kysymällä, mistä sitaatti oli. (Weldon, 1989: 103) ['And all is well...in heaven as on earth']

The scene in the ST occurs when Helen has just given birth to Clifford's child. She had planned to have an abortion, but Clifford had prevented this. Helen's words express the feelings of both parents: Clifford has forgiven her, and the child is a promise of future happiness. The longer extract used in the questionnaire (ST: Text Q, Appendix 6) contains many emotionally charged words (corresponding to *pain and pleasure; the drive to protect; the warm reassuring glow; the recognition of privilege; ungrudging love; Helen glowed in his forgiveness*). A literal translation of St Julian's words (*'Kaikki on*

hyvin, ja kaikki tulee olemaan hyvin, ja kaikenlaiset asiat tulevat olemaan hyvin')
is unrecognisable as an allusion as well as intolerably clumsy (because of
the repetitions and the special future forms, rarely used in Finnish) so that
to use it would disturb the heightened emotionality of the scene.

The translator's choice of words was perceived as religious by most of
the Finnish readers. They were asked: 'What does Helen mean? Does this
allude to anything?' (See Table 20.)

Table 20   GRT 2 reader responses to Example 15: All be well

Peace, happiness, forgiveness	36
Mention of source only	16
Other answers	3
No answer	2
Total	57

Readers were, however, uncertain about the precise source.[41] They referred to the Lord's Prayer ($N = 19$), the nativity ($N = 3$), Revelations ($N = 1$)
or simply the Bible ($N = 8$). Some saw a combination of a religious and a
secular source (either the saying *Loppu hyvin kaikki hyvin = All's well that
ends well* or the cry of medieval night watchmen combined with the Lord's
Prayer or a vaguely 'biblical' source). One suspected this might be a Shakespearean allusion. Ten respondents suggested no source at all but two of
these did explain the meaning of Helen's words.

The explanations varied from assurances of happiness ever after or at
least for the time being to more analytical ones, involving awareness of past
controversies and the need for reconciliation and the probability that the
present euphoria will be short-lived.

One of the students gathering data wrote that she thought the remark in
the extract about *asking for the source of the quotation* unmotivated in Finnish
as the source was so familiar. The results, however, show that there was a
degree of uncertainty among the TT readers about the exact source; hence,
the remark is not out of place. (It is of course better motivated in the ST;
while St Julian's words can be found in reference works and are recognisable as religious, two of the three NS colleagues consulted on this example
could not place them.)[42]

This exploration of reader responses to allusions in translation supports
the hypothesis that literal translations of unfamiliar allusions pose problems of understanding for TT readers. In other words, they are culture

bumps. To say this is not to underestimate the TT readers: there was evidence of reading competence both in the responses to the test allusions and in the common recognition of the modified *to be or not to be* in the original Finnish text used as a test (Appendix 3). It should also be borne in mind that many respondents were, to some extent, bilingual, as they were in the habit of reading texts in foreign languages including English. Still, the degree of biculturalism required both to recognise the presence of source-cultural allusions in a TT through the veil of the TL as it were, in literal translation, and to see their meanings, would seem to be too much to expect. Readers who are bicultural to that degree will probably prefer to read foreign books untranslated anyway. Responses to Examples 11 to 15 suggest that cultural mediation through more interventional strategies has a better chance of enabling TT readers to grasp the point of an allusive passage.

It is difficult to give an exact quantitative conclusion as the questions were open-ended, not multiple-choice, and hence more difficult to assign to particular categories. However, by way of conclusion, an attempt is made to reduce the previous data to simpler figures. The totals in Table 21 include only one answer per respondent, unlike some of the earlier tables where totals occasionally surpass the number of respondents, as alternative or complementary answers have been listed separately (see notes to individual examples). The number of respondents per question varies.[43] 'NS-like response' means a response comparable to those of competent native-speakers as indicated by the written responses of the NS respondents and information on sources and connotations in reference works. It is of necessity a relative concept – cf. the discussion earlier in this Chapter. (See Table 21.)

Table 21   GRT reader responses to allusions in literal translation

Example 1 *(The White Rabbit)*	
NS-like response	3
Other	16
No answer	4
Total	23
Example 2 *(The Walrus and the Carpenter)*	
NS-like response (= link to sea noted)	5
Other	17
No answer	13
Total	35

Table 21   continued

Example 3 (A light-blue body stocking)	
NS-like response (= named Superman)	40
Other	16
No answer	1
Total	57

Example 4 (An olive branch)	
NS-like response	53
Other	2
No answer	2
Total	57

Example 5 (With my body I thee worship)	
NS-like response (= religion)	4
Other	15
No answer	4
Total	23

Example 6 (Pumpkins at midnight)	
NS-like response (= Cinderella)	15
Other	19
No answer	1
Total	35

Example 7 (A woman works from sun to sun)	
NS-like response (= reversal of roles)	1
Other	21
No answer	1
Total	23

Table 21   continued

Example 8 (*That Visigoth realtor her mother*)	
Link between Visigoth and Barbarian noted	13
Not noted	56
No answer	<u>11</u>
Total	80
Example 9 (*Some corner of an English field*)	
NS-like response (= ironical, putdown)	4
Other	13
No answer	<u>6</u>
Total	23
Example 10 (*Where are the Imps of yesteryear*)	
NS-like response (= nostalgia)	1
Other	12
No answer	<u>10</u>
Total	23

An analysis of these figures shows that basically, the examples can be put into two categories: (1) culture bumps, to which few readers reacted in the way an analysis of the ST extract based on source cultural background knowledge suggests as appropriate. This category includes the examples with a low occurrence of NS-like responses (Examples 1, 2, 7, 9 and 10) and a high number of no answers; (2) transcultural examples which clearly communicated their meaning: the majority of readers had no difficulty understanding them (Examples 3 and 4). (As indicated in Note 25, it is possible that some of those who did not specifically name Superman took this identification for granted; if so, the answer of NS-like responses would be even greater for Example 3.) Three further examples (Examples 5, 6 and 8) are to some degree (3) inconclusive. Many of the 'other answers' for Example 5, while not specifically mentioning religious reasons, yet spoke of respect and commitment and thus sensed much of what the issue was; in Example 6, the denotative meaning of the allusion (no taxis available) was clear even to those who failed to see the point of the mention of pumpkins. For Example 8, few of the native-speakers made overt mention of the link between calling one woman the Barbarian, another a Visigoth, so that strictly speaking, an NS-like response apparently did not involve this identification. It is worth noting, however, that the number of no answers was quite high for Example 8: this can be thought to indicate reader puzzlement.

A similar reduction to simpler figures for Examples 11–15 is given in Table 22.

Table 22   GRT reader responses to more interventional translations

Example 11 *(Rebecca/Pollyanna)*	
NS-like response (= positive attributes)	26
Other	18
No answer	<u>13</u>
Total	57
Example 12 *(Carry Nation/A 1920s suffragette)*	
NS-like response (= unattractive)	16
Other	6
No answer	<u>0</u>
Total	22
Example 13 *(Tangled webs)*	
NS-like response (= difficult to unravel)	13
Suspicion of crime	4
Other	3
No answer	<u>2</u>
Total	22
Example 14 *(There's gold in them thar quarters/A veritable gold mine)*	
NS-like response (= rich and/or naive)	49
Other	2
No answer	<u>6</u>
Total	57

Table 22 continued

Example 15 (All be well)	
NS-like response (= peace etc.)	36
Source only	16
Other	3
No answer	_2
Total	57

An analysis of the figures for Examples 11–15 shows a distribution which does not indicate culture bumps: the clear majority of readers show an NS-like response, and the numbers of no answer are low. The number of examples is too small to allow for generalisation, but at least with these examples, the allusions can be said to have 'worked' for the respondents: their meaning did not prove very difficult to get.

The following chapter, which reports on some experimental data involving university students of English, may give us some indication of how easily the necessary degree of biculturalism required of translators is acquired by students of a foreign language.

Notes

1. Empirical studies of reading concerning real readers have been carried out in the context of literary studies, focusing on reactions to given texts, such as poems (Richards, 1929). Sociologically oriented studies have looked for data for example on literacy or the lack of it in a given segment of society, such as school-leavers (cf. Hirsch, 1988, Pattison, 1982), or national, cultural, gender or age group differences in reader responses (cf. Eskola, 1990: 170–1). Cultural differences in a wide sense are considered when the cognitive orientation of non-native readers is assumed to colour their responses to literary texts in another language, beyond mere language difficulties or unfamiliar realia (Watts, 1991: 28).
2. The first Finnish-language newspaper was issued in 1776 but discontinued the same year; it did not have successors till the 1820s.
3. A British visitor to Finland a century ago reports that 12 of Shakespeare's plays had been translated and performed in Finnish by 1896 (Tweedie, 1989: 138).
4. In 1994 Finland had a population of 5,098,800; discounting those under seven years of age, the size of the school-age and adult population was 4,644,400. Of these, 2,488,000 or 49.2% were borrowers of books from public libraries, borrowing 102,010,000 books in all, or an average of 41 books per borrower that year (*Statistical Yearbook of Finland*, 1995: 475). The combined weekday circulation of newspapers issued 4–7 days a week in Finland was 2.4 million, or 473

copies per 1000 inhabitants, in 1994 (*Statistical Yearbook of Finland*, 1995: 473). The figure does not include newspapers with a circulation of below 8000.

5. The only group in Finland to read more foreign books than Finnish ones are urban readers under 30 years of age (Eskola, 1987).

6. It is not my intention to denigrate any such choices, only to point out that they are likely to have an effect on a reader's attitude to reading and responses to texts later in life.

7. Eight lecturers teaching at Finnish universities.

8. 'Sufficiently' was not quantified but there was no real disagreement about meanings with the examples chosen. (In a different selection of texts, particularly if they represented more challenging literature, there would undoubtedly have been more differences of opinion.) Besides, as Schaar (1975) notes, while associations are subjective, similarities between texts can be verified by comparison. The allusions in the reader-response tests were also verified by consulting reference works.

9. This could possibly also be taken to mean 'turned the train upside down', but Kelletat does not mention this potential but rather perverse translation.

10. That is, that trains from Helsinki to Northern Finland leaving Tampere (a city largely surrounded by water) used to go back along the tracks they had come in by before resuming their northbound way. An inexperienced passenger might think the train was returning to Helsinki.

11. The use not of extracts but of complete short texts such as short stories might have been a way of resolving the last difficulty. (The published TTs of the corpus were over 250 pages long on the average.) Contemporary short stories are so rarely published in Finnish translation, however, that a selection of available ones was unlikely to offer enough variety in types of allusions and translation strategies used.

12. A translation may make sense without reproducing the sense of the ST, and this is sometimes a legitimate translation strategy (for instance with jokes and wordplay).

13. The strategy of omission removes the culture bump but may at the same time remove much or part of what the ST tries to convey. It may therefore be an effective strategy from one point of view but rarely an optimal one.

14. Finnish not being an Indo-European language, there is more of an initial language barrier for learners to overcome.

15. For reasons of space, all examples given in this chapter are shorter than the extracts given to the respondents. The Finnish target texts are not included in this volume, but see Appendix 6 for the ST extracts.

16. The others used the words 'nervous, harassed'; 'blank and harried'; 'preoccupied'; 'worried, hurried, bothered'.

17. All readers answered in Finnish; my translations.

18. Cf. Pocheptsov (1991: 89), who notes in a review of Urdang and Ruffner (1986) that the hare, presented by them as 'sexual desire incarnate', is rather a symbol of cowardice in Russian culture. Pocheptsov's comment applies to Finnish culture as well: Finns traditionally think of the hare as a timid, easily frightened animal (cf. the slurs *jänishousu* 'hare pants' = coward; *menikö pupu pöksyihin? 'Have you got a bunny in your pants?'* = Are you afraid?).

19. Rabbits (*Oryctolagus cuniculus*) are generally thought of as pets in Finland, not creatures out in the wild which they can be for instance in Britain. Of hares, both

Lepus europaeus 'rusakko' and *Lepus timidus* '[metsä]jänis' are commonly glimpsed in Finnish woodlands. The layperson may think of all three as representing roughly the same species.

20. There were also some suggestions that this was a different literary allusion. Among those mentioned were John Updike (whose best-known character is called Rabbit Angstrom), *Winnie-the-Pooh* (where one of the characters is called Rabbit), an unnamed children's picture book about a black hare or rabbit and a white one, and Richard Adams's *Watership Down* (where all the characters are rabbits).

21. In *Through the Looking Glass*, the Walrus and the Carpenter go for a walk with oysters, inviting them to lunch, and eventually eat the oysters for lunch: 'Now if you're ready, Oysters dear,/We can begin to feed' (Carroll, 1981: 241).

22. This respondent used the words *Mursu ja Nikkari* (see later).

23. The other respondent offered a guess only: 'Would this be a reference to *Alice in Wonderland*?'

24. Additionally, three respondents also mentioned the habit of giving English pubs odd names as a possible explanation, but as these suggestions were secondary to their main answers, they are not shown on the table.

25. It is possible that some of the respondents who gave contextual interpretations rather than brief explanations on the lines of 'he is comparing himself to Superman' had in fact recognised the reference to Superman, but thought this was self-evident and that the question focused on the purpose of Spenser's words. The need for such speculation shows a weakness in the test question.

26. The familiarity of this character in Finland was proved later in 1992, as Finnish newspapers included items on the death of Superman when it occurred in the American strip cartoon.

27. This information was given to the respondents.

28. The lack of a larger context was, however, more of a problem than anticipated: two highly experienced NS readers commented on an earlier presentation of this example saying that while they recognised the allusion as being to the marriage ceremony, they thought it was being used ironically. In the ST, the scene is highly charged emotionally, and very serious. (It may be relevant that the author was born as early as 1904.)

29. 85.9% of Finns are Lutherans (1994). 12% are not members of any religious association.

30. As this group of respondents had limited time at their disposal, all of them may not have had sufficient time to come to a conclusion.

31. A reference to race relations; see p.73.

32. Another example deleted from discussion here as superfluous is a reference to the *Miller of Dee* (an old song) in Lurie (ST: Text I, Appendix 6), which proved to be totally unknown to GRT 1 respondents.

33. One of them also wondered whether presentation of the roles of victim and accomplice in a certain work of popular psychology was being referred to. — The Visigoths sacked Rome in AD 410.

34. One GRT 2b respondent referred to Asterix as a source of familiarity with Goths.

35. *Hymyillen* 'smiling' sounds mostly positive in Finnish. The extract used in the test does not contain one of the recurrent references in the ST to Edwin's *Cheshire Cat* appearance; judging by the other responses to allusions to *Alice*, however, it is quite likely that even the Cheshire Cat would have been little

known to these readers. The names used for the Cheshire Cat in the Swan and Kunnas and Manner translations (*Irvikissa, Mörökölli*), however, have negative associations (with grimaces or sulking), so that if those names were used in the TT, readers of the whole text would be prepared for Edwin to say something unfriendly. The associations of the translator's choice of *Virnukissa* (cf. Chapter 4, Note 19) are milder ('Grinning Cat').

36. Rossetti's translation is the one quoted in all dictionaries of quotation consulted except for the Penguin one, which translates Villon's words literally.

37. The penultimate stanza contains the lines: 'Where have all the soldiers gone? In the graveyards, every one.'

38. In the KLA test (Chapter 4) the name of Carry Nation was unfamiliar to all the respondents.

39. This could perhaps be due to cultural differences. In Finland, the wearing of make-up may be less of a sign of a woman who has internalised the traditional view of a woman's role.

40. In Great Britain, where the term is associated with the Pankhursts, women were granted limited suffrage in 1918 and equal voting rights in 1928 (PCE). Emmeline Pankhurst founded her organisation in 1903.

41. The Finnish form of the Lord's Prayer contains the words *Tapahtukoon sinun tahtosi myös maan päällä niinkuin taivaassa* 'Thy will be done in earth, as it is in heaven' (Matt. 6: 10).

42. Nor did the author remember the source offhand, when asked (Weldon interview, 1989).

43. KLA responses are not included in Tables 21 and 22 as students and teachers of translation cannot, strictly speaking, be thought general readers. If KLA responses (available for Examples 1 and 5) were included, they would be grouped as follows: Example 1: NS-like response 19, other 26, no answer 6; Example 5: NS-like response 6, other 15, no answer 30. Total 51.

6 Allusions in the Classroom (The Novice Translator Stumbles)

The experiment discussed in Chapter 5 showed that allusions – particularly those to unfamiliar sources – do not cross cultural barriers easily. Translators therefore need to acquire sufficient cultural and metacultural competence to meet the needs of their readers, who may understandably well lack it. But is this competence automatically acquired as part of the language skills taught at school and university? Non-native students of a foreign language are, by definition, also undergoing a process of biculturalisation. Will students then, after learning the language itself well, also demonstrate a familiarity with foreign allusions when they read texts in the foreign language? Or is their biculturalisation in this respect incomplete, so that they do not fully understand the function and meaning of allusions in such texts, or even do not notice that the SL author is using preformed material? To get a clearer view of what might be expected of novice translators, I did some empirical work with Finnish university students of English.

Empirical Data on Student Recognition of Source-text Allusions

There were a number of interlinked questions on which data were wanted. First, how well would the students notice allusions in English texts, and what factors might have an effect on visibility? Second, to what extent would students see what the allusions convey beyond denotation? Third, what translation strategies would students outline; and fourth, would their reading competence, as revealed by their understanding of the meaning of allusions, be reflected in their translations? This section addresses the first question while the others are discussed in the next.

In this test of students of English (TSE) as in the general reader and KLA tests discussed in Chapter 5, extracts of texts had to be used. The students

178

were given nine English-language extracts roughly one page long each to read (Texts A to J in Appendix 7; for reasons of space the extracts are not reproduced in this discussion). They were asked to read them through at their own pace and to underline any allusions they noted. A sheet of instructions included several standard definitions of the term (Appendix 5). They were also asked to write down any source they were able to identify, including guesses and vague recollections. After this they handed the papers to the teacher conducting the experiment, and received another copy of the same pages, with certain allusions ($N = 14$) underlined. Their instructions were then to explain the meaning of those allusions in the context shown and to draft a translation for each of the marked sections. The students continued to work at their own pace, aware that they did not necessarily have to complete the test. All students completed the first task of the test, but none explained and translated all of the set sections (task two).[1] The students were also encouraged to evaluate alternative strategies and to note down any thoughts occurring to them concerning the translation of the allusions. No dictionaries or reference works were available, nor could students consult each other or the teacher. The language of the texts was not particularly difficult for the students. Answers could be given in either English or Finnish.[2]

The test was conducted at the department of English of the University of Helsinki in 1991.[3] The respondents ($N = 33$) were 20 students attending their compulsory one-term Stage II translation (English into Finnish) course and 13 students attending a then new, non-credit course in culture-bound translation problems which was not linked to any particular stage of studies.[4] The latter group was tested after the introductory lecture, before any discussion of allusions had taken place. Four of the students in the two groups tested differed from the rest because of family background or more experience in translation: one Stage II student had lived in Britain for several years, and another had a parent who was a native-speaker of English; two of the Stage III respondents were professional translators, one of fiction and the other of non-fiction. With the exception of the translator of non-fiction, the scores of these students with special backgrounds were the highest achieved.

Answers for the first task, finding allusions and giving their sources, were graded as follows.

0 = not underlined (that is, not noted)

1 = underlined but either no source or an incorrect source given

2 = vague or incomplete answer (for example 'literary' for 'Macbeth' [Text B, Appendix 7]; 'Bible' for 'Prodigal Son' [Text E])[5]

3 = full identification (for example 'Macbeth' for B; 'Robert Frost' for Ha)

Table 23   Scores of individual students in TSE

Score (Sums of points scored by students)	Number of students with the score
34	1
30	1
27	1
25	1
24	2
23	2
22	1
20	2
19	1
18	1
17	1
16	2
15	2
14	2
13	2
12	1
11	4
10	1
9	2
8	1
7	1
5	1
Total	33

If the results of both groups are considered as a whole (see Table 23), it can be seen that the scores of individual students for the 14 allusions considered varied a great deal. The potential maximum score was 42; the highest score achieved was 34 and the lowest 5.

The top three scores were achieved by the translator of fiction, the student who had lived in England and the student with a NS parent. The average score was 16.5 points. The averages for the two groups were practically identical, and hence the groups will not be differentiated in further discussion. When scores were counted, points were not taken off for underlining other, in my view non-allusive, words or phrases, but it could be noted that students who did this the most were all students with average to low scores. Some of the 'false alarms' (see later) appeared to indicate a hazy conception of the term allusion itself.

Table 24 shows the distribution of scores for seven key-phrase (KP) allusions. It shows how visible the allusions were, in other words, whether or not they were noted by the students, and also degrees of familiarity, that is, how well they were identified. (See Table 24.)

Table 24 The visibility and familiarity of seven KP allusions in TSE. (The distribution of scores among 33 respondents showing allusions noted and identified: absolute figures)

Allusion	0	1	2	3
A	18	10	4	1
E	4	14	5	10
F	0	20	1	12
G	5	19	9	0
Ha	30	0	0	3
Hb	23	6	4	0
J	28	2	2	1

With the KP allusions, close to half of the answers (47%) given by the students were graded as zero. Approximately 30% of the answers consisted of just an underlining (and possibly an incorrect source reference), showing that the allusion had been spotted but that its source was unknown. Approximately 11% had some idea of the source, and full identification was given only in c. 12% of the answers. The percentages of misses and identifications varied a great deal from allusion to allusion, as was expected. It is of some interest next to see which KP allusions were easy to spot, and which were easy to miss. This links up with the question of recognisability (see Chapter 3).

There was only one clearly visible KP allusion: *an old goose begetting a swan* (F). No student overlooked it, and c. 36% identified it as an allusion to H.C. Andersen.[6] Two other allusions were noted by the majority, namely *Oh! withered is the garland of war! The soldier's poll is fallen* (G)[7] and *fatted calves* (E). The latter, a biblical allusion, was confidently identified as referring to the prodigal son by 30%, while an additional 15% identified it more loosely as 'biblical'. The actual Shakespeare play alluded to in G, *Antony and Cleopatra*, on the contrary, was not identified by any of the respondents, but 27% suggested 'Shakespeare' or 'literary' (some with question marks attached) and 57% spotted it without knowing its source. Thus when both visibility (how easily an allusion is spotted) and familiarity (how well its source is known) are taken into account, it can be seen that they do not necessarily correlate. An allusion can be highly visible (easy to spot) without being familiar.

What the top three visible KP allusions in the test share is that they are all metaphorical. The nature of metaphor is such that readers understand that a metaphorical statement is not to be taken literally (for instance readers do not assume that the father in E regrets not having actual fatted calves to offer). Passages recognised by common sense and world knowledge as non-literal appear to be more easily suspected of being allusions than passages which can be understood in the literal sense; this claim is reinforced by many of the 'false alarms' discussed later. For instance the less commonly noted *corner of an English field* (A) can also be taken in its surface sense, as a simple reference to a burial spot. Also, the allusion in A is modified (see Chapter 3) as *foreign* is replaced by *English* and *England* by *Tulsa*; the modification may be a contributory factor to its lack of visibility. (As it is the only modified allusion in the test, this point cannot be established.) G, the longest literary quotation in the test, may have been highlighted because of its length and unusual word order; there is no parallel example in the test. Among the less visible allusions (Hb, Ha and J), the shared characteristics are lack of familiarity (under 10% identified the source), brevity (4–5 words), common vocabulary and, in the case of Ha and J, ellipsis. These would seem to be factors which tend to hide an allusion. (See Table 25.)

Table 25 The visibility and familiarity of seven PN allusions in TSE. (The distribution of scores among 33 respondents showing allusions noted and identified: absolute figures)

Allusion	0	1	2	3
B	0	21	2	10
Ca	12	20	2	1
Cb	12	8	0	13
D	3	4	0	26
Hc	3	13	2	15
Hd	11	11	0	11
He	12	14	4	3

Proper name (PN) allusions as a rule seem to be more visible than KP allusions. PN allusions in this test were missed by only one in four on the average compared to nearly half for KP allusions – and if two cases where a number of students left familiar names (*Sherlock Holmes and Nero Wolfe*, Cb; *David Attenborough*, Hd) unmarked, unsure whether or not they should be considered allusions, are omitted, the percentage of zeros goes even further down, to c. 18%.[8] Full identifications were given in one-third of the PN answers on the average, compared to 12% for KP allusions.

As regards familiarity, *Alice* (D) was by far the most familiar, being a set book in the department. The phrase *perfumes of Arabia*[9] (B) was noted by all, though 60% could not identify it, or saw just the denotation ('refers to Oriental perfumes'). The least familiar name was *Dick Butkus* (Ca), an American football player of the 1970s, whose name none of the informants knew (the sole three-point answer was based on the clue of a football metaphor in the context). The old story of the geese saving the Capitol (He) was surprisingly little known – though in the discussion which followed the test in class, some students remembered meeting the story in their Latin reader.

Figures 4 and 5 show the visibility of the different KP and PN allusions; in other words, how many of the 33 respondents noted each allusion. The figures also show how many respondents fully identified (= score 3) the same allusions.

The test thus shows that PN allusions are both more visible and – in the case of most of the examples used – more familiar. Visibility and familiarity may thus be linked to a certain degree (at least with the names studied), but further examination of the results also shows that the mere presence of a proper name in the test often led to a decision to underline it (even with names such as *Sellotape*; see the discussion later on false alarms). There were actually no instances of low visibility (i.e. over 40% misses) for PN allusions. We can therefore add one more factor to those leading to high visibility for allusions: the presence of a proper name.

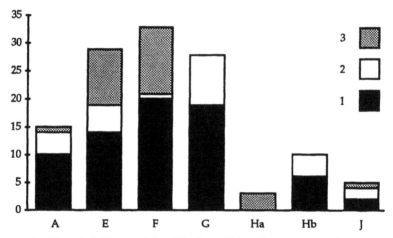

Figure 4   The visibility and familiarity of KP allusions in TSE

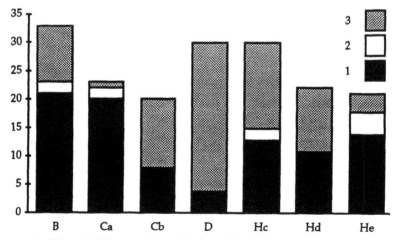

Figure 5   The visibility and familiarity of PN allusions in TSE

The following conclusions are drawn on the basis of the data previously discussed; due to the small number of examples, the conclusions are necessarily tentative.

Factors leading to higher visibility appear to include:

- familiarity (E, F, D, Hc),
- presence of a proper name (B, D, Hc),
- metaphorical statements (F, E, G),
- ? length (A, G),
- ? stylistic contrast (G),

Factors tending to hide allusions, on the other hand, would include:

- lack of familiarity (A, Ha, Hb, J),
- absence of proper name (Ha, Hb, J),
- common vocabulary (A, Ha, Hb, J),
- brevity (Ha, Hb, J),
- ellipsis (Ha, J),
- ? modifications (A).

There were also a great number of words or phrases marked by TSE respondents, which possibly rang a bell for some of them, but which more experienced readers have failed to confirm as allusions. It is true that allusions in a sense do not exist for a reader who does not see them; conversely, it may be argued that if a reader claims that a certain phrase is allusive, it *is* a private or personal allusion for that reader (but its associations would depend on that individual reader's experiences). Most of the 'false alarms', however, did not seem to belong to a category of personal allusions as no sources were given for them. False alarms are relevant to some degree as a hypersensitive translator who sees allusions where none are intended is likely to waste time in trying to track them all down, or may in any event feel unsure about which ones need to be tracked down and which do not. This would be contrary to the minimax strategy (Levý, 1967), greatly increasing the translator's workload but adding little to the quality of his/her translations.

The tendency for the students to see allusions in proper names is partly explained by the fact that the texts used were extracts – the students could not always know if the names used referred to people and places in the novel or whether they had allusive significance. For instance, the place name *Wiltshire* (in Text A) was thought by several students to have allusive significance (one referred to Stonehenge). Some students felt impelled to explain such brand names as *Clorox* (B) and *Sellotape* (D) ('a detergent', 'a brand of sticky tape'), as well as *the NHS* (J).

Some metaphors attracted underlinings from several students. Among them were *digging for ancestors* (A), *fireworks* (C), the battle metaphors in G and *crucified* in H. Even dead metaphors like the verbs in *fished a pack of cigarettes* (E), *the door swung open* (F), *red flame-like spots burned in her cheeks* (G) were underlined by one student. This tendency for non-literal expressions to attract notice was commented on earlier where it was suggested that a non-literal allusion is more easily noticed than one which can be taken literally. Apparently, for some students the tendency went further so that when a student was requested to look for allusions, non-literal expressions in general were suspected of being allusive.

Some of the underlinings highlighted words and phrases which may well not have been part of the student's vocabulary: *malodorous shoes* (B), *bawled me out* (E), *absorbent* (G), *pounded sorghum and water from a stinking goatskin bag* (J). They may have been underlined on the principle that what one cannot make sense of is possibly an allusion – particularly as sources or explanations as to why these should be allusions were not offered by the students for these phrases. This may also mean that some students' conceptions of allusion were hazy despite the definitions given, or that the definitions themselves were too vague to be helpful.

Student Interpretations and Suggestions of Strategies

In the second part of TSE the student respondents were asked to explain the meanings of the allusions in the context shown, and to suggest translations or to comment on possible translation strategies. Fewer answers were given in this part of the test, and some passages in particular were provided with very few explanations or translations.[10]

This part of the test sheds further light on the students' reading competence: to what extent did they see beyond denotation? Another, related point of interest is the translations offered: is the 'point' of the allusions transmitted or not in the translations of those who did not specifically speak of connotations in their explanations; and conversely, do those who expressed awareness of connotations suggest different translations or outline other translation strategies in order to transmit more of the meaning?

With some of the allusions, of course, there was little hidden meaning. Everybody who offered an explanation to F (*goose/swan*) saw that the allusion refers to an ugly man and his lovely daughter (apart from one careless reader who thought the metaphor referred to the daughter alone who, like the duckling of Andersen's story, could have changed from a plain child to a beauty). Likewise, the reference to *Alice* (D), though explained variously as referring to a reader who was bored by her book, or spoilt, or lonely, did not seem to require any deeper analysis in the extract shown.[11] The use of extracts no doubt impeded full understanding of some of the passages: for instance in A (cf. the discussion of this example as Example 9 in Chapter 5), only a couple of respondents sensed the irony in the speaker's use of the allusion – though in a page-long extract, without knowledge of the relationships between characters, this was perhaps hard to infer. Similarly, B (*not all the perfumes of Arabia*), while recognised as alluding to *Macbeth* by ten (see Appendix 7 for the extract), had only four mentions of blood and guilt. The other Shakespearean allusion, G, was said by all who commented on it to refer, denotatively, to the death of a soldier. Again, the shortness of the extract may have obscured the contrast in the novel between the everyday expression of the young widow's grief and the poetry of Cleopatra's grief for the slain Antony.

But even where the relationships between characters were clearly set out and the allusion could be thought transcultural, connotations were not necessarily recognised. An example were the comments on *fatted calves* (E), where only one respondent out of three referred to the important return-of-the-prodigal-son motif. The rest treated the allusion on the surface level, as a reference to some type of delicacy or just as a general term for food. The classical myth in He was also mysterious to practically all of the respondents, one even doubting whether the reference was to actual birds at all: 'Hawks? flags? planes? war? nature?'. The wordplay in J (*unkindest cut*) defeated all but the the professional translator of fiction.

Connotations in all the passages, then, were often missed or at least not overtly stated, though the use of extracts undoubtedly made it more difficult to see what the function of the allusions might be in a larger context. The remaining questions concern the translations offered: do the students who saw allusions involving connotative meanings transfer this awareness to their translations or are their translations similar to those offered by the majority? Or, do the students who did not specifically mention connotations nevertheless try to convey them in their translations? It must be remembered that the students did not have much time, and their translations are therefore first drafts only; they were also told that they could simply outline translation strategies for the various allusions instead of or in addition to actually verbalising them.

In the unproblematic F, many of the students decided to change *goose* into *duck*, in accordance with their assumption that the expression was an allusion to 'The Ugly Duckling'. Some deleted all reference to birds, speaking of father and daughter without metaphor.

In D, practically everybody used *niin kuin Liisa ihmemaassa* 'like Alice in

Wonderland' for *like another Alice*, this being the Finnish title of Carroll's book. *Niin kuin toinen Liisa* 'like another Liisa' was not thought (with one exception) to refer clearly enough to Carroll's book, which is perhaps less commonly read in Finland than in Britain; and of course the name of the character in the text used is Alice, not Liisa. One student left in a mysterious reference to *eräs toinen Alice*, a literal translation of *another Alice*.[12] She had not underlined the allusion in part one of the test, and the reference was still obscure to her when she translated it, which led to this impenetrable translation. One student, while recognising the allusion, chose to delete it, speaking of pictures and conversation unallusively.

In Ca, the single student who suspected (on the basis of clues in the context) that *Dick Butkus* might be a football player used an American football term ('quarterback') to describe his approach. Those who thought him a fictional detective nevertheless saw the intended contrast between two types of approaches to problems and managed well enough to describe *the Dick Butkus approach* with a variety of words of action ('attack, direct action', etc.). One student wondered if the name should be replaced by that of a better known detective, such as Marlowe.

There was some doubt among respondents as to the actual words for *fatted calf* in the Finnish Bible. Among those who recognised the reference to the biblical story of the prodigal son, the phrase was translated variously as *syöttövasikka, juottovasikka, lihotettu vasikka* (all of these mean a calf not butchered but left to eat, drink and grow fat), etc. Of those who recognised the allusion more vaguely as biblical, most used one of these terms, but also other expressions about food like 'enough food to feed an army'. The Finnish New Testament (Luke 15: 23) has *syötetty vasikka*, a term not used by any of the students but occurring in Sinnemäki (1989: 429), a Finnish dictionary of quotations. Several students wrote that they were uncertain of the precise term and would look it up if they were translating the text 'for real'. This uncertainty suggests that the archaic terms *syöttövasikka, juottovasikka* are thought by many to be the standard biblical expression; if this uncertainty is common among general readers as well, they would seem to be adequate translations.

The translations of A as a rule left something to be desired. Only a couple of students 'marked' their translations as poetry by using a special rhythm (*siispä ikuisesti jokin niityistämme* ...) or a poetic phrase (*ikiajoiksi*). Of the two who recognised the irony, only one attempted a translation, and she did try to convey the irony by suggesting, instead of *Tulsa* (which does not immediately signify America in contrast to England to a Finnish reader; cf. the difficulties of general readers with this allusion, Chapter 5), alternative terms like *cowboy* or the *Wild West*. Otherwise the translations were flat, simply stating that 'one place in England will always remind us of Tulsa'.

Similarly, the use of the *Macbeth* allusion in B conveyed denotation only ('the smell is so bad that not even good Arabian perfumes would help remove it') to most of the students, despite the use of the word *guilty* some lines earlier in the extract. The main character had resorted to some questionable methods – burglary – in her detective work and forgotten about a dinner date. When criticised on both scores by her date, she angrily turns to washing first her running shoes, which smell of vomit, and then her hands. She thus has relatively little reason to feel like Lady Macbeth, and the effect of the allusion is partly humorous, though this did not come through in the suggested translations. Three students suggested looking up the passage in published translations of *Macbeth*; one would have added *kuten Macbeth totesi* 'as Macbeth said' as guidance to her use of the 'official translation'; another, *siteerasin Shakespearea* 'said I, quoting Shakespeare'. One chose innovatively to use *mirhami* 'myrrh', an Oriental substance never discussed in everyday contexts but known to smell sweet. The rest, more or less elliptically, transferred the denotation only ('I rubbed lemon juice on them, not fine Arabian perfumes'). The idea of an active modern woman contemplating rubbing 'fine Arabian perfumes' on her hands after cleaning her dirty trainers might puzzle some readers, though.

In G (*Oh! withered is the garland of war* ...), many of the translations retained the inverted word order of the ST. This minimum change strategy conveyed the poetry, which was useful. Three students wanted to establish the wording of the 'official translation' first. One planned to find something to the same effect in Finnish literature; as the death of a soldier is the topic, she suggested looking for a suitable phrase in Väinö Linna's classic war novel *The Unknown Soldier*, which is, however, so different from Shakespeare stylistically that it is unlikely to provide a replacement poetic enough to convey the contrasting styles of expressing grief.

The translations of the elliptical Ha (*lovely, dark and deep*) were literal, usually with a head word added; this was the *shadows* of the preceding sentence, not the *woods* of Frost ('Under the trees there were lovely, deep, dark shadows'). Of the two who recognised the source, one chose to delete the allusion, the other planned to check whether there is a Finnish translation of the poem. A third, who suspected the source might be literary, saw the function of the allusion and noted that a literal translation would ruin the effect.

Of the translations of Hb (*Only man is vile*), the intended contrast was conveyed by the three students who brought the words *peto* 'beast' or *eläin* 'animal' into their translations, as in *Ihminen on pahin peto* 'man is the worst of beasts'.

With He (*its ancestors had saved the Capitol*), the word *Capitol* caused problems for those who understood it to refer to Capitol Hill in Washington, DC ('Hard to believe that its ancestors had saved the United States Parliament'). In Finnish, the Capitol in Rome is known by the Latin form of the name, *Capitolium* ; this required change was made by one student only, who remembered the story well and suggested it might be 'reader-friendly' to name the species of bird in the translation.

As for J (*the unkindest cut of all*), 'obscure, obscure' was one student's only comment. J is an example of a stereotyped allusion reanimated in its context:

> 'That's the trouble with today's Government,' she said. 'These cuts are doing so much damage.'
> She flourished a box of mints about in a way that defied you to take one. Penny plucked up her courage. In the Sudan, she'd seen a child die from an infected insect bite because no antibiotics had been available. The unkindest cut of all. (Moody, 1985: 64)

As *cut* means budget cuts to the first speaker and a mortal wound (as in *Julius Caesar*) to the second, and there is no precise equivalent in Finnish, it is difficult to work out a solution. The few translations suggested by the students either repeated the word *leikkaus* 'operation, cut' or replaced it where it occurs on the last line by *supistus* 'financial cut, contraction' or the less specific *hirveä tilanne* 'ghastly situation'. The professional translator of fiction suggested either checking if the 'official translation' of *Julius Caesar* has anything at all usable to offer, but pointed out the difficulty caused by the wordplay. Alternatively, he suggested sacrificing Shakespeare in favour of a more familiar allusion within the same genre.[13]

This test thus allowed us some insight into what was going on in the minds of the novice translators (with less precision than in think-aloud protocol studies like Krings [1986], but with considerably more informants than Krings' eight) and to compare what they knew and sensed with what they produced. The use of students instead of professionals was partly dictated by practical concerns (the students being a captive population of a sort while professionals might see little reason to participate in such a test), but also because of my interest in language teaching and translator training, which meant that people in the process of becoming language professionals were a more interesting object of study than those who already possess the skills. Also, the published translations examined in

Chapter 4 were the work of professionals. The considerable differences among TSE respondents (cf. their scores in finding allusions and giving their sources, Table 23) showed that some were competent and sensitive readers biculturalised to a considerable extent, but that the highest scores were achieved by the few who had either professional experience in translating fiction or prolonged personal experience of British culture. The biculturalised students had a wider variety of strategies in mind when drafting translations, and attempted to bring in the connotations they had perceived. The others were much less able to grasp the point of allusive messages and even of spotting allusions in the extracts (or they suspected all kinds of striking phrases of being allusions); they usually limited themselves to fairly literal translations (many of which would, in my view, have been culture bumps), made mistakes and usually did not comment on or evaluate their own offerings. As many of the students took much longer than expected to complete the first task, they had less time for the second, which meant that fewer explanations, translations and comments were produced than had been hoped for, particularly for the last texts of the test, G, H and J. Only tentative conclusions can, of course, be drawn on the basis of these data. Nevertheless, with the allusions used in the test, many of which have important connotations which should not be lost in translation, it can be seen that

- in 47% of the answers to KP allusions, the allusion was missed;
- few students showed that they understood the meaning of the allusions and their function in the context shown;
- understanding the function and meaning did not necessarily spontaneously lead to a satisfactory translation (as evaluated by the student him/herself and also by myself);
- but without such recognition and an awareness of what was implied, in most cases the drafted translations were flat and failed to convey what the writer's choice of words would convey to a competent reader of the ST.

Implications for Translator Training

The results of TSE[14] suggest that non-native university students of English, even after a dozen years or more of learning the language, are not necessarily all sufficiently competent readers of English-language fiction nor biculturalised enough to recognise allusions and their connotations in a test situation. (Cf. the estimates of the interviewed translators in Chapter 4 that allusions might occasionally be missed by novice translators – this would appear to be an understatement.) It is clear that the degree of biculturalisation required of competent translators had not been acquired by all of the students who participated in the test, despite their c.10 years of English at school in a country where Anglo-American culture is highly visible and accessible, and their further years at a university department of English.[15] It would seem, therefore, that familiarity with the type of socio-cultural elements focused on in this study is not automatically acquired in the course of advanced language studies. What, then, are the implications of this for translator training and for the teachers of future language professionals?

We need to ask questions both about the syllabus and about the work that goes on in the classroom. As teachers, do we rely solely on a kind of os-mosis, or is the acquisition of biculturalism built into the programme? Are students made aware of the goal at the outset? It is, of course, a lifelong project to learn more and more about a foreign language culture, and we need to be open about this so that students will not be unduly downcast when they realise how many gaps they must fill before they can claim to be more than superficially familiar with the source culture, including allusion-generating texts. To achieve this realisation, which can serve as a motivator, we need to present authentic examples of allusions in all sorts of texts, not only literary ones. (The many examples in this book can perhaps provide exercise materials for teachers who work with English as the source language – see especially the last section of Chapter 4, in particular the flow-charts.) Students can be made more aware of the use of preformed material by presenting for discussion different types of both SL and TL al-lusions, including modified ones, and by talking about the types of sources that provide allusions in a particular language culture. The effect of formal properties on recognisability can be explored. Above all, we need to study the function and effect of allusions in context, so that students see how much can be conveyed when the author and the reader meet halfway in the creation of meaning. Thematic allusions and allusive wordplay should be particularly rewarding material in the classroom. And to encourage stu-dents to solve problems caused by unfamiliar allusions, exercises can involve the use of dictionaries of quotations and allusions as well as other reference works, not forgetting the powerful electronic search engines, to develop problem-solving faculties. Increased demand for better works of reference might even lead to the production – and purchase – of works with more helpful formats.

If the work in the classroom is done as an intellectual challenge – a way of solving puzzles – and if teachers can accept that an intergenerational learning experience can go both ways: that authors of source texts may also allude to materials that are more familiar to the students than to the teacher (many allusions to popular-culture sources might well fall in this category), it will greatly enhance the learning process. My experience of students who work with English as the SL suggests that students find work on allusions relevant and useful and feel that it adds significantly to their language skills.

There is, of course, a limit to how much language learning can be done in class as opposed to individual learning for which students, and later, language professionals, are themselves responsible. The process of biculturalisation also involves other activities than reading, though first-hand familiarity with both 'great works' and children's classics is clearly valuable, showing how long-lived some of the literature is and how much effect it continues to have on the language. But students also need to know what films and television programmes people see, what they listen to on the radio, what slogans are used in advertising and political campaigns, etc.; this requires foreign travel and ideally even extended stays abroad, not only when they are students but throughout their working lives.

In addition to learning more about allusions in the SL, translation students – and practising translators in their in-service training – would need specifically to consider the translation of allusions, recognising the responsibility of translators to TT readers. Examples of various strategies adopted in TTs and alternatives to these can be discussed and evaluated. Through such discussions novice translators will learn that if they translate a text without spotting or understanding its allusions, then the meanings of allusive passages are lost for the mass of TT readers, irrespective of the TT readers' own reading competence, with the exception of readers who are themselves sufficiently bicultural to be able to backtranslate the culture bumps and to recognise the meaning behind the words despite the translator as it were.

To return to our conception of the translator as a competent reader, a responsible text producer and a cultural mediator, we can summarise as follows. In order to be competent readers of SL texts, novice translators need to learn to be aware of the possible presence of allusive material in STs and of their function and meaning in those texts. To be responsible text producers, they need to consider the various strategies available in individual cases in order to avoid culture bumps and instead choose strategies that best serve the needs of their actual or potential readers (one such need, depending on the text type, may well be the need to follow the author's thought processes and imagination as far as these are revealed by the allusions s/he chooses to use). And as cultural mediators, translators need to be familiar with the cultural differences between ST and TT audiences and to take these into account when making choices. At various stages in translator training, with appropriate materials and planning, students can be guided and encouraged to learn more about all of these things.

Notes

1. The number of extracts was deliberately high so that no student would leave before the end of the time reserved, thus possibly disturbing the concentration of others and decreasing their motivation to complete the test. The students worked more slowly than expected, though.
2. Translations of answers given in Finnish by the author.
3. In Finland, some translators have studied in foreign language departments, others in translation departments.
4. See Appendix 2 for details on the respondents. (An MA usually takes six to eight years to complete in Finland, partly because the students cannot afford to study full-time.)
5. Some answers had question marks attached, indicating doubt, but the answers were graded without regard to the question marks. Question marks were found attached to both correct and incorrect answers.
6. True, Andersen's story has ducks, not geese: nevertheless, 'The Ugly Duckling' was the only named source suggested by the students. I am unaware of an alternative source that could explain Rendell's use of *goose*. A NS informant notes that 'old duck' is an endearment. 'Old goose' is used primarily of an unattractive old woman; here, by extension, of a man.
7. Few students (N = 8) marked the whole of the two lines of poetry. If only *the garland of war* was marked, zero points were given (N = 3).
8. The exclusion of Cb and Hd from some of the statistics seems advisable, as an equal number of students left them unmarked or gave the identification, some saying the Cb pair of names was known to 'everybody'. This suggests the decision whether or not to underline them was not based on whether or not the names were recognised as having allusive potential, but on each student's view of what the term allusion was supposed to cover. The examples are indeed marginal, and were included only because of their proximity to less familiar allusions (*Dick Butkus* in Ca and the other various allusions in H).
9. This phrase and the *geese of the Capitol* (He) are included among PN phrases: when responses were analysed, the criterion was that if there was any proper name in a phrase, it was listed under PNs.
10. The allusions that were most often commented on were A, B, Ca, Cb, D, E and F, where the number of explanations varied from 11 to 17 for each; that of translations and comments from 16 to 27 for each. (The number of respondents was 33.) The least often commented on were G, Ha, Hb, He and J, with three to six explanations and interpretations and six to ten translations and comments for each. (Hc and Hd were excluded from this part of the test to avoid repetition as the translation problem in them is similar to that in Cb.) The dearth of comments on the last few examples suggests that the students ran out of time.
11. This is different on the macro-level of the novel, where the character Alice finds herself in a nightmarish situation where ordinary events may have a sinister interpretation, and eventually 'wakes up' from her 'dream'.
12. The most recent Finnish translation of *Alice's Adventures in Wonderland* (by Alice

ALLUSIONS IN THE CLASSROOM

Martin, 1995) does not change the heroine's name into *Liisa* but keeps *Alice*. TSE was carried out before this translation was published.

13. He had in mind a detective story by Joyce Parker with this allusion in its title (*Dover and the Unkindest Cut of All*), which has been translated into Finnish as *Dover ja tukala leikkaus* 'Dover and a painful/embarrassing operation' (the reference is to castration).

14. And of other, informal quizzes carried out over the years in the course of my translation teaching.

15. It is true that these were students of English and not of translation, so that the majority may well have been planning to use their education in other fields than translation. Still, their decision to take a non-credit course in culture-bound translation problems indicates that at least 13 of the respondents took a special interest in translation; and the averages for these students were practically identical with those of the other student respondents. It is also a fact that many Finnish translators working in commercial as well as literary and media translation are former students of language departments.

7 Concluding Remarks

This book has focused on a particular problem in intercultural communication, the translation of source-cultural allusions for readers in another language culture. It has looked at three stages in the translation process: source-text analysis, reverbalisation and reception. The roles of the main participants involved in the process, translators and target-text readers, are necessarily interlinked since what readers *can* do is ultimately dependent on what choices translators have made; and conversely, translators always need to consider the expectations and cultural context of the target-text readership. As competent readers and responsible text producers, translators develop translation strategies and try to determine which will work best in a particular context, while readers, as end-users of the products, or as co-authors, if we accept a more dramatic interpretation of their role, receive and respond to the results of the translators' endeavours.

Translation being a real-life phenomenon, this book could not focus on theoretical issues only. They needed to be viewed at all times against the reality of translation practice and reception. Hence real translators and real readers (who are often absent from studies of translation) had to be approached and heard, and this gave useful insights both into the way professional translators deal with allusions and the way their readers understand the results. Indeed, the empirical findings presented in this book indicate that real readers are not infrequently puzzled by passages in target texts if cultural differences have not been taken into account at the stage of reverbalisation.

Further empirical data suggests that the biculturalisation expected of translators is a very slow process, as even at university level and with good foreign-language skills in general, novice translators frequently found it difficult to spot allusions and to see their function in the source text. In other words, their source-cultural reading competence was not yet sufficient to enable them to cope with this aspect of source-text analysis.

A different point of interest was to see if it would be possible to systematise potential strategies in a way that would be helpful in translation classes and possibly also in translation practice. This resulted in a 'minimax' ordering of strategies in the form of flow-charts, which may serve as a reminder of the range of strategies available, and counteract the tendency observed in the descriptive part of the study, that translators all too frequently opt for minimum change when dealing with allusions.

It is the conclusion of this book that the use of the predominant strategy in the target texts studied – minimum change of key-phrase allusion, retention of proper-name allusion – can be questioned on the basis of the results of the reader-response tests. The tests support the hypothesis that translating the words of the allusions but ignoring their connotative and pragmatic meaning often leads to culture bumps, in other words, renderings that are puzzling or impenetrable from the target-text reader's point of view. This conclusion can be read as a recommendation for translators to take the needs of receivers into account when choosing translation strategies for allusions, and for university-level language teaching and translator training to pay more attention to the biculturalisation of their students. Clearly, target-text readers are entitled to translations which work — successful translations are those that give readers the materials needed for participation in the communicative process.

It is to be hoped that future work in translation studies will bring in more data on how translated texts are received and how their reception varies over time and from culture to culture. After all, few translators translate for themselves. It is their crucial role to act as mediators between cultures in the service of their readers.

Bibliography

I. Examples Used

A. Fiction

Aird, C. (1990) *The Body Politic*. London: Pan Books.
Allingham, M. (1986, 1963) *The China Governess: A Mystery*. London: Chatto & Windus.
Ashford, J. (1986) *A Question of Principle*. London: Collins.
Babson, M. (1988, 1984) *Trail of Ashes*. Glasgow: Fontana/Collins.
Bawden, N. (1987) *Circles of Deceit*. London: Macmillan.
Cross, A. (1985, 1984) *Sweet Death, Kind Death*. New York: Ballantine.
Cunningham, E.V. (1987, 1986) *The Wabash Factor*. London: Gollancz.
Dickens, C. (1906) *A Tale of Two Cities*. London: Everyman.
Dickinson, P. (1985, 1972) *The Lizard in the Cup*. London: Hutchinson/Arrow Books.
Francis, D. (1971, 1967) *Blood Sport*. London: Pan Books.
— (1990, 1989) *Straight*. London: Pan Books.
George, E. (1989) *A Great Deliverance*. London: Bantam.
Godwin, G. (1985, 1984) *Mr Bedford and the Muses*. London: Pan Books.
Gosling, P. (1992, 1991) *Death Penalties*. London: Pan Books.
Haymon, S.T. (1984) *Stately Homicide*. London: Constable.
Hill, R. (1991, 1990) *Bones and Silence*. London: Grafton.
— (1993, 1992) *Recalled to Life*. London: Grafton.
— (1995, 1994) *Pictures of Perfection*. London: HarperCollins.
King, S. (1991, 1978) *The Stand*. New York: Penguin/Signet.
Lodge, D. (1979, 1975) *Changing Places*. Harmondsworth: Penguin.
— (1985, 1984) *Small World*. Harmondsworth: Penguin.
— (1988) *Nice Work*. London: Secker & Warburg.
Lurie, A. (1986, 1985) *Foreign Affairs*. London: Michael Joseph/Sphere Books.
MacLeod, C. (1980, 1979) *The Family Vault*. New York: Avon Books.
Marlow, J. (1986, 1985) *Kessie*. London: Coronet/Hodder & Stoughton.
McBain, E. (1984, 1976) *Bread*. London: Hamilton/Pan Books.
Moody, S. (1984) *Penny Dreadful*. London: Macmillan/Futura.
— (1985) *Penny Post*. London: Macmillan.
Paretsky, S. (1987) *Bitter Medicine*. London: Gollancz.
Parker, R. B. (1987a, 1980) *Looking for Rachel Wallace*. Harmondsworth: Penguin.
— (1987b, 1983) *The Vanishing Gyre*. Harmondsworth: Penguin.
— (1990, 1989) *Playmate*. London: Penguin.
Peters, M. (1977, 1975) *Unquiet Soul*. London: Collins.

Piercy, M. (1987) *Gone to Soldiers.* New York: Ballantine/Fawcett Crest.
Pym, B. (1979, 1961) *No Fond Return of Love.* London: Jonathan Cape.
Rendell, R. (1970, 1965) *To Fear A Painted Devil.* New York: Beagle Books.
— (1981, 1969) *The Best Man to Die.* New York: Ballantine.
— (1984, 1966) *Vanity Dies Hard.* London: Hutchinson/Arrow Books.
Rule, A. (1988, 1987) *Small Sacrifices.* London: Corgi Books.
Sayers, D.L. (1987, 1935) *Gaudy Night.* London: Hodder & Stoughton/New English Library.
Seth, V. (1993) *A Suitable Boy.* Boston: Little, Brown.
Spark, M. (1988) *A Far Cry From Kensington.* London: Constable.
Tindall, G. (1983) *Looking Forward.* London: Hodder & Stoughton.
Tweedie, J. (1983) *Letters from a Faint-Hearted Feminist.* London: Pan Books/Picador.
Valin, J. (1987, 1980) *Final Notice.* London: Macdonald/Futura.
Weldon, F. (1988, 1987) *The Hearts and Lives of Men.* Glasgow: Heinemann/ Fontana.

B. Non-fiction

Ang, S. (1989) Eyeless in Gaza. *The Guardian* 28–29 Jan., 1–4.
Barrett, L. I. (1988) Congeniality wins. *Time* 10 Oct., 16–7.
Carlson, M. (1989) The battle over abortion. *Time* 17 July, 32–3.
Clemons, W. (1988) The Grimm reaper. *Newsweek* 19 Dec., 48–50.
Cohen, R. (1988) This junior partner is not fit to step up. *International Herald Tribune* 24 Aug, 3.
Domum, D. (1989) The emperor's boarding pass. *The Guardian* 28–9 Jan., 6.
Dyer, G. (1988) Life in the Faust lane. *New Statesman and Society* 7 Oct., 14.
Ellman, L. (1989) Judicial violation of a mother's fight for right. *The Guardian* 23 Jan., 25.
Fernand, D. (1988) US firm puts a smile in Irish workers' eyes. *The Sunday Times* 11 Sept.
Fussell, P. (1989) The brutal cut-off. *The Guardian* 1 Sept., 27.
Gleckman, H. (1989) Tax paranoia is causing gridlock on the Hill. *Business Week* 29 May.
Hadfield, G. (1988) Rote learning was a winner. *The Sunday Times* 11 Sept.
Ivins, M. (1988) Beulah Mae Donald. *Ms.* Jan., 52+.
Iyer, P. (1988) South Korea: an ancient nation on the eve of a modern spectacle. *Time* 5 Sept., 16.
Leith, Prue (1989) Unkind cuts come close to the bone. *The Guardian* 28–9 Jan., 10.
Lurie, A. (1990) *Don't Tell the Grown-ups.* London: Bloomsbury.
Maddox, J. (1992) Language for a polyglot readership. *Nature* 359 (8 Oct.), 475.
Peterson, P.G. (1994) Remember cost control. *Newsweek* July, 30–1.
Pravdic, V. (1992) Plight of Bosnia and Croatia. *Nature* Vol. 359 (15 Oct), 571.
Russell, G. (1988) Smiling Irish eyes. *Time* 5 Dec., 16–8.
Shapiro, W. (1988) How it plays in Toledo. *Time* 17 Oct., 48–9.
Steinem, G. (1989) A basic human right. *Ms.* July/ Aug., 38–41.
Steiner, G. (1991) A nation saved by philistinism. *The Guardian* 1 Oct., 25, 27.
New Statesman and Society (1988) The ghosts of Christmas Present (caption to picture by Omar Assad). 23/30 Dec., (cover).
The Sunday Times (1988) Hidden truths about child sex abuse. 11 Sept.
Time (1989) Beauty and her many beasts. 29 May, 47.

The Guardian (1989) Boom at the top. 5 July, 2.
Time (1989) Dread My Lips. 1 May, 31.
The Daily Telegraph (1989) Merry has no Wigan peer for sprint title. 7 July, 31.
Newsweek (1989) See no evil. 20 March, 21.
Guardian Weekly (1989) Voodoo economics – Mark II. 19 Feb., 12.
Glamour (1995) To pee or not to pee. Aug., 162.
Wallace, J. (1988) Translation theories and the decipherment of Linear B. In W. Frawley (ed.) *Translation: Literary, Linguistic and Philosophical Perspectives* (pp. 188–218). London: Associated Universities Press.

II. Target Texts

Allingham, M. (1990) *Kohtalokas kotiopettajatar*. Trans. Eeva Heikkinen & Pirkko Haljoki. Porvoo: WSOY.
Cross, A. (1990) *Ihana kuolema, hellä kuolema*. Trans. and abridged Anna-Laura Talvio. *Anna*, no. 30–2.
Lodge, D. (1990) *Mukava homma*. Trans. Eila Salminen. Hämeenlinna: Karisto.
Lurie, A. (1988) *Ulkomaansuhteita*. Trans. Elsa Carroll. Helsinki: Tammi.
McBain, E. (1981) *Verirahat*. Trans. Kalevi Nyytäjä. Helsinki: Tammi.
Parker, R. B. (1988) *Kovaa peliä Bostonissa*. Trans. Erkki Jukarainen. Porvoo: WSOY.
Weldon, F. (1989) *Rakkauden ilot ja surut*. Trans. Liisa Hakola. Helsinki: Otava.

III. Works Cited

Aaltonen, A. (1989) Näin mies kääntyy. *Ruumiin kulttuuri* 1, 4–11.
Abrams, M.H. (1984, 1981) *A Glossary of Literary Terms*. Holt-Saunders International Edition. New York: Holt, Rinehart and Winston.
Archer, C.M. (1986) Culture bump and beyond. In J.M.Valdes (ed.) *Culture Bound. Bridging the Cultural Gap in Language Teaching* (pp. 170–8). Cambridge: Cambridge University Press.
Armstrong, P.B. (1988) Pluralistic literacy. In P. Franklin (ed.) *Professions 88* (pp. 29–32). New York: MLA.
Arnott, P. (1971, 1961) Greek drama and the modern stage. In W. Arrowsmith and R. Shattuck (eds) *The Craft and Context of Translation* (pp. 83–94). Austin, TX: The University of Texas Press.
Arrowsmith, W. and Shattuck, R. (eds) (1971, 1961) *The Craft and Context of Translation*. Austin, TX: The University of Texas Press.
Bakhtin, M. (1988, 1967) From the prehistory of novelistic discourse. Trans. C. Emerson and M.Holqvist. In D. Lodge (ed.) *Modern Criticism and Theory: A Reader* (pp. 125–56). Harlow: Longman.
Bassnett-McGuire, S. (1980) *Translation Studies*. London: Methuen.
Bassnett, S. (1991) Preface to the revised edition. *Translation Studies*. Revised edition. London: Routledge.
Beaugrande, R-A. de and Dressler, W.V. (1988) *Introduction to Text Linguistics*. London: Longman.
Benjamin, A. (1989) *Translation and the Nature of Philosophy: A New Theory of Words*. London: Routledge. Cited in van den Broeck (1992) p.117.
Ben-Porat, Z. (1976) The poetics of literary allusion. *PTL: A Journal for Descriptive Poetics and Theory of Literature* 1, 105–28.

The Holy Bible. King James Version (1991) New York: Ivy Books/Ballantine.

Blake, N.F. (1992) Translation and the history of English. In M. Rissanen, O. Iha-
lainen, T. Nevalainen and I. Taavitsainen (eds) *History of Englishes: New Methods
and Interpretations in Historical Linguistics* (pp. 3–24). Berlin: Mouton de Gruyter.

Bloomsbury Thematic Dictionary of Quotations (TDQ) (1989, 1988) London: Bloomsbury.

Boller, P.F. Jr and George, J. (1989) *They Never Said It. A Book of Fake Quotes, Mis-
quotes, and Misleading Attributions*. New York and Oxford: Oxford University
Press.

Bradbury, M. (1988, 1987) *Cuts*. London: Arrow Books.

Bradley, H. (1957, 1904) *The Making of English*. London: Macmillan.

Briere, E. (1988) In search of cultural equivalences: translations of Camara Laye's
L'Enfant Noir. Translation Review 27, 34–9.

Broeck, R. van den (1992) Translation theory revisited. *Target* 4(1), 111–20.

Brooke-Rose, C. (1958) *A Grammar of Metaphor*. London: Secker & Warburg.

Brown, P. and Levinson, S.C. (1987, 1978) *Politeness. Some Universals in Language
Usage*. Cambridge: Cambridge University Press.

Bödeker, B. (1991) Terms of material culture in Jack London's *The Call of the Wild* and
its German translations. In H. Kittel and A.P. Frank (eds) *Interculturality and the
Historical Study of Literary Translations* (pp. 64–70). Berlin: Erich Schmidt.

Carroll, L. (1970, 1960) *The Annotated Alice. Alice's Adventures in Wonderland and
Through the Looking Glass*. Ed. M. Gardner. London: Penguin.

— (1981, 1865, 1872) *Alice's Adventures in Wonderland and Through the Looking Glass*.
Harmondsworth: Penguin.

— (1984) *Liisan seikkailut ihmemaassa*. Trans. A. Swan (1906). Porvoo: WSOY.

— (1972) *Liisan seikkailut ihmemaassa ja Liisan seikkailut peilimaailmassa*. Trans. K.
Kunnas & E-L. Manner. Jyväskylä: Gummerus.

— (1995) *Alicen seikkailut ihmemaassa*. Trans. A. Martin. Porvoo: WSOY.

Catford, J.C. (1965) *A Linguistic Theory of Translation*. London: Oxford University
Press.

Chesterman, A. (1993) From 'is' to 'ought': laws, norms and strategies in translation
studies. *Target* 5 (1), 1–20.

Churchill, W. (1958, 1930) *My Early Life. A Roving Commission*. London: Odhams
Press.

Coindreau, M.E. (1974) Interview by Jean-Louis de Rambures. Comment travail-
lent les écrivains. *Le Monde* 4 Oct., 22. Cited in Briere (1988), p.36.

Coleridge, S.T. (1906) *Biographia Literaria*. London: Everyman's Library/J.M. Dent.

Concise Oxford Dictionary of Current English. (1946, 1934). Third edition. Oxford:
Clarendon.

Concise Dictionary of Quotations (1986, 1961). N.p.: Collins.

Corcoran, B. (1990) Reading, re-reading, resistance: versions of reader response. In
M. Hayhoe and S. Parker (eds) *Reading and Response* (pp. 132–46). Buckingham:
Open University Press.

Cordero, A.D. (1984) An experiment on loss in translation. *ATA Silver Tongues:
American Translators' Association Conference 1984* (pp. 471–76). Proceedings of the
25th Annual Conference of the ATA. New York: Learned Information.

Dagut, M. (1987) More about the translatability of metaphor. *Babel* 33 (2), 77–83.

Davison, C. (1989) Eggs and the sceptical eater. *New Scientist* 11 March, 45–9.

Dejean Le Féal, K. (1987) Putting translation theory into practice. *Babel* 33 (4), 205–11.

Delabastita, D. (ed.) (1996) *The Translator* 2 (2), special issue 'Wordplay in Translation'.

Delisle, J. (1988) *Translation: An Interpretive Approach*. Ottawa: University of Ottawa Press.

Di Jin (1989) The great sage in literary translation: transformations for equivalent effect. *Babel* 35 (3), 156–74.

Dittgen, A.M. (1989) *Regeln für Abweichungen. Funktionale sprachspielerische Abweichungen in Zeitungsüberschriften, Werbeschlagzeilen, Werbeslogans, Wandsprüchen und Titeln*. Frankfurt am Main: Lang.

Eco, U. (1988, 1984). *Casablanca*: cult movies and intertextual collage. In D. Lodge (ed.) *Modern Criticism and Theory: A Reader* (pp. 446–55). Harlow: Longman.

Eisel, D.D. and Reddig, J.S. (eds) (1981) *Dictionary of Contemporary Quotations*. N.p.: John Gordon Burke.

Encyclopedia Americana (1979) International edition. Danbury, CN.: Americana Corp.

Encyclopaedia Britannica (1974). Chicago: Encyclopaedia Britannica Inc.

Enkvist, N.E. (1991) On the interpretability of texts in general and of literary texts in particular. In R.D. Sell (ed) *Literary Pragmatics* (pp. 1–25). London: Routledge.

Enkvist, N.E. and Leppiniemi, G. (1989) Anticipation and disappointment: an experiment in protocolled reading of Auden's 'Gare du Midi'. In L. Hickey (ed.) *The Pragmatics of Style* (pp. 191–207). London: Routledge.

Eskola, K. (1987) Nykysuomalaisten suuret kertomukset. In T. Hoikkala (ed) *Kieli, kertomus, kulttuuri* (pp. 134–54). Helsinki: Gaudeamus.

— (1990) Kaunokirjallisuuden vastaanoton analyysi ja tulkinta. In K. Mäkelä (ed.) *Kvalitatiivisen aineiston analyysi ja tulkinta* (pp. 162–91). Helsinki: Gaudeamus.

Everyman's Encyclopedia (1978) Vol. 12. Sixth edition. London: J.M. Dent.

Fish, S.E. (1980) *Is There a Text in This Class? The Authority of Interpretive Communities*. Cambridge, MS.: Harvard University Press.

Fontanier, P. (1968, 1821–30) *Les Figures du Discours*. Paris: Flammarion.

Frank, B. (1988) Reculturing, or the kimono won't go in Oshkosh. *Translation Review* 26, 27–9.

Franklin, P. (ed.) (1988) *Professions 88*. New York: MLA.

Fraser, A. (1989, 1988) *The Warrior Queens. Boadicea's Chariot*. London: Mandarin.

Fraser, J. (1996) The translator investigated. Learning from translation process analysis. *The Translator* 2 (1), 65–79.

Freund, E. (1987) *The Return of the Reader. Reader-Response Criticism*. London: Methuen.

Genette, G. (1980) *Narrative Discourse: An Essay in Method*. Trans. J.E. Lewin. Ithaca, NY.: Cornell University Press.

Gilbert, S.M. and Gubar, S. (1984, 1979) *The Madwoman in the Attic: The Woman Writer and the Nineteenth-Century Literary Imagination*. New Haven: Yale University Press.

Gordon, I. A. (1966) *The Movement of English Prose*. London: Longmans.

Green, J. (1982) *A Dictionary of Contemporary Quotations*. London: Pan Books.

Grice, H.P. (1975) Logic and conversation. In P. Cole and J.L. Morgan (eds) *Syntax and Semantics III. Speech Acts* (pp. 41–58). New York: Academic Press. Cited in Brown and Levinson (1987).

Gutt, E-A. (1990) A theoretical account of translation – without a translation theory. *Target* 2 (2), 135–64.
— (1991) *Translation and Relevance. Cognition and Context.* Oxford: Blackwell.
Hall, W.F. (1971) Hawthorne, Shakespeare and Tess: Hardy's use of allusion and reference. *English Studies* 52, 533–42.
Harrison, G.B. (1954) *Introducing Shakespeare.* Harmondsworth: Penguin/ Pelican.
Hatakka, J.J.M. (1990) Letter to the author. April 1990.
Hatim, B. and Mason, I. (1990) *Discourse and the Translator.* Harlow: Longman.
Hazlitt, W. (1919) *Lectures on the English Poets and the Spirit of the Age.* London: Dent. Cited in Engler, B. (1991) Textualisation. In R.D. Sell (ed.) *Literary Pragmatics* (pp. 179–89). London: Routledge.
Heibert, F. (1993) *Das Wortspiel als Stilmittel und seine Übersetzung am Beispiel von sieben Übersetzungen des 'Ulysses' von James Joyce.* Kodikas, Code: Supplement 20. Tübingen: Gunter Narr.
Hewson, L. and Martin, J. (1991) *Redefining Translation: The Variational Approach.* London: Routledge.
Hickey, L. (ed.) (1989) *The Pragmatics of Style.* London: Routledge.
Hirsch, E.D. Jr (1988, 1987) *Cultural Literacy: What Every American Needs to Know.* New York: Random House/Vintage Books.
Hlebec, B. (1989) Factors and steps in translating. *Babel* 35 (3), 129–41.
Holmes, J.S. (1972) The name and nature of translation studies. In J.S. Holmes (1988) *Translated! Papers on Literary Translation and Translation Studies* (pp. 67–80). Amsterdam: Rodopi.
— (1988) *Translated! Papers on Literary Translation and Translation Studies.* Approaches to Translation Studies 7. Amsterdam: Rodopi.
Holz-Mänttäri, J. (1984) *Translatorisches Handeln. Theorie und Methode.* Annales Academiae Scientiarum Fennicae. B:226. Helsinki: Suomalainen Tiedeakatemia.
hooks, b. (1982) *Ain't I A Woman? Black Women and Feminism.* London: Pluto Press.
House, J. (1989) Translation quality assessment. In A. Chesterman (ed.) *Readings in Translation Theory* (pp. 157–61). Helsinki: Finn Lectura.
Hrala, M. (1989) Criteria for translation evaluation. In I. Sorvali (ed.) *Papers in Translation Studies* (pp. 28–44). Kouvola: University of Helsinki.
Hämäläinen, H. (1988) Enkelin sormenjälki. In H. Karjalainen (ed.) *Löytöretki lapsuuteen* (pp. 113–37). Porvoo: WSOY.
Hönig, H.G. and Kussmaul, P. (1984, 1982) *Strategie der Übersetzung.* Tübinger Beiträge zur Linguistik 205. Tübingen: Gunter Narr.
Hönig, H.G. (1993) Review of S. Hervey and I. Higgins (1992) *Thinking Translation. A Course in Translation Method,* London: Routledge. *Target* 5:1, 119-123.
Ingo, R. (1992) Käännöstutkimuksen ongelmia. Paper presented at the seminar 'Tiedon ja taidon dialogia kääntämisen ja tulkkauksen opetuksessa,' 18–19 November, Kouvola, Finland.
Iser, W. (1974) *The Implied Reader: Patterns of Communication in Prose Fiction from Bunyan to Beckett.* Baltimore: Johns Hopkins University Press.
— (1978) *The Act of Reading: A Theory of Aesthetic Response.* Baltimore, MD: Johns Hopkins University Press.
Jalonen, O. (1985) *Kansa kulttuurien virroissa. Tuontikulttuurin suuntia ja sisältöjä Suomessa itsenäisyyden aikana.* Helsinki: Otava.
Jauss, H.R. (1982) *Toward an Aesthetic of Reception.* Trans. T. Bahti. Minneapolis: University of Minnesota Press.

Johnson, A.L. (1976) Allusion in Poetry. A review of Gian Biagio Conte (1974), *Memoria dei poeti e sistema letterario: Catullo, Virgilio, Ovidio, Lucano,* Turin: Einaudi. *PTL: A Journal for Descriptive Poetics and Theory of Literature* 1, 579–87.

Juva, K. (1993) Sayersin suomentamisen ihanuus ja ihanuus. In L. Lehtolainen (ed.) *Kuka ja miksi? Dorothy L. Sayers 100 vuotta* (pp.69–92). Espoo: Suomen Dekkariseura.

Jääskeläinen, R. and Tirkkonen-Condit, S. (1991) Automatised processes in professional vs. non-professional translation: a think-aloud protocol study. In S. Tirkkonen-Condit (ed) *Empirical Research in Translation and Intercultural Studies* (pp. 89–110). Tübingen: Gunter Narr.

Jääskeläinen, R. (1993) Investigating translation strategies. In S. Tirkkonen-Condit and J. Laffling (eds) *Recent Trends in Empirical Translation Research* (pp. 99–120). University of Joensuu, Faculty of Arts.

Kahila, S. (ed.) (1990) *Suhteeni kieleen.* Hämeenlinna: Karisto.

Kallio, J. (1993) Neljän vapauden kielellinen liikkuminen. *Kielikello* 4, 10–16.

Karvonen, P. (1995) Säädöskieli takaisin tsaarinaikaan? *Hiidenkivi* 1, 3.

Kelletat, A.F. (1991) Was mir beim Übersetzen durch den Kopf geht – Ein Werkstattmonolog über eine Erzählung des Finnen Antti Tuuri. In J. Stenfors (ed.) *Erikoiskielet ja käännösteoria,. VAKKI-seminaari XI, Vöyri 9-10 Feb.* (pp. 97–113). University of Vaasa.

Kernan, A. (1989) Literary crises, old and new: information technologies and cultural change. *Language and Communication* 9 (2/3), 159–73.

Kilpi, E. (1983) *Elämän evakkona.* Porvoo: WSOY.

Koller, W. (1989) Equivalence in translation theory. In A. Chesterman (ed.) *Readings in Translation Theory* (pp. 99–104). Helsinki: Finn Lectura.

Kovala, U. (1989) Englantilaisen kirjallisuuden tulo Suomeen: kaunokirjallisuuden kääntämisen ja kustantamisen historiaa. *Kulttuuritutkimus* 6 (3), 24–9.

Krings, H.P. (1986) *Was in den Köpfen von Übersetzern vorgeht. Eine empirische Untersuchung zur Struktur des Übersetzungsprozesses an fortgeschrittenen Französischlernern.* Tübinger Beiträge zur Linguistik 291. Tübingen: Gunter Narr.

Kristeva, J. (1969) *Semeiotikè: Recherches pour une sémanalyse.* Paris: Seuil.

Kulick, D. (1992) Finding the culture: theories and methods for delineating cultural dimensions of language acquisition. In H. Nyyssönen and L. Kuure (eds) *Acquisition of Language — Acquisition of Culture* (pp. 142–58). Jyväskylä: Kopi-Jyvä.

Kussmaul, P. (1991) Creativity in the translation process. Empirical approaches. In K.M. van Leuven-Zwart and T. Naaijkens (eds) *Translation Studies: The State of the Art* (pp. 91–101). Amsterdam: Rodopi.

Lakoff, R.T. (1982) Some of my favorite writers are literate: the mingling of oral and literate strategies in written communication. In D. Tannen (ed.) *Spoken and Written Language: Exploring Orality and Literacy* (pp. 239–60). Norwood, NJ: Ablex.

Lambert, J. (1991) Shifts, oppositions and goals in translation studies: towards a genealogy of concepts. In K.M. van Leuven-Zwart and T. Naaijkens (eds) *Translation Studies: The State of the Art* (pp. 27–37). Amsterdam: Rodopi.

Lambert, J. and van Gorp, H. (1985) On describing translations. In T. Hermans (ed.) *The Manipulation of Literature. Studies in Literary Translation* (pp. 42–53). London: Croon Helm.

Larson, M.L. (1984) *Meaning-Based Translation: A Guide to Cross-Language Equivalence.* Lanham, MD: University Press of America.

Lass, A.H., Kiremidjian, D. and Goldstein, R.M. (1987) *The Facts on File Dictionary of Classical, Biblical and Literary Allusions*. New York: Facts on File Publications.

Lawrence, D.H. (1957). *The Complete Poems of D.H. Lawrence*, Vol. II. London: Heinemann.

Lefevere, A. (1981) Programmatic second thoughts on 'literary' and 'translation' or: where do we go from here. *Poetics Today* 2 (4), 39–50.

— (1992) *Translation, Rewriting, and the Manipulation of Literary Fame*. London: Routledge.

Leppihalme, R. (1989) Allusions: a cross-cultural translation problem. In G. Caie, K. Haarstrup, A.L. Jakobsen, J.E. Nielsen, J. Sevaldsen, H. Specht and A. Zettersten (eds) *Proceedings from the Fourth Nordic Conference for English Studies*. Vol. I. (pp. 357–66). Helsingør, 11–13 May, Department of English. University of Copenhagen.

— (1990) 'Crossing a cultural barrier: allusions and their translation.' Unpublished Licentiate thesis. Department of English. University of Helsinki.

— (1994) *Culture Bumps: On the Translation of Allusions*. English Department Studies 2. Helsinki: University of Helsinki.

Levine, S.J. (1975) Writing as translation: *Three Trapped Tigers* and *A Cobra*. *MLN* 90, 265–77.

Levý, J. (1967) Translation as a decision process. In *To Honour Roman Jakobson*, Vol. II (pp. 1171-1182). The Hague: Mouton.

Lively, P. (1992) *City of the Mind*. London: Penguin.

Loponen, S. (1993) Selityksiä Joel Kontiselle. *Kääntäjä* 3, 6.

Lörscher, W. (1991) *Translation Performance, Translation Process, and Translation Strategies. A Psycholinguistic Investigation*. Tübingen: Gunter Narr.

Lurie, A. (1990) *Don't Tell the Grown-ups*. London: Bloomsbury.

Lyytikäinen, E. (1995) *Bikinirajaus. Näkökulmia kieleen*. Helsinki: SKS.

Maddox, J. (1992) Language for a polyglot readership. *Nature*, 359 (8 Oct.), 475.

Makkonen, A. (1991) Onko intertekstuaalisuudella mitään rajaa? In A. Viikari (ed.) *Intertekstuaalisuus: suuntia ja sovelluksia* (pp. 9–30). Helsinki: SKS.

Masnerová, E. (1989) Cross-cultural aspects in translated fiction. In I. Sorvali (ed.) *Papers in Translation Studies Prague - Kouvola* (pp. 66–73). Kouvola: University of Helsinki.

Meyer, H. (1968, 1961) *The Poetics of Quotation in the European Novel*. Trans. T. and Y. Ziolkowski. Princeton, NJ: Princeton University Press.

Morier, H. (1961) *Dictionnaire de Poétique et de Rhétorique*. Paris: Presses Universitaires de France.

Mäkelä, K. (1990) Kvalitatiivisen analyysin arviointiperusteet. In K. Mäkelä (ed.) *Kvalitatiivisen aineiston analyysi ja tulkinta* (pp. 42–61). Helsinki: Gaudeamus.

Nash, W. (1985) *The Language of Humour*. London: Longman.

Nedergaard-Larsen, B. (1993) Cultural factors in subtitling. *Perspectives: Studies in Translatology* 2, 207–41.

Neubert, A. and Shreve, G.M. (1992) *Translation as Text*. Kent, OH: Kent State University Press.

Newmark, P. (1988) *A Textbook of Translation*. New York: Prentice Hall.

Nida, E.A. and Taber, C.R. (1969) *The Theory and Practice of Translation*. Leiden: E.J. Britt.

Nikula, H. (1991) Texte sind keine Botschaftsträger. Ein Beitrag zur Theorie des literarischen Übersetzens. In J. Stenfors (ed.) *Erikoiskielet ja käännösteoria.* *VAKKI-seminaari XI. Vöyri 9-10 Feb. 1991* (pp. 234–43). University of Vaasa.

Nord, C. (1991) *Text Analysis in Translation. Theory, Methodology, and Didactic Application of a Model for Translation-Oriented Text Analysis.* Trans. C. Nord and P. Sparrow. Amsterdam: Rodopi.

Nortamo, S. (1992) Sanojen solmuja 4. *Helsingin Sanomat* 11 March, B6.

Oxford Dictionary of English Proverbs (1970) Third edition. Revised by F.P. Wilson. Oxford: Clarendon.

The *Oxford English Dictionary* (1933) Ed. J.A.H. Murray, H.Bradley, W.A. Craigie, C.T. Onions. Oxford: Clarendon.

Oksala, T. (1990) Vänrikit – suurta runoutta vai roskaa? *Kanava* 2, 94–102.

O'Neill, M. (1990) Molesting the text: promoting resistant readings. In M. Hayhoe and S. Parker (eds) *Reading and Response* (pp. 84–93). Buckingham: Open University Press.

Östman, J-O. (1982) Pragmatic particles in an applied perspective. *NM* LXXXIII, 135–53.

Paloposki, T.J. (1986) Vapauden aika. In P. Avikainen and E. Pärssinen (eds) *Suomen historia* Vol. 4. (pp. 8–181). Espoo: Weilin & Göös.

Partridge, E. (1962, 1940). *A Dictionary of Clichés with an Introductory Essay.* London: Routledge and Kegan Paul.

— (1977) *A Dictionary of Catch Phrases British and American, from the Sixteenth Century to the Present Day.* London: Routledge and Kegan Paul.

Pasco, A.H. (1973) A study of allusion: Barbey's Stendhal in *Le Rideau cramoisi.* *PLMA* 88, 461-471.

Pattison, R. (1982) *On Literacy. The Politics of the Word from Homer to the Age of Rock.* Oxford: Oxford University Press.

Penguin Concise Columbia Encyclopedia (1987) Ed. J. S. Levey and A. Greenhall. Harmondsworth: Penguin.

Penguin Dictionary of Proverbs (1983) Ed. R. Fergusson. London: Penguin.

Penguin Dictionary of Quotations (1960) Ed. J.M. Cohen and M.J. Cohen. London: Penguin.

Penguin Dictionary of Modern Quotations (1980) Ed. J.M. Cohen & M.J. Cohen. Second edition. Harmondsworth: Penguin.

Perri, C. (1978) On alluding. *Poetics* 7, 289–307.

Perri, C., Carugati, G., Costa, P.W., Forndran, M., Mamaeva, A.G., Moody, E., Seligsohn, Z.L., Vinge, L. and Weinapple, F. (eds) (1979) Allusion studies: an international annotated bibliography, 1921-1977. *Style* 13 (2), 178–225.

Pocheptsov, G.G. (1991) Review of L. Urdang and F.G. Ruffner Jr (eds) (1986) *Allusions – Cultural, Literary, Biblical, and Historical: A Thematic Dictionary.* Second edition. Detroit: Gale. *American Speech* 66 (1), 87–9.

Preminger, A. (ed.) (1965) *Encyclopedia of Poetry and Poetics.* Princeton, NJ: Princeton University Press.

Pyhä *Raamattu,* Vanha Testamentti yhdennentoista, vuonna 1933 pidetyn yleisen kirkolliskokouksen käytäntöön ottama suomennos. Uusi Testamentti kahdennentoista, vuonna 1938 pidetyn yleisen kirkolliskokouksen käytäntöön ottama suomennos (1967) Pieksämäki: Suomen kirkon sisälähetysseura.

Ratinen, S. (1992) Kirjallisuudenkääntäjät Suomessa – ammattikuvatutkimus. *Kääntäjä* 7, 10–11.

Reader's Digest Pocket Treasury of Great Quotations (1988, 1978) London: The Reader's Digest Association.

Redfern, W.D. (1984) *Puns*. Oxford: Blackwell.

Rees, N. (1989) *Why Do We Quote?* London: Blandford.

— (1991) *Bloomsbury Dictionary of Phrase and Allusion*. London: Bloomsbury.

Reiss, K. and Vermeer, H.J. (1984) *Grundlegung einer allgemeinen Translationstheorie*. Tübingen: Max Niemeyer.

Richards, I.A. (1929) *Practical Criticism*. New York: Harcourt, Brace. Cited in Freund (1987).

Rissanen, M. (1971) *Problems in the Translation of Shakespeare's Imagery into Finnish*. Helsinki: Société Néophilologique.

Schaar, C. (1975) Vertical context systems. In H. Ringbom, A. Ingberg, R. Norrman, K. Nyholm, R. Westman and K. Wikberg (eds) (1975) *Style and Text. Studies Presented to Nils Erik Enkvist* (pp. 146–57). Stockholm: Scriptor.

— (1991) On free and latent semantic energy. In R.D. Sell (ed.) *Literary Pragmatics* (pp. 164–78). London: Routledge.

Schogt, H.G. (1988) *Linguistics, Literary Analysis and Literary Translation*. Toronto: University of Toronto Press.

Scott, A.F. (1965) *Current Literary Terms: A Concise Dictionary of Their Origin and Use*. New York: Macmillan.

Seidl, J. and McMordie, W. (1978) *English Idioms and How to Use Them*. Oxford: Oxford University Press.

Séguinot, C. (1989) The translation process: an experimental study. In C. Séguinot (ed.) *The Translation Process* (pp. 21–53). Toronto: H.G. Publications, School of Translation, York University.

— (1991) A study of student translation strategies. In S. Tirkkonen-Condit (ed.) *Empirical Research in Translation and Intercultural Studies* (pp. 79–88). Tübingen: Gunter Narr.

— (1992) Where angels fear to tread ... in defence of translation theory. *Language International* 4 (4), 40–1.

Sell, R.D. (1991) Literary pragmatics: an introduction. In R.D. Sell (ed.) *Literary Pragmatics* (pp. xi–xxiii). London: Routledge.

Shakespeare, W. *Antony and Cleopatra*. The Arden edition of the Works of William Shakespeare (1954) Ed. M.R. Ridley. London: Methuen.

— *Antony and Cleopatra*. New Swan Shakespeare Advanced Series (1985, 1971) Ed. John Ingledew. Harlow: Longmans.

— *The Complete Works*. The Tudor edition (1951) Ed. P. Alexander. London: Collins.

— *Kootut draamat*. Vol. VIII (1950) Trans. P. Cajander. Porvoo: WSOY.

— *Suuret draamat*. Vol. III (1962) Trans. Y. Jylhä. Second edition. Helsinki: Otava.

Shaw, H. (1976, 1972) *Dictionary of Literary Terms*. New York: McGraw-Hill.

Simon, R. (1989) Ballad of an ace café. *The Spectator* 28 Jan., 35–6.

Sinnemäki, M. (1989) *Lentävien lauseiden sanakirja*. Helsinki: Otava.

Smith, B.D. (1987) Language power. In I.M. Zawala, T.A. Van Dijk and M. Diaz-Diocaretz (eds) *Approaches to Discourse, Poetics and Psychiatry* (pp. 1–12). Amsterdam: John Benjamins.

Snell-Hornby, M. (1988) *Translation Studies: An Integrated Approach*. Amsterdam: John Benjamins.

— (1990) Linguistic transcoding or cultural transfer? A critique of translation theory in Germany. In S. Bassnett and A. Lefevere (eds) *Translation, History and Culture* (pp. 79–86). London: Pinter.

— (1991) Translation studies – art, science or utopia? In K.M. van Leuven-Zwart and T. Naaijkens (eds) *Translation Studies: The State of the Art* (pp. 5–12). Amsterdam: Rodopi.

Sorvali, I. (1990) *Studier i översättningsvetenskap*. Uleåborg: Institutionen för nordiska språk vid Uleåborgs universitet.

Spiegelman, A. and Schneider, B. (eds) (1973) *Whole Grains. A Book of Quotations*. New York: Douglaslinks.

Statistical Yearbook of Finland 1995 Vol. 90 (new series). Helsinki: Valtion painatuskeskus.

The Story of British People in Pictures. S.a. London: Odhams.

Straight, H.S. (1981) Knowledge, purpose and intuition: three dimensions in the evaluation of translation. In M.G. Rose (ed.) *Translation Spectrum. Essays in Theory and Practice* (pp. 41–51). Albany, NY: State University of New York Press.

Tanner, L.B. (comp. and ed.) (1971) *Voices from Women's Liberation*. New York: New American Library/Signet.

Toury, G. (1980) *In Search of A Theory of Translation*. Tel Aviv: The Porter Institute for Poetics and Semiotics, Tel Aviv University.

— (1991) Experimentation in translation studies: achievements, prospects and some pitfalls. In S. Tirkkonen-Condit (ed.) *Empirical Research in Translation and Intercultural Studies* (pp. 45–66). Tübingen: Gunter Narr.

— (1992) Everything has its price: an alternative to normative conditioning in translator training. *Interface, Journal of Applied Linguistics* 6 (2), 60–72.

Troupp, H. (1987) Onko Wodehouse suomennettavissa? *Lääkäri ja vapaa-aika* 3, 32–7.

Turk, H. (1991) The question of translatability: Benjamin, Quine, Derrida. In H. Kittel and A.P. Frank (eds) *Interculturality and the Historical Study of Literary Translations* (pp. 120–30). Berlin: Erich Schmidt.

Tweedie, Mrs A. (1989) *Matkalla Suomessa 1896*. Trans. A.T.K. Lahtinen. Helsinki: Otava.

Urdang, L. and Ruffner, F.G. Jr (eds) (1986) *Allusions – Cultural, Literary, Biblical, and Historical: A Thematic Dictionary*. Second edition. Detroit: Gale.

Venuti, L. (1995a) *The Translator's Invisibility: A History of Translation* (pp. 26–31). London: Routledge.

— (1995b) Preliminary remarks to the debate. In C. Schäffner and H. Kelly-Holmes (eds) *Cultural Functions of Translation*. Clevedon: Multilingual Matters.

Watts, R.J. (1991) Cross-cultural problems in the perception of literature. In R.D. Sell (ed.) *Literary Pragmatics* (pp. 26–43). London: Routledge.

Weisgerber, J. (1970) The use of quotations in recent literature. *Comparative Literature* 22 (1), 36–45.

Weldon, F. (1985, 1984) *Letters to Alice on First Reading Jane Austen*. London: Coroner/Hodder and Stoughton.

Williamson, D. (1991) *Kings and Queens of Britain*. Enderby: Promotional Reprint.

Wilss, W. (1983) Translation strategies, translation method and translation technique: towards a clarification of three translational concepts. *Revue de Phonétique Appliquée* 66–67–68, 143–52.

— (1989) *Anspielungen. Zur Manifestation von Kreativität und Routine in der Sprachverwendung*. Tübingen: Max Niemeyer.

— (1990) Cognitive aspects of the translation process. *Language and Communication* 10 (1), 19–36.
— (1992) *Übersetzungsfertigkeit. Annäherungen an einen komplexen übersetzungsprak-tischen Begriff*. Tübingen: Gunter Narr.
WSOY (1992) Letter to the author from the publishing house Werner Söderström Oy, 16 January, unpublished.
Ylikangas, H. and Koivusalo, E. (Signed HY, EK) (1994) Lainvalmistelun kieli. *Hiidenkivi* 4/1994, 2.

IV. Interviews

Elsa Carroll, Interview in writing, April 1992.
Liisa Hakola, Interview in writing, March 1992.
Erkki Jukarainen, Interview in writing, April 1992.
Kalevi Nyytäjä, Personal interview, February 1992.
Eila Salminen, Personal interview, February 1992.
Anna-Laura Talvio 'Elone, Personal interview, January 1992.
Fay Weldon, Personal interview, March 1989.

Appendixes

Appendix 1 The Translator Interviews

Translation of the questionnaire used. The questions were formulated both for oral interviews and for sending to translators if they preferred to answer in writing. (Translation of this and the questionnaires in the other appendixes by the author.)

ALLUSION STUDY / TRANSLATOR INTERVIEW

I. *Background*
   1. How many books have you translated?
   2. When did you start working as a translator?
   3. What was your educational background and training?
   4. What had your training NOT given you (i.e. what knowledge and skills did you find you lacked to begin with)?

II. *The translation problem*
   1. What is your view of translation studies (research on translation) at present?
   2. Have you yourself found allusions difficult to translate? Would you call them a translation problem?
   3. What principles do you follow when you translate them?
   4. Are you in the habit of thinking about such questions on a general level, or do you approach them on a case-by-case basis?

III. *The readers*
   1. Do you think of your future readers when translating?
   2. Do you see them as your readers or as the ST author's?
   3. How do you see the people who read your translations? Do you have an idea of your 'typical reader'?
   4. Does this idea change from one text to another?

5. Has this concept of reader changed during the years you have been working as a translator and have gained experience?
6. Do you think a translator needs to consider his/her readers? Is it of any use?
7. Do you ever think: this is something *Finnish* readers will not understand?
8. If so, does this have an effect on the solution you choose?

IV. *Finding and recognising allusions*

1. When you read a ST, how do you know you have come across an allusion?
2. Do you think you miss any?
3. Do you ever set out to trace an allusion? How do you do it? How common is this?
4. Does understanding the meaning of an allusion (= why this has been used here?) ever cause you difficulty?

V. *Translation strategies*

1. In your view, is a translator allowed to explain?
2. In what kind of circumstances would you omit an allusion?
3. What are your principles on replacing one allusion by another or on explaining things in a footnote?
4. How do you react as a rule when you spot an allusion in a text?
5. How do you feel about the idea that a translator is a cultural mediator?
6. Do you think of your own work as cultural mediation?

VI. *Further*

1. Do you remember any illuminating examples regarding any of the issues touched on here?
2. Is there anything else you would like to say regarding this topic?
3. What was it like translating the text which is now part of my corpus?

Thank you!

Appendix 2   Details on Respondents (GRT, KLA, TSE)

The GRT 1 test

Respondents: general readers ($N = 23$)

Sex		Age	
Female	20	20–29	5
Male	2	30–39	3
Not stated	1	40–49	6
Total	23	50–59	6
		60+	3
		Total	23

Foreign-language reading

The respondents estimated their frequency of reading foreign-language (Swedish is included as a foreign language if a respondent so named it) texts (newspapers/magazines or books) as follows:

(a) English

Often (= every week)	4
Sometimes (= once or twice a month)	6
Rarely (= a few per year)	9

(b) Other foreign languages but not English

Often	0
Sometimes	1
Rarely	1
(c) No foreign languages	2
Total	23

The 'Hamlet' test

Respondents were asked to underline and give the source of any allusions they noticed in text 0, an extract from a novel by Eeva Kilpi (1983) (see p.141 for part of the extract). The most obvious allusion in the Finnish text was a modification of *To be or not to be*.

Source given	13
No source, but standard Finnish form given	2
No source, but underlined	5
Not marked	3
Total	23

The GRT 2 Test

Respondents: general readers (*N* = 57)

Sex		*Age*	
Female	20	19	2
Male	36	20–29	31
Not stated	1	30–39	13
Total	57	40–49	5
		50–59	3
		60+	3
		Total	57

Foreign-language reading

(a) *English*

Often (= every week)	13
Sometimes (= once or twice a month)	17
Rarely (= a few per year)	19

(b) *Other foreign languages but not English*

Often	2
Sometimes	0

Rarely	1
(c) No foreign languages	5
Total	57

The 'Hamlet' test

Source given	50
No source, but standard Finnish form given	2
No source, but underlined	1
Not marked	4
Total	57

The KLA Test

Respondents: students and teachers of translation at the Kouvola department of translation studies, University of Helsinki ($N = 51$)

Sex

Female	32
Male	9
Not stated	10
Total	51

Age

(a)   *Students working with English*

19	2
20–29	16
30–39	4

(b)   *Students working with other languages*

19	3
20–29	20
30–39	2

(c)   Teachers (one working with English)

40–49	2
50–59	_2
Total	51

The TSE Test

Respondents: students at the department of English, University of Helsinki
(*N* = 33)

Sex

Female	30
Male	3
Not stated	_0
Total	33

Age

20–29	30
30–39	0
40–49	2
50–59	0
60+	_1
Total	33

Stage of studies (after c. 10 years of English at school)

I (basic)	1
II (intermediate)	23
III (advanced)	8
Postgraduate	_1
Total	33

Appendix 3   The GRT Questionnaire

Translation of the instructions to readers participating in GRT, and of the questions to each extract. (The target texts used are not reproduced in this book. For source text extracts, see Appendix 6.)

READER INQUIRY

Dear reader,

I am writing a dissertation on the translation of allusions and need information on how Finnish readers respond to what they read.

---

allusion = an often short, either direct or indirect reference e.g. to a person, book, event or saying which is assumed to be familiar to the reader. Allusions are culture-bound, so that some of them are familiar only in one's native language, while others are familiar in more than one language (e.g. through the influence of translated books or films).

For instance: 'Would you like Finland to stay in her <u>Impivaara</u> for ever?' (an allusion to Aleksis Kivi's *Seven Brothers)*

'The teacher promised the sixth-formers <u>blood, sweat and tears</u> – but then, <u>it's through difficulties that one achieves victory.</u>' (The former is an allusion to one of Winston Churchill's speeches during the second world war, the latter to the Latin saying *per aspera ad astra.)*

I would like you to read the enclosed extracts and to answer the questions. Please answer on the basis of what you yourself know and feel without consulting other people or works of reference. Please return the questionnaire even though you may feel that you have said very little. It will still be useful to me.

For processing the information I shall also need the following data on the respondent: (fill in, underline, mark with a circle or a cross ...)

I am a woman/man, aged _____ years.

I also read newspapers and magazines in foreign languages: yes/no

Likewise books: yes/no

Approximately every week/one or two per month/a few per year

in which languages? _____

Further information available [phone number].

Thank you for your help!

[*Example: an extract from a Finnish novel; not reproduced in this book*]

The enclosed extract from a novel by Eeva Kilpi contains an allusion (the underlined words). It alludes to a hymn and may suggest for example that the characters in the extract are of a religious turn of mind; or a reader may find the combination of everyday matters and a line from a hymn amusing.

If you notice allusions in the texts of this questionnaire, please underline them and write down what they bring to mind. There are also phrases or sentences in the texts that have already been underlined. Answer the questions on those phrases or sentences in your own words.

Please note that this is not a test on what you know. It deals with the way you as a reader respond to what you read.

Text 0 : an extract from a Finnish novel, Kilpi (1983) (used to check whether the respondents were able to notice a presumably familiar but modified allusion used in an original text in their native language. See p.141 for part of the extract; for the results of this 'Hamlet' test, see Appendix 2.)

Target texts used

GRT 1

- Lodge (Where are the Imps of yesteryear)

  Instruction: Underline any allusions you may find.

- McBain (A woman works from sun to sun)

  Question: What do you think this means? What does it mean in this context?

- McBain (Separate but equal)

  Question: What do you think this means? What does it mean in this context?

- Allingham (With my body I thee worship)

  Question: How do you understand the young man's argument?

- Lurie (The White Rabbit)

  Question: What kind of expression is this (and what makes you think so)?

- Lurie (The Miller of Dee)

Question: What does this comparison suggest to you?

- Lurie (That Visigoth realtor her mother)

Question: How do you understand the reference to Barbie's mother?

- Lurie (Some corner of an English field)

Background information given: The scene of the novel is England. Vinnie, a middle-aged woman researcher, is telling her old acquaintance Edwin, an Englishman, that Chuck, a 'typical American' whom they both knew, has suddenly died of a heart attack. What Vinnie does not reveal is that she and Chuck had had a brief love affair just before this happened.

Question: How do you interpret Edwin's words? (the thought, the tone of voice)

Source texts in Appendix 6.

GRT 2

- Parker (Rebecca/Pollyanna)

Background information given: Ticknor is inviting the narrator, Spenser, to become the bodyguard of the feminist writer Rachel Wallace for some time.

Question: How do you understand the underlined requirement? What should an ideal bodyguard be like and how should he behave?

- Parker (Carry Nation/A 1920s suffragette) (in version (a) of the test)

Question: Describe what Rachel Wallace did NOT look like, ie. what kind of image the words 'a suffragette of the 1920s' gives rise to.

- Parker (The Walrus and the Carpenter) (in version (b))

Question: Why was the place called the Walrus and the Carpenter? What if it had been called 'Mursu and Nikkari'? ('Nikkari' is another possible term for 'carpenter')

- Parker (A light-blue body stocking)

Question: How do you understand Spenser's words?

- Allingham (There's gold in them thar quarters/A veritable gold mine)

Question: What does the exclamation 'A veritable gold mine!' mean?

- McBain (Tangled webs) (in version (a))

Question: What do the underlined words mean to you in this context?

- Lurie (Pumpkins at midnight) (in version (b))

Question: What is the meaning of the underlined words? (= what does Vinnie mean?) Do you see an allusion to something here? How do you understand Mr Mumpson's words: 'Huh? Oh. Ha-ha'?

- Lurie (An olive branch)

Question: What do the images used in the second paragraph make you think of? What could they be an allusion to?

- Lurie (That Visigoth realtor her mother)

Question: How do you understand the reference to Barbie's mother?

- Weldon (All be well)

Background information given: Helen has just had a baby.

Question: What does Helen mean? Is something being alluded to here?

Source texts in Appendix 6.

Appendix 4   The KLA Questionnaire

Translation of the questionnaire used in the KLA test

READER INQUIRY

Information on the respondent

— female/male, aged _____
— student/teacher/translator
— working with English: Y/N
— mother tongue (if not Finnish): _____

(1) Do you know the following names? Underline those that are familiar to you and give a few words of description.

Example: <u>Little Red Riding Hood</u> *went to see her grandmother, eaten by wolf*

Agag
Boadicea (Boudicca)
Daisy Buchanan

Thomas Gradgrind
Carry Nation
Pollyanna
Nero Wolfe
the geese of the Capitol

(2)   Read the following extracts and answer the questions briefly:

  • Lurie (The White Rabbit)

    Question: What kind of expression is this (and what makes you think so?)

  • Allingham (With my body I thee worship)

    Question: How do you understand the young man's argument?

Thank you for your help!

Target texts not reproduced in this book. Source texts in Appendix 6.

Appendix 5   The TSE Questionnaire

Translation of the instructions to students participating in TSE

ALLUSION TEST

This test attempts to discover how much difficulty allusions in English-language texts cause to Finns. The aim is to see how easily a student of English will spot allusions in an English text, recognise their sources (i.e. what they allude to) and understand their meaning. A further aim is to map the various types of translations offered.

Two handouts containing the same texts will be given to you. You may proceed at your own speed, and you need not have dealt with all of the texts by the end of the test.

DO THIS:

  • First read the definitions of *allusion* given and answer the questions below.
  • Read all the texts in the first handout and underline the allusions that you spot. Write down their sources (i.e. what they allude to) if you recognise them. You may also base an answer on a vague recollection or a guess. Answers in either Finnish or English.

- Exchange the first handout for the second. In the second one, certain allusions to be dealt with are underlined. Irrespective of which ones you underlined on the first round, consider (a) the content of each in the context shown and give an explanation in writing (on a separate sheet or on the back of the page), as if you were explaining the passage to someone who knows English less well than you do. Also explain the significance of the allusion (i.e. answer the question: Why is it used here?). Then (b) translate the marked section containing the allusion into Finnish. You may outline more than one translation, and evaluate and comment on your translations.

'ALLUSION. Latin *alludere*, to play with, to jest, to refer to. A reference to characters and events of mythology, legends, history.' (Scott, *Current Literary Terms*, 1965)

'ALLUSION. Tacit reference to another literary work, to another art, to history, to contemporary figures, or the like.' (Preminger, *Encyclopedia of Poetry and Poetics*, 1965)

'A reference, usually brief, often casual, occasionally indirect, to a person, event, or condition presumably familiar but sometimes obscure or unknown to the reader.' (Shaw, *Dict. of Lit. Terms*, 1976)

'An allusion is a figure of speech that compares aspects or qualities of counterparts in history, mythology, scripture, literature, popular or contemporary culture.' (Lass *et al.* 1987)

Participant:

— code name

— age

— female/male

— stage of studies I/II/III

— family background, education (answer only if eg. a parent is a native speaker of English, or you went to an English school or the like)

Source texts used:

- Lurie (Some corner of an English field)
- Paretsky (Not all the perfumes of Arabia)
- Paretsky (Dick Butkus)
- Rendell (Like another Alice)
- Bawden (Fatted calves)

- Rendell (Goose/swan)
- Rendell (Oh! withered is the garland of war)
- Moody (Lovely, dark and deep)
- Moody (Unkindest cut)

Source texts reproduced in Appendix 7.

Appendix 6   Source Text Extracts (GRT, KLA)

Text A: Lurie (The White Rabbit)

The studio, when he finds it, is discouraging – not the place anyone would choose for a lovers' meeting. Fred would have preferred the BBC building in Portland Place, where he once went with Rosemary: a comic temple of art deco design with a golden sunburst over the door and a bank of gilded elevators. Behind them was a warren of corridors down which eccentric looking persons hurried with White Rabbit ex-pressions. The sound rooms were cosy burrows furnished with battered soft leather chairs and historical-looking microphones and switchboards; the Battle of Britain still seemed to reverberate in the smoky air.

The commercial station is cold and anonymous and ultra contemporary; its glass-fronted lobby is decorated in Madison Avenue minimalism. A dozen or so teenagers slump on plastic divans, chewing gum and jiggling their knees to the pounding beat of rock music. (Alison Lurie, *Foreign Affairs*)

Text B: Parker (The Walrus and the Carpenter)

Susan and I were at the raw bar in the middle of Quincy Market eating oysters and drinking beer, and arguing. Sort of.

'So why didn't you keep out of it?' Susan said. 'Rachel had asked you to.'

'And stand there and let them drag her out?'

'Yes.' Susan slurped an oyster off the shell. They don't offer forks at the raw bar. They just serve oysters or clams or shrimp, with beer in paper cups. There are bowls of oyster crackers and squeeze bottles of cocktail sauce. They named the place the Walrus and the Carpenter, but I like it anyway.

'I couldn't do that,' I said. Under the vaulted ceiling of the market, people swirled up and down the main aisle. A bearded man wearing a ski cap and a green turtleneck sweater eyed Susan and whispered something to the man with him. The man with him looked at Susan and nodded. They both smiled, and then they both caught me looking at them and looked away and moved on. I ordered another beer. Susan sipped a little of hers.

'Why couldn't you do that?' Susan asked.

'It violated something.'

'What?'

I shrugged. 'My pride?' (Robert B. Parker, *Looking for Rachel Wallace*)

Text C: Parker (A light-blue body stocking)

'I told you before, I have no sense of humor. Do you agree or disagree?'

'Agree.'

'Finally, except when you feel my life is in danger, I want you to stay out of my way. I realise you will have to be around and watchful. I don't know how serious the threats are, but you have to assume they are serious. I understand that. But short of a mortal situation I do not want to hear from you. I want a shadow.'

I said, 'Agree,' and drank the rest of my beer. The waiter came by and removed the empty peanut bowl and replaced it. Rachel Wallace noticed my beer was gone and gestured that the waiter should bring another. Ticknor looked at his glass and at Rachel Wallace's. His was empty, hers wasn't. He didn't order.

'Your appearance is good,' she said. 'That's a nice suit, and it's well tailored. Are you dressed up for the occasion or do you always look good?'

'I'm dressed up for the occasion. <u>Normally I wear a light-blue body stocking with a big red S on the front</u>.' It was dim in the bar, but her lipstick was bright, and I thought for a moment she smiled, or nearly smiled, or one corner of her mouth itched.

'I want you presentable,' she said.

'I'll be presentable, but if you want me appropriate, you'll have to let me know your plans ahead of time.'

She said, 'Certainly.' (Robert B. Parker, *Looking for Rachel Wallace*)

Text D: Lurie (An olive branch)

The other weight on Fred's mind is heavier, though it consists not of a stack of books but of an airletter almost lighter than air. The letter is from his estranged wife Roo, and is her first in four months – though

Fred has written her several times: asking her to forward on his mail, returning her health insurance card, and inquiring for the address of a friend who's supposed to be at the University of Sussex. Roo, as he might have expected, hasn't forwarded the mail, acknowledged the card, or provided the address.

But now, like a tardy bluebird of peace returning late to a deserted ark after three times forty days and nights, this blue airletter has flapped across the ocean to him. In its beak it holds, no question about that, a fresh olive branch. (Alison Lurie, *Foreign Affairs*)

Text E: Allingham (With my body I thee worship)

He left her without speaking, shut the door of the staircase carefully behind him, turned on the switch which lit the bedroom above and ran up into it, to come to a sudden halt on the threshold. Someone was there, lying on the bed, the shadows of the high footboard hiding her face. He knew who it was before he went over and looked down.

Julia was lying on her back, her hands behind her head, her eyes wide open and very dark. There was no expression whatever on her face and he got the impression that she was not breathing. She watched him silently, only her grave eyes, dark with exhaustion from the emotional struggle she had lost, flickering to show that she was alive.

Timothy stood looking a moment and then made as if to turn away from her, his face working, and she put up her arms and pulled him down.

For a little while he let the tide of relief and peace close over him but as the surge rose in his blood he took hold of himself and pushed her away as he struggled to get up.

'No. Stop it,' he whispered fiercely. 'Not here I tell you. Not in this hole and corner. I won't let you. You're mine as well as your own. We've got something to lose. 'With my body I thee worship' and don't forget it, my – my *holy* one.' (Margery Allingham, *The China Governess*)

Text F: Lurie (Pumpkins at midnight)

Something. What? Well, she could go back into the terminal and try to telephone for a minicab, though they are notorious for not turning up when promised. And for overcharging. And if they do overcharge, does she have enough English money?

No use worrying about that, not yet. Taking a couple of deep breaths to calm herself, Vinnie shoves her luggage back toward the terminal, hoping for the miraculous apparition of a taxi. There is none, of course;

only a mob of Sun Tourists and their luggage waiting to board a char-
tered bus. She is about to retreat when Mr Hobbs/Mumpson hails her.
He is now wearing a tan cowboy hat trimmed with feathers and a
fleece-lined sheepskin coat, and is hung about with cameras, making
him look even more than ever like the caricature of an American tour-
ist, Western division.

'Hi there! What's the trouble?'

'Nothing,' says Vinnie repressively, realising that her state of mind
must be engraved upon her countenance. 'I was just looking for a taxi.'

Mr Mumpson stares out across the empty, rain-sloshed, light-
streaked pavement. 'Don't seem to be any here.'

'No.' She manages a brief defensive smile. 'Apparently they all turn
into pumpkins at midnight.'

'Huh? Oh, ha-ha. Listen, I know what. You can come on the bus with
us. It's going right into town: centrally located hotel, said so in the bro-
chure. Bet you can get a cab there.'

Over her weak, weary protests, he plunges into the crowd and
returns a minute later to report that it is all fixed up. Luckily, since Vinnie and Mr Mumpson are the last to board, they have to sit separately,
and she is spared any more of his conversation. (Alison Lurie, *Foreign
Affairs*)

Text G: McBain (A woman works from sun to sun)

If you know the marks a gun can leave, and if you know where to
look for them on a spent cartridge case, why then, all you have to do is
fire some shells from the suspect gun, retrieve them, and mark them for
identification. Then you take the shell found at the scene of the crime,
and you also mark *that* for identification, since any normal Ballistics
Section has a lot of loose shells around, and you don't want to spend all
your time playing the shell game when you've got more important
matters to consider – like homicide, for example. Then you wash (yes,
that's right, *wash*) all the shells in your favorite detergent (a woman
works from sun to sun, but a man's work is never done) and you are
now ready to compare them. You do this with a microscope, of course,
and you photograph your findings under oblique light to bring the
marks into sharp relief, and then you paste up an enlargement of the
suspect shell alongside an enlargement of the comparison shell, and
you record the marks on each the way you would record the whorls
and tents and loops and ridges of a fingerprint – and there you are.

Where you are, if you are Michael O. Dorfsman, is in that euphoric
land known as Positive Identification. It is very nice when all those

marks and scratches line up like separate halves of the same face. It makes a man feel good when he's able to pick up the telephone and call the investigating detective to report without question that the gun delivered to Ballistics was definitely the gun that fired the bullets that killed somebody. (Ed McBain, *Bread*)

Text H: McBain (Separate but equal)

At a quarter past nine Rosalie Waggener asked if it was all right if she went home. The detectives told her it was not all right. The detectives told her that they were charging Hemmings, Worthy, and Chase with arson and homicide, and Grimm, Chase, and herself with attempting to smuggle dope into the country.

'I had nothing to do with any dope,' Rosalie said.
'You paid for it,' Carella said.
'I was only a messenger.'
'For a jig pusher,' Ollie said.
'Knock off that kind of talk, will you?' Carella said.
'What kind of talk?'
'That bigoted bullshit,' Hawes said.
'Bigoted?' Ollie said. 'White or black, they're all the same to me, they *all* stink. That's bigoted?'

'That's not even equal but separate,' Carella said, and Ollie burst out laughing. He slapped Hawes and Carella on their backs, simultaneously, with both beefy hands, almost knocking over Carella, who was off balance to begin with. 'I like you guys,' he said, 'you know that? I really enjoy working with you guys.' (Ed McBain, *Bread*)

Text I: Lurie (The Miller of Dee)

Presumably Chuck is still away in Somerset, which must mean that he's found more relatives, possibly even some aristocratic ones. But in that case, why hasn't he called to tell her all about it? Because he's angry at her, or tired of her, and/or because he's met somebody he likes better. Well, she might have foreseen it. As the old rhyme puts it,

She that will not when she may,
When she would she shall have nay.

Vinnie feels an irritability rising to anger at Chuck and at herself. Until she took up with him, she had been content in London, almost happy, really. Like the Miller of Dee, as long as she didn't really care for anyone, the fact that nobody cared for her could not trouble her. She's just as well off now as she was before Chuck got into her life, but she feels miserable, hurt, rejected, and sorry for herself.

Vinnie imagines the long sitting room of a large expensive country house, far away in the southwest of England in a town she has never seen. There, at this very moment, Chuck Mumpson is having tea with newly discovered English cousins named De Mompesson, who have a rose garden and hunters. Charmed by his American naiveté and bluntness of speech, they are plying him with watercress sandwiches, walnut cake, raspberries and heavy cream. (Alison Lurie, *Foreign Affairs*)

Text J: Lurie (That Visigoth realtor her mother)

'They took care of everything, really. Except for the cremains. That was kinda weird and awful, y'know. Professor Gilson had them saved for me. I thought they'd be in a big heavy silver urn or something, but it wasn't anything like that.' Barbie snuffles, stops.

'Nothing like that,' Vinnie prompts.

'Naw. They were in a, I don't know, a kinda waxed cardboard carton like you get with store-packed ice cream, about that size. Inside it was a plastic bag full of this kinda pale gritty gray stuff. I couldn't believe that was all that was left of Dad, just a coupla pounds of what looked like health-food soy mix.' Barbie snuffles again, swallows.

'Then I didn't know what to do with it,' she continues. 'I didn't know if it was legal to take cremains on a plane. I mean, suppose there was a customs inspection? I couldn't see putting that carton in the suitcase with my clothes anyhow, y'know?' She begins to tear up again. 'Sorry. I'm so stupid.'

Barbie's continual assertion of her lack of intelligence has begun to annoy Vinnie. Stop telling me how stupid you are, she wants to say. You graduated from the University of Oklahoma, you can't be all that stupid.

'That's all right,' she says instead. 'I think you've done very well, considering everything.' Almost against her will she reclassifies The Barbarian as an innocent peasant – the victim rather than the accomplice of <u>that Visigoth realtor her mother</u>, who is no doubt responsible for Barbie's low opinion of her own intelligence.

'Anyhow, when I phoned home next, Mom said not to bother,' Barbie resumes presently. 'She said what I should do was scatter the cremains somewhere. So Professor Gilson drove me out in the country to a place he said Dad had liked... ' (Alison Lurie, *Foreign Affairs*)

Text K: Lurie (Some corner of an English field)

'... She'd have to be an awfully gifted actress.'

'Oh, she's gifted,' Edwin agrees, carefully skinning a ripe peach with one of his ivory-handled Victorian fruit knives. 'She can imitate just about anyone. You should hear her do your cowboy friend, Chuck what's-his-name. How is what's-his-name, by the way?' he adds, changing the subject with his customary deftness. 'Is he still digging for ancestors down in Wiltshire?'

'Yes – no,' Vinnie replies uncomfortably. Though she has been at Edwin's for nearly two hours, and spoken to him earlier on the phone, she hasn't dared to mention Chuck. She knows it will be nearly impossible for her to tell the story without falling apart as she has been falling apart at intervals for the past ten days. But she plunges in, beginning with Barbie's telephone call.

'So the wife and son couldn't make it to England,' Edwin remarks presently.

'No. Of course, it's just a convention that when someone dies you have to hurry to the fatal spot. It doesn't actually do them any good.'

'I suppose not. Still, it does give one a certain opinion of Chuck's relatives.'

'It does.' Vinnie continues with her story. Several times she hears a tell-tale wobble in her voice, but Edwin seems to notice nothing.

'So there's some corner of an English field that is forever Tulsa,' he says finally, smiling.

'Yes.' Vinnie strangles the cry that rises in her.

'Poor old Chuck. Rather awful to go out like that, so unprepared and sudden and far from home.' (Alison Lurie, *Foreign Affairs*)

Text L: Lodge (Where are the Imps of yesteryear)

Vic is all in favour of backing Britain, but there are times when the *Mail*'s windy chauvinism gets on his tits. He takes a drag on his cigarette and taps the ash between his legs, hearing a faint hiss as it hits the water. 100 M.P.G. FAMILY CAR LOOKING GOOD IN TESTS.

Trials have been started by British Leyland of their revolutionary lightweight aluminium engine for a world-beating family car capable of 100 miles per gallon.

When was the last time we were supposed to have a world-beating aluminium engine? The Hillman Imp, right? Where are they now, the

<u>Hillman Imps of yesteryear? In the scrapyards, every one</u>, or nearly. And the Linwood plant a graveyard, grass growing between the assembly lines, corrugated-iron roofs flapping in the wind. A car that nobody wanted to buy, built on a site chosen for political not commercial reasons, hundreds of miles from its component suppliers. He turns to the City Pages. HOW TO GET UP A HEAD OF ESTEEM.

> What has been designated Industry Year has got off to a predictably silly start. Various bodies in Manufacturing Industry are working themselves into one of their regular lathers about the supposed low social esteem bestowed upon engineers and engineering.

Vic reads this article with mixed feelings. Industry Year is certainly a lot of balls. On the other hand, the idea that society undervalues its engineers is not. (David Lodge, *Nice Work*)

Text M: Parker (Rebecca/Pollyanna)

'The only reservation I have,' Ticknor said when the waiter had retreated, 'is the potential for a personality clash.'

I leaned back in my chair and folded my arms.

'You look good in most ways,' Ticknor said. 'You've got the build for it. People who should know say you are as tough as you look. And they say you're honest. But you work awfully hard sometimes at being a wise guy. And you look like everything Rachel hates.'

'It's not hard work,' I said.

'What isn't?'

'Being a wise guy. It's a gift.'

'Perhaps,' Ticknor said. 'But it is not a gift that will endear you to Rachel Wallace. Neither will the muscles and the machismo.'

'I know a guy would lend me a lavender suit,' I said.

'Don't you want this work?' Ticknor said.

I shook my head. 'What you want, Mr. Ticknor, is someone feisty enough to get in the line of someone else's fire, and tough enough to get away with it. And <u>you want him to look like Winnie-the-Pooh and act like Rebecca of Sunnybrook Farm</u>. I'm not sure Rebecca's even got a gun permit.'

He was silent for a moment. The other table cleared, and now we were alone in the upstairs dining room, except for several waiters and the maitre d'.

'God damn it,' Ticknor said. 'You are right. If you'll take the job, it's

yours. Two hundred dollars a day and expenses. And God help me, I
hope I'm right.'
'Okay,' I said. 'When do I meet Ms. Wallace?' (Robert B. Parker, *Looking for Rachel Wallace*)

Text N: Parker (Carry Nation/A 1920s suffragette)

I met Rachel Wallace on a bright October day when Ticknor and I
walked down from his office across the Common and the Public Garden through the early turn-of-fall foliage and visited her in her room at
the Ritz.
She didn't look like Carry Nation. She looked like a pleasant woman
about my age with a Diane Von Furstenburg dress on and some lipstick, and her hair long and black and clean.
Ticknor introduced us. (Robert B. Parker, *Looking for Rachel Wallace*)

Text O: McBain (Tangled webs)

'What's Alfie's business with Erhard Bachmann?'
'I don't know.'
'Was Bachmann expecting you when you got to Germany?'
'Yes. But I used a phony name. Alfie told me to use a phony name.'
'What did Bachmann say when you gave him the money?'
'He said *"Danke sehr."'*
That was the end of their little chat with Rosalie Waggener. They fig-
ured, by that time, that she had either told them all she knew or all she
was willing to tell. They thanked her very much (in English), and asked
her to wait in the room down the hall. From what they could gather,
Chase and Grimm seemed to be equal partners in the little-wooden-
animal business. Without Worthy and Hemmings knowing about it,
Chase had paid $500,000 of his own money to Grimm's packer in Ger-
many, and Grimm (before the devastating warehouse fire) had been
ready to pay *another* $500,000 for the cargo when it reached America.
According to Grimm's own estimate, the resale value of the cargo was
one million dollars. The three cops investigating the case knew very
little about high-level business transactions involving astronomical
figures. They knew only that tangled are the webs we weave when first
we practice to deceive, and they further knew that nobody invests a
million bucks hoping merely to break even.
It looked like time for a little game of poker. (Ed McBain, *Bread*)

Text P: Allingham (There's gold in them thar hills/
A veritable gold mine)

Mr. Campion continued to be dubious.

'You are telling me seriously that young Kinnit was responsible for wrecking the council flat? Have you any proof of this at all?'

'I don't want any. I don't want anything to do with it, and don't forget anything I'm telling you now is off the record.'

Joe Stalkey's face, unattractive to start with, was not improved by an expression of obstinate prejudice. 'Of course he is. Ron reports that he is babbling about having been locked in his college at Oxford at the hour in question, but that only proves he has some useful friends or enough money to employ a few hooligans. What one might be able to prove is one thing but what we know must be the truth is another. Be your age, Campion. Who are you working for? The little lad himself?'

'No. I belong to the other side of the family. I am protecting the interests of the girl friend.'

'Are you indeed? Quite a client!' He was openly envious. '<u>There's gold in them thar quarters</u>. Oh well, good luck to you. You're welcome to everything we've got – at the right price, of course. Happy to oblige you. But in this particular case we don't want to work with you. We've come out and we're staying out, especially after this morning's performance. That kind is decadent and dangerous. It never pays to take a youngster out of his normal environment and bring him up in something plushy.'

'Do you know what his normal environment was? I thought that was the object of the exercise.' (Margery Allingham, *The China Governess*)

Text Q: Weldon (All be well)

He picked the baby up.

'Careful,' said Helen, but there was no need. Clifford was accustomed to handling objects of great value. And there and then he felt, to his surprise, and acutely, both the pain and pleasure of fatherhood – the piercing anxious needle in the heart which is the drive to protect, the warm, reassuring glow which is the conviction of immortality, the recognition of privilege, the knowledge that it is more than just a child you hold in your arms, but the whole future of the world, as it works through you. More, he felt absurdly grateful to Helen for having the baby, making the feeling possible. For the first time since he had rescued her from the de Waldo clinic, he kissed her with ungrudging love. He had forgiven her, in fact, and Helen glowed in his forgiveness.

'<u>All be well,</u>' she shut her eyes and said, quoting something she had
read, but not quite sure what '— <u>and all will be well, and all manner of
things will be well,</u>' and Clifford did not even snub her by asking for
the source of the quotation. And so it was, very well indeed, for a time.

Until she was nearly a year old, then, Nell lived in the cocoon of happiness created by her parents. Leonardo's flourished under Clifford
Wexford's guidance – an interesting Rembrandt was acquired, a few
tedious Dutch masters sold, the putative Botticelli labelled and hung as
such, to the Uffizi's astonishment, and in the new contemporary section, the price of a David Firkin, now required to paint no more than
two paintings a year, lest he spoil his own market, soared to five figures. Helen lost a whole stone and worshipped Clifford and baby Nell
in turns. It is even pleasanter – if more difficult – to love, than to be
loved. When both happen at once, what higher joy can there be? (Fay
Weldon, *The Hearts and Lives of Men*)

Appendix 7   Source Text Extracts (TSE)

The students had the texts twice, first unmarked, then with a section or sections marked and some words underlined. This Appendix shows the
markings and underlinings.

Text A: Lurie (Some corner of an English field)

See Appendix 6, Text K.

Text B: Paretsky (Not all perfumes of Arabia)

Peter seemed to think this was sound advice. He caught up with me
as I started up the stairs. 'Sorry, Vic. Didn't mean to criticise. The thing
is, I've been drinking more than I should. These the documents? Here,
let me carry 'em for you.'

He took the books from me and followed me up the stairs. I carried
my malodorous shoes into the kitchen and began pouring water and
Clorox on them. I was really furious, both with his criticism, and also
with myself for having said anything. It's never a good idea to let people know that you've been obtaining information through
questionable means. If I hadn't been startled, guilty, feeling at ease
with Mr. Contreras, and pissed as hell with Dick, I wouldn't have said
one word about it. Goes to show.

Peter gave me a tentative, alcoholic kiss behind my ear. 'C'mon, Vic.

Scout's honor, I won't say anything more about your – uh – business
methods. Okay?'
'Yeah, okay.' I finished rinsing my shoes. / My hands now smelled
of Clorox, not as bad as vomit, but not good. I rubbed lemon juice into
them. Not all the perfumes of Arabia. / 'No one likes being criticised,
Peter.' (Sara Paretsky, *Bitter Medicine*)

Text C: Paretsky (Dick Butkus)

'Rawlings?' Murray asked. 'Why bring in the police? They'll spoil
everything.'
'I don't know if he'll come,' I said impatiently. 'But I'd like him to see
the story with his own eyes. It's too unbelievable otherwise. Will you
do it, Max?'
'Certainly. And I want to be there in person. If there are to be fireworks, why should I not see them? Anyway, this will be a fine
opportunity for me to watch you at your detective work. I have always
been curious.'
/ 'It's not the thrill you're expecting, Loewenthal,' Murray said. 'Vic
favors (Ca) the Dick Butkus approach to detection – hit the offense hard
– you know, just so they know they met you at the line of scrimmage –
then see who's left on the ground when she gets done. If you're looking
for (Cb) Sherlock Holmes or Nero Wolfe doing some intellectual foot-
work, forget it.' /
'Thank you for the testimonial,' I said, bowing over the table. 'All are
appreciated and may be sent to our head office in Tripoli, where an appropriate response will be generated. Anyway, Murray, you don't
have to come. I was just asking Max to include you out of courtesy.'
'Oh, no. I'm coming. If this story is going to start breaking on Friday,
I want to be there. Anyway, I'm going to have the thing keyed in, ready
to transmit, the moment your pal Burgoyne looks at you with his honest but troubled eyes and says, "Vic, you've persuaded me to turn
myself in." Or does he just call you "sweetheart" or "Victoria" or "She-
Who-Must-Be-Obeyed"?' (Sara Paretsky, *Bitter Medicine*)

Text D: Rendell (Some other Alice)

For a moment or two, feeling a faint recurrence of malaise, she held
the book unopened in her hands. The brown and blue cover was
slightly torn. Andrew could bring her the Sellotape when he came up
again and she would mend it for him.
If they were really to leave tomorrow she must make an effort, not

just lie here listlessly. To see her reading would please him; he would understand that she was beginning to relax again, to take an interest in something apart from her own health.

Were Victorian women really attracted by husky men in Norfolk jackets, men with great bushy fair beards? She smiled at the delicate Huskinson drawings, lingering over them. Here was a winsome crino-lined girl standing in front of a Gothic mansion and here a painfully real illustration of a hunting accident. The pictures were amusing but the text looked dreadfully political. How would she ever plough through all that stuff about the Ballot and the Irish Reform Bill? Besides the illustrations were few and the text vast, nearly three hundred and sixty pages in the first volume. / She sighed. <u>Like another Alice she wanted pictures and conversation.</u> /

Snuggling down in the warm bed, she turned back to the list of con-tents. The characters and the place names in the chapter headings were all new to her. 'Phineas Finn Takes His Seat', she read abstractedly, 'Lord Brentford's Dinner', 'The New Government', 'Autumnal Pros-pects'. Her eyes were beginning to close ... Then, with a little gasp, suddenly wide awake, she struggled up, first rubbing her eyes, then bringing the print close to them.

No, it couldn't be! It must be a hallucination, a delusion. She shut her eyes tightly and frightened by the darkness and the drumming in her head, opened them again to stare and stare. Every number, every line on that page swam together into a greyish blur except two words in italics: *Saulsby Wood*. (Ruth Rendell, *Vanity Dies Hard*)

Text E: Bawden (Fatted calves)

'Oh, Dad,' he said. 'Don't go *on*.'

A familiar, agonised cry. And he looked agonised. He was a dirty grey colour; there was hardly any flesh on his face; his cheeks were sucked in, his jaw jutted. He fished a squashed pack of cigarettes out of the pocket of his filthy red leather jacket. I grabbed a box of matches from beside the stove and lit his cigarette before he could get out his lighter. He smiled his gratitude, not for this gesture, but for the reason behind it. He inhaled deeply and started coughing again. When he could speak, he said, 'I couldn't stay with Mum. She's got someone there.' He glanced at me, hesitating. 'A *friend*,' he said, delicately. 'And she was angry anyway. Bawled me out.'

'You understand why, I hope?'

'Yes, Dad. I suppose so.' Eyes downcast. Very humble.

/'Good. Well, forget that for a minute. I don't know that we've got

any <u>fatted calves</u> in the cupboard, but you look as if you ought to eat something. And you could do with a bath.'/
He said, 'I smell bad because my body is rotting.'
He spoke flatly and calmly; stating a fact he believed absolutely.
No point in telling him it wasn't true. I had learned that much. I said, as casually as I could, 'A bath won't do any harm, all the same. For my sake, if not yours. Fiona is in your room, she's staying the night because we weren't sure how late we'd be home this evening. You'll have to share my bed with me. So a bath, if you please.'
He trailed up the stairs after me; stripped off his clothes while I ran the bath and shook in pine essence. I tried not to look at his body, not because he appeared to be modest, or even self-conscious, but because it tore at my heart to see the ravages it had suffered. His buttocks and thighs were like an old man's: shrunken and withered. He sank under the green, scented water with a grunt of what I hoped might be pleasure, and then, as I began to gather his clothes, shot up with a look of alarm. (Nina Bawden, *Circles of Deceit*)

Text F: Rendell (An old goose)

... rather like that, Wexford thought. 'I had the pleasure of a visit from your daughter the other day,' he heard the dentist say. 'What a lovely girl she is.'
'I'm told she's much admired,' Wexford said dryly. The compliment slightly displeased him. He interpreted it as spurious and ingratiating. / Also there had been a note of incredulity in Vigo's voice as if he marvelled at such an old <u>goose begetting a swan</u>./
The front door swung open and Mrs. Vigo came in, holding the child. For the first time since his arrival, Wesford remembered that there was another child, a mongol, confined somewhere in an institution.
The baby which Vigo now took in his arms was perhaps six or seven months old. No one could have doubted its paternity. Already it had its father's jaw and its father's athletic limbs. Vigo lifted the boy high, laughing as he chuckled, and there came into his face an intense besotted adoration.
'Meet my son, Mr. Wexford. Isn't he splendid?'
'He's very like you.' (Ruth Rendell, *The Best Man To Die*)

Text G: Rendell (Oh! withered is the garland of war)

'Mrs. Hatton, did your husband ever receive any callers in this flat that you didn't know? Strangers, I mean, that he wanted to talk to alone?'

'No, he never did.'

'Perhaps when you were out? Can you ever remember your husband asking you to go out and leave him alone with anyone?'

The handkerchief was torn now, sopping wet and useless as an absorbent. But she put it to her eyes and brought it away streaked black and green. 'When he was home,' she said, 'I never went out. We always went out together. We was like – like inseparable. Mr. Wexford ... ' She gripped the arms of her chair and two red flame-like spots burned in her cheeks. 'Mr. Wexford, I've heard all you've said and I've got to believe it. But whatever my Charlie did, he did it for me. /He was a husband in a million, a good kind man, a wonderful man to his friends. You ask anyone, ask Jack ... He was one in a million!'

Oh! withered is the garland of war! The soldier's poll is fallen ... . Strange, Wexford thought, that when you considered Charlie Hatton you thought of war and soldiers and battles. / Was it because life itself is a battle and Hatton had waged it with unscrupulous weapons, winning rich spoils and falling as he marched home with a song on his lips?/

How sentimental he was getting! The man was a blackmailer and a thief. If life was a battle and Charlie Hatton a soldier of fortune he, Wexford, stood in the position of a United Nations patrol whose job it was to prevent incursions on the territory of the defenceless. (Ruth Rendell, *The Best Man To Die*)

Text H: Moody (Lovely, dark and deep)

Emerald stopped at a wide barred gate let into the wire. The path carried on between clumps of hazel to a lane. Penny guessed it led back towards the Manor's stableyard. The ground into the wood was pitted and churned up, as though heavy machinery passed through quite often.

Underfoot there were leaves which crackled like cornflakes as they walked. The air was warm with residual heat. Beneath the trees were shadows. (Ha) Lovely, dark and deep.

'Country living,' said Emerald. 'I never knew I was a deprived child until Kendal brought me here.' She scuffed up leaves. She breathed deeply.

'Good grief,' said Penny.

A square of ground had been fenced off. Thin white posts. Barbed wire. It was grotesquely upholstered with the corpses of small creatures. Grey squirrels were tied in rows by their tails, paws curled against their chests. Crows hung upside down, wings spread, beaks open. There was a weasel, its sharp white teeth bared as though sucking back a scream. Rats and voles and rabbits lay crucified on the wire. More crows swung from the branches of nearby trees like broken umbrellas.

'Fun, isn't it?' Emerald sounded apologetic.

(Hb) '<u>Only man is vile</u>,' said Penny. She tried not to look at a vixen spread like a jumble-sale tippet along the barbs, tail threaded between the wire strands. There was a long-dried drop of blood at the corner of the half-open mouth. Here and there, white bone showed through rotting flesh.

'It's meant to be a warning to the other vermin.'

'Doesn't seem to be working.'

'If you saw what foxes do to pheasant poults you'd think they were pretty vile too.'

'Kill them if you have to,' said Penny. 'But why string them up?'

'It's Old Mayhew's idea, not mine.'

'Who is this guy, (Hc) the Marquis de Sade?'

Penny stomped off. The wood was full of atmospheric stuff. Rotting stumps. Sprouting fungi. Long taproots vicious with thorns. It only needed a BBC camera crew and (Hd) David Attenborough cuddling a baboon.

/ A large grey bird was wiping its beak on a log. When it saw them, it came running. It held its wings out to balance itself. One wing was higher than the other. Every now and then it gave a little skip to keep up with itself. Hard to believe that (He) <u>its ancestors had saved the Capitol</u>./

'He knows to expect me,' said Emerald.

'For gosh sakes,' said Penny. 'They're almost human, aren't they?' (Susan Moody, *Penny Post*)

Text J: Moody (Unkindest cuts)

Priscilla poured wine into long-stemmed glasses and told them how broke the Cassidys were. She wiped lipstick from her eye-tooth and said prices these days were so high they could hardly afford to eat. Penny wondered how she'd enjoy pounded sorghum and water from a stinking goatskin bag.

Priscilla suggested they go into the drawing room for coffee. Through the hatch she suggested the same thing in less kindly tones. She started on about the NHS and how she'd waited nine months to have a non-malignant mole removed from her foot.

'That's the trouble with today's Government,' she said. 'These cuts are doing so much damage.'

She flourished a box of mints about in a way that defied you to take one. Penny plucked up her courage. /In the Sudan, she'd seen a child die from an infected insect bite because no antibiotics had been available. <u>The unkindest cut of all.</u>/

'You're making a film over here, I believe,' Martin Cassidy said to Oliver, when Priscilla left the room.

'Not quite,' said Oliver. 'I'm scouting locations in Europe.'

'If you want to use our house, dear boy, you're welcome,' Cassidy said. He laughed as if it was only a joke. 'Film companies usually pay handsomely for that kind of thing, don't they?'

'Not mine,' said Oliver. 'I'm an independent.'

Priscilla returned. 'I've never seen any of your films,' she said. She sounded glad.

'You missed out,' said Emerald.

'I've read reviews, of course.' People like Priscilla always had. (Susan Moody, *Penny Post*)

Index

Lightning Source UK Ltd.
Milton Keynes UK
UKHW021807081218
333681UK00021B/660/P

9 781853 593734